IN SEARCH OF JERUSALEM

J IN SEARCH OF ERUSALEM

Religion and Ethics
in the Writings of
A. M. Klein

G. K. FISCHER

McGILL — QUEEN'S UNIVERSITY PRESS
MONTREAL AND LONDON 1975

This book has been published with the help of
a grant from the Humanities Research Council of Canada,
using funds provided by the Canada Council.

© MCGILL-QUEEN'S UNIVERSITY PRESS 1975
ISBN 0 7735 0227 0
LEGAL DEPOSIT SECOND QUARTER 1975
BIBLIOTHÈQUE NATIONALE DU QUÉBEC

DESIGN BY ANTHONY CROUCH MGDC

PRINTED IN CANADA BY JOHN DEYELL COMPANY

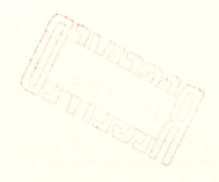

For Arnošt and Anny Kraus

Acknowledgements

I thank especially Professor Louis Dudek for his suggestions and editorial help. He directed my doctoral thesis, on which this book is based, and his criticism has been invaluable. I thank also Professor Alec Lucas, Professor Hugh MacLennan, and the anonymous readers for critical comments which prompted me to make a number of revisions.

I am greatly indebted to Mr. Colman Klein and Mr. Sandor J. Klein for permission to quote from material in which they hold copyright. I thank the firm of Faber and Faber Limited and the firm of Harcourt Brace Jovanovitch, Inc. for permission to quote lines from T. S. Eliot's "The Fire Sermon." Excerpts from *The Collected Poems of A. M. Klein*, compiled by Miriam Waddington (copyright 1974), are printed by permission of McGraw-Hill Ryerson Limited.

I am grateful to Mrs. Tema Lewin, formerly Librarian at the Jewish Community Centre in Ottawa, who generously made available to me her knowledge of Judaica; to Mr. David Rome, formerly Librarian of the Jewish Public Library in Montreal, particularly for allowing me to consult his manuscripts of bibliographical material on A. M. Klein; and to Mr. Usher Caplan for valuable bibliographical information he assembled while preparing his doctoral thesis. I am indebted to the late Rev. S. Ralph Collins, who, in some instances, made available to me his superior knowledge of Scripture. Further, I thank the staff of the National Library and of the Public Archives of Canada for their ever-ready, friendly efficiency and promptness in providing me with the research material I needed; and I thank the staff of the Ottawa Public Library for the friendly efficient help I received whenever I approached them with a request. I also take this opportunity to thank my friends who have provided me with valuable background information. Further, I acknowledge with much appreciation the attention given my book by the editor, Ms. Sylvia Haugo.

Most of all, I thank Hugo for accepting cheerfully the inevitable turbulence of my student years, the time of preparation that made possible the writing of this book.

Contents

Introduction

Since modern science has to a large extent destroyed the faith in revealed religion, man has been deprived of a touchstone by which to measure human actions and of an important source of consolation and hope. He may turn to philosophy for guidance. Yet, in the face of perennial anxieties and fears, what spiritual defences have twentieth-century philosophers to offer? Many, perhaps even most of them, reject the belief in ethical absolutes and hold either that the concepts of good and evil refer merely to the variable norms of society or that the individual is the sole arbiter of his own morality. To victims of oppression and persecution, such theories must needs appear diabolical. Unlike the traditional religions of western society, most secular theories have no answers for those who are concerned with the problem of ultimate moral purpose. For many human beings, however, life can only be meaningful when there is consciousness of a purpose that transcends our existence.

It is not surprising that in this intellectual predicament there are those who see a need for a religious philosophy rooted in the laws of observable nature (beyond the challenge of human opinion) and attended by a system of ethics beneficial to the individual as well as to the community. The longing for such a creed has inspired philosophers and theologians since antiquity, and it is still alive today.

In order to reach a wide audience, poetry rather than philosophical writing has usually been employed to disseminate religious ideas; and attempts to find a religion adequate for the needs of modern man have been mirrored in the literature of the past three hundred years. A public not trained in philosophy had access to many unfamiliar currents of thought, and became acquainted with the ideas of men like Toland and Newton, Volney and Schelling, because these ideas reverberated in the writings of Pope, of the Romantic poets, and of the Transcendentalists. Men whose orthodoxies had been shattered by the discoveries of Lyell and Darwin found in the works of Tennyson and Shaw that the new knowledge could furnish a basis for modern religious thought. Philosophies that seek God in nature continue to influence the world view of creative artists, and their effect can be discerned, for instance, in the writings of D. H. Lawrence, Dylan Thomas, and Kathleen Raine.

In Canadian literature, a new and ardent concern with religious systems that conceive of divinity in the natural universe is apparent in the poetry of Abraham Moses Klein. This writer was interested in a wide spectrum of creeds which, dissimilar though they are in some fundamental concepts, seem yet to agree in this important aspect: life in the universe is equated with divine life. Within the current of Judaic ideas, Klein seems to have been drawn irresistibly to wherever such thinking flourished.

We find in his writings a burst of youthful enthusiasm for the monism of Spinozan philosophy.[1] In an ecstatic moment of joy, he embraced Spinoza's proposition, "Besides God no substance can be granted or conceived,"[2] equating God with the totality of existence. It was an experience which, in some respects, seems to have had a lasting effect on his attitude. It roused his creative energies, and it inspired lines whose echo can still be discerned in pages he wrote at the end of his working life.

But Klein's work is filled also with an abiding affection for the Chassidic movement, especially for its originator, Israel ben Eliezer (the Baal Shem Tov, "Master of the Good Name") and his great grandson, Rabbi Nachman of Bratzlav, who spread their teaching in the eighteenth century among the Jews of eastern Europe. These religious leaders were loyal to the traditional Judaic dualism, which teaches that the Deity differs essentially from His creation. Nevertheless, writers seem to agree that the early Chassidim were conscious of a degree of God's immanence not usually admitted in the non-Chassidic mainstream of Jewish tradition.[3] The rabbis of the *Talmud* have held that the power and love of God permeate the universe, but that He is not within it except in rare and very special circumstances. The actual presence of the Lord Himself is thought to have appeared to Moses and, later, to have dwelled in the Temple in Jerusalem. Some of the Jewish sages believed that the divine presence appeared on specific occasions, when people worshipped, loved, or were in great need.[4] On the whole, however, the rabbis have taught the doctrine of a Deity "who is himself different from and removed from every human faculty."[5] They have not envisaged a world in which God Himself dwells in all things. The early Chassidic teachers, on the other hand, believed—as some of the Romantic writers believed several decades later—in a transcendent, enlivening Principle that permeates the universe, "a beyond that rolls through nature."[6]

Sporadically in Klein's writings, one may also detect sympathies with Cabalistic ideas, and at the end of his poetic prose narrative, *The Second Scroll*, one comes to realize how fervently committed he was to Cabalistic thought. Here, it seems, beckoned a possibility that monistic theology might be harmonized with traditional dualism. Of greatest renown among the works of the older Cabala is probably the *Zohar* (The Book of Splendour). After long controversy, the most reliable authorities now ascribe this book to Moses de Leon, a Spanish Cabalist of the thirteenth century. It is a work of immense poetic force. In the main, it consists of commentaries on the Pentateuch, and an elaborate emanation theory emerges from its explications of certain words in Genesis. It seems to suggest that all creation ultimately derives from one primeval source. An energy, proceeding from the hidden recesses of supernal ether, produced the first rung of creation "from itself."[7] Also of great significance in the Cabalist current of ideas and, as we shall see, of special importance to the present study, is *Maaseh Merkabah*. Based on Ezekiel's vision of the heavenly chariot, *Merkabah* mysticism originated in the first and second centuries of the Christian era and continued among the Jewish mystics of the Middle Ages. It too appears to suggest that the universe is an emanation of the Deity.

Almost inevitably, such theories invite monistic interpretations: if creation emanates from a source, then it may be assumed to be of the same essence as the source. One may well understand why, in certain respects, Klein would find this Cabalist form of pantheism more attractive than Spinozan philosophy. In the Cabala, differentiations in the degree of divinity are readily admitted: as one rung of creation leads to another, created existence progresses further and further away from the creative centre that is the Deity, and there is, then, a difference between God and the universe. The mind that may tremble before the boldness of the Spinozan vision will thus find the world view of the Cabalists less harrowing. At the same time, the Cabalist doctrine is still pantheistic; the implication remains that all existence is of one essence, and that it is divine. Clearly, the ethics inherent in a religious philosophy that seeks God at the centre of purely creative strength and divinity within the natural universe has a great deal to offer.

Two of the best-known Jewish philosophers of the twentieth century, Martin Buber and Mordecai M. Kaplan, believe that God is immanent in the world. Martin Buber, in *I and Thou* (1923), speaks of "meetings with the Spirit which blows around us and in us."[8] Mordecai M. Kaplan, the founder of the Reconstructionist movement, said in his main work, *Judaism as a Civilization* (1935): "Our knowledge of God is determined by our knowledge of reality."[9] According to his teaching, "God as a helper and protector may be identified with the powers of nature which maintain life, and with the intelligence that transforms environment by subjugating and controlling the natural forces for the common good of humanity."[10] Kaplan thus provided a theology which was in keeping with twentieth century ideas that do not conceive of supernatural reality, and he related to it the essential structure of traditional Judaic moral law. When man places himself on the side of the powers of nature which maintain life, he is in harmony with the Divine; he is obeying cosmic laws, not the dictates of personal opinion or social expediency. Kaplan's thinking tends toward ideas of evolution and there it ultimately becomes indistinguishable from the Judaic Messianic idea in which is envisaged the universal establishment of redeemed life. In one of his later books, *Questions Jews Ask: Reconstructionist Answers* (1956), he calls God "the Power that makes for salvation," and holds that "if we take into account the infinite duration of Godhood, it is possible to conceive that the evil which now mars the cosmos will ultimately be eliminated."[11]

As an active member of Jewish organizations, and as editor of *The Judaean*, *The Canadian Zionist*, and *The Canadian Jewish Chronicle*,[12] journals dedicated to popularizing Jewish learning, Klein had to be well acquainted with the currents and cross-currents of contemporary Jewish thought. Ideas much like those of Buber permeate *The Second Scroll*, and there is in Klein's thinking also evidence to link him with Kaplan; but how far Klein developed his ideas on his own and how much he absorbed from his readings, remains uncertain.

The greater part of Klein's work is devoted to propagating his religious and moral thought. For him, the poet "is part of the fighting forces, as much so, indeed, as is the trumpeter, marching into the fray."[13] Writing, for Klein, has always meant involvement. To write a page was to perform an act of immense responsibility. He once remarked that he was influenced by everything he read, and that he did not "distinguish reading from living."[14] But the degree of influence that can be brought to bear through a work of art depends to a considerable extent on its success as art. If it is to teach, it has to be attractive, it has to excite; and it does this largely through form: the values to be conveyed have to be made palatable.

It is probable that artistry for Klein has always been subordinate to content; but this does not mean that form is of no importance in his writings. He has always been interested in technique.[15] It may, then, be asked to what degree he was successful in making his art serve his moral purpose, what stature he attained as an artist. In the present volume, I am not attempting to answer this question, although I have, on occasion, allowed myself to include a critical comment. Others have treated this subject more fully, and Klein's writings will, no doubt, receive a great deal of critical attention in the future. At the time of his death, in 1972, they have been the subject of many articles, two books, and a number of theses. So far, favourable comments have outweighed the negative criticism.[16] A French-Canadian critic, Guy Sylvestre, has called Klein "un des plus grands poètes juifs du monde . . . un des meilleurs poètes de la langue anglaise au Canada."[17]

As to my own approach to Klein's work, I have tried to clarify lines which seemed obscure and to draw attention to ideas which seem to be present in his writings, but which, so far, have not been discussed, or have not been fully interpreted. I hope that my book will help readers to enter Klein's world and to feel at home in it; for Klein was a great advocate of friendships. His reputation, at present, appears to be chiefly that of a parochial poet, an author who writes primarily for a Jewish public[18] and for those whose interest is focused on the Quebec scene.[19] I hope to prove that his work is significant beyond these confines. It seems to me that his was the archetypal quest of a human being who emerges from the shelter of orthodox certainty and struggles toward a redeeming philosophy and intellectual peace.

No clearly defined theory emerges from Klein's writings; but it becomes evident that, eventually, he found in the religion of his fathers a strain of thought that allowed him to cleave to the old faith and, at the same time, to proceed in the direction of a progressive religious philosophy. In his work we find the quest for a modern faith, one that renews trust in the destiny of mankind and confirms the traditional ethical verities without which civilized existence cannot be sustained.

Orthodoxy, Emancipation, and Early Writings

Children brought up in a household regulated by religious orthodoxy enjoy a sense of security which is denied to offspring in a more free-thinking home. They are born into a world without insoluble problems. Good and evil are defined for them. They know what to expect. If their relatives, teachers, or friends should fail to respond to their virtues or peccadilloes, there is the all-loving Father who watches over them and will punish or reward their conduct according to merit. Fate is in one's hands. The good child is reassured.

Those who are growing up in an atmosphere of such settled values are in many ways to be envied; or rather, they would be deservedly the object of envy if there were not in store for them the almost inevitable eventual expulsion from this kind of childhood Eden. Usually, such an experience is more deeply uprooting than the process of gradual enlightenment to which children of progressive-minded parents are exposed when they outgrow the fairytale and the fable. To find out that daddy is the supplier of goodies and that Santa Claus is a myth may be temporarily upsetting, but the children of rationalist parents, if they have access to the imagination's Eden at all, will soon recuperate: they will be used to disappointments of this kind; they will not expect too much. Never having known the tranquility of absolute faith, they will know how to cope with the occasional minor disenchantment.

It is very different with young people who have grown up in

an orthodox environment. Some few, of course, may continue into adulthood unshaken in the belief of their forefathers. They will carry on the old practices and will probably be happier and almost certainly less beset with problems than their free-thinking fellow citizens. They will follow their law; they will live a life of devotion. It will be regulated by considerations which may have been vital in bygone ages but which now have little relevance in the larger society of which they are a part. They will live a life that has form, steadfastness, and a centrality which is often painfully lacking in the existence of their non-orthodox contemporaries; but they will remain strangers in the modern world whose premises they do not acknowledge.

Most children of orthodox parents are drawn into the mainstream. Those who want to take part in the making of modern society will usually be estranged from the mores of their early years. They will be exiled from a paradise where faith was unclouded by doubt, and their fall, when it happens, will in some cases spell a crippling experience, one from which complete recovery is not always possible. How the crisis is weathered depends largely on personal propensities and on the type of orthodoxy that is perforce abandoned. If the life to which the child has been exposed was hemmed in by stern and manifestly outdated rules which no one bothered to explain, if the spirit of the old religion had long been replaced by superstition, by a joyless clinging to rituals which are unexplainable and unacceptable in terms of modern thought, the reaction is likely to be violent. The old values will be rejected in their entirety. There will be a rift which will leave the individual detribalized and disillusioned. If, on the other hand, orthodoxy was related to convictions which modern thought cannot entirely deny, if the orthodox regime brought not only freedom from doubt but also love, warmth, and joy, the intellect that finally strains away from it will remember with nostalgia, will forever seek a synthesis of ideas, some mode that will allow the recreating of the lost Eden on new and firmer foundations.

The Americas have shown hospitality to numerous and widely differing forms of orthodoxy. Some of the orthodox immigrants, the Doukhobors, for instance, or the Hutterites—whose religion is closely linked with the building of self-sufficient rural communities—have been able to transmit their faith to successive American generations; but orthodox Jews, who have come from the eastern parts of Europe and settled in American cities, are, to a large extent, losing their young people to the greater freedom and opportunities which are the rewards of emancipation. The changing attitudes of their American-born children are reflected in American literature to which Jewish writers are contributing in disproportionate quantity.

Among Canadians whose writings are affected by the process of emancipation, we find, for instance, Irving Layton with his fiery indictment of petrified custom. It produced the early short story, "Piety,"[1] in which a mother, a Jewish immigrant from Poland, savagely beats her little boy because he refuses to go to synagogue, and then goes off to the synagogue herself, somewhat in the manner of the chimney-sweeper's parents in Blake's *Songs of Experience*, who "are gone to praise God and His Priest and King" while their little son languishes in misery. The situation which Layton describes is, to say the least, non-typical; yet it is informative, not in regard to Jewish family life, but in regard to Layton's frame of mind. Perhaps we should not be astonished. According to the available biographical notes, orthodoxy in the Layton household was not tempered with joy. A learned but introverted father was unable to instil in his son any love for the ritual which he was expected to observe,[2] and what remained in the memory was merely the cold, meaningless compulsion. Layton's approach to his heritage in these early pages is one of shrill aversion.

At the other end of the scale, we have the writings of Jack Ludwig, the Winnipeg author who is prone to sentimentalizing the very smell of the fishcounters on St. Lawrence Boulevard, once the Montreal "ghetto."[3] To Ludwig, the loss of orthodoxy means the loss of a way of life where ritual gave dignity and meaning to humble, daily activities. In "Celebration on East Houston Street," he tells us of a thoroughly emancipated man-about-town, a frequenter of chic brasseries in New York, who belatedly finds a spiritual haven in a dingy orthodox synagogue and as he drives away from it finds "a new world new risen."[4] Ludwig does not seriously suggest that a man can return to the old way of life once he has left it. All he can hope for is a momentary encounter, the fleeting touch; but even this, Ludwig feels, is beneficial, ennobling, refreshing.

Between the two extremes of Layton and Ludwig are others of varying nuances. We have Mordecai Richler and Leonard Cohen, for instance, both straining to prove that they have left orthodoxy behind, with all its restrictions and inhibitions. In Richler's early novel, *Son of a Smaller Hero*, we meet a young man of thoroughly disreputable ethics, who seems to feel he can claim the world's sympathies simply because he managed to break away from a stifling milieu. In this book, the notion that a man's loyalty to his faith may be strong enough to make him endanger his life is bitterly derided: the hero's father who, according to popular rumour, plunged into a burning building to save the Torah scrolls, did so only to rescue hoarded money. There is, however, a remarkable shift in outlook in Richler's later novels. In his best book, *The Apprenticeship of Duddy Kravitz*, he subtly differentiates between those manifestations of orthodoxy which make for dignity, for tranquility, and those which persist without adequate spiritual vitality. Indeed, Duddy's ability to distinguish between the two appears as a redeeming trait in an otherwise repulsive character.

In some of Leonard Cohen's poetry, and in *The Favourite Game*, there is evidence of a strong sense of attachment to the Jewish heritage. But in *Beautiful Losers* we see a compulsive drive to leave behind, not just orthodoxy, but every kind of restricting influence. In the writings of Richler and Cohen we thus find both acceptance of Judaism and critical rejection of traditional mores. What we do not find is an effort to reform, to revitalize the old beliefs. No positive suggestion is made that would adapt traditional attitudes to modern life. For this we have to go to Adele Wiseman and A. M. Klein.

Adele Wiseman sees with compassion, with an objectivity which is still close to involvement, the difficulties which orthodoxy imposes on the faithful. She does not simply reject the old mores. In her novel, *The Sacrifice*, she analyses the way in which orthodoxy has failed to keep alive the spirit of the Law. The plot of this novel concerns a New Canadian, named Abraham, who has brought up his son Isaak to venerate the Torah scrolls to such a degree that Isaak feels compelled to plunge into a burning synagogue to rescue them. The motif which in Richler's *Son of a Smaller Hero* is treated with such flippancy receives here serious attention. Neither father nor son can understand why a heroic action, instead of being rewarded, results in Isaak's death. They cannot see that they have misunderstood a fundamental principle of their faith.

In the Bible, Abraham is prevented from sacrificing Isaak: God does not want human sacrifice; man thus becomes aware of the holiness of life. Adele Wiseman's Isaak acts counter to the will of God when he risks his life for a book, even though it is a sacred book. The importance of the letter of the Law has become an overriding obsession; its spirit is obscured. Isaak cannot see that the spirit of his faith is not contained in pieces of parchment and printers' ink. Tradition, upbringing, obedience to superficial ideas have replaced true comprehension of the living religion.

At the end of the book, Abraham, for the second time, causes disaster because of his blind obedience to tradition. When Laiah, a woman of jaded character, embraces him, he pushes her away and by this, inadvertently, causes her death. Her dubious past disgusts him; and yet one feels that this disgust is merely an automatic reaction brought about by a stern moral upbringing, by an environment of narrowly defined values. One realizes that Abraham's natural inclinations, more in keeping with the Golden Rule of Leviticus than with the pilpul of moralizing rabbis, would have led him to respond to Laiah's love, would have allowed him to make a better existence for her and for himself. The strong link of the novel with the Abraham and Isaak story in the Bible suggests that we are to look at the man's moral rejection of the woman as a sacrifice. The result of his sacrificial gesture is disaster. Adele Wiseman seems to imply that not only religious orthodoxy but all moralistic thinking is contrary to the will of God if it is in opposition to life. What we find in Adele Wiseman's book is a plea for purification of religious and moral thinking. Hers is a call for a return to fundamental principle unencumbered by the exegeses of the centuries.

A. M. Klein alone was able to reinterpret and to transform in his writings the orthodox faith into which he was born, to make it live rejuvenated, not merely by discarding what was a dried-up shell, the chaff that had collected around the eternal verities during centuries of isolation in the pale of eastern Europe, but through adaptation, through fusion with the experience of twentieth-century man. He neither resented the hardships which his father's orthodoxy may have inflicted on his childhood, nor did he later regret the passing of formalities which can have only a spectral existence in the cities of North America. He abandoned orthodox practices tactfully, without ostentation, careful not to give offence to his more conservative friends,[5] and he retained the spiritual values he had been taught. He gleaned from orthodox religion moral strength and a formidable amount of learning, and this he combined with ideas more in keeping with the modern age. Such maturity of approach was not achieved at once, of course. It was the result of a struggle which began in the 1920s, when Klein was in his teens, and appears to have ended only in the 1940s.

Klein's early years were spent in a home which afforded him spiritual tranquility and the security of a family where a simple faith was combined with a great deal of affection and good humour. His parents, Kalman and Yetta Klein, came from

Ratno near Kamenets. According to Palnick,[6] Kalman was a widower with three children when he married Yetta, a widow and a mother of two. Their marriage was blessed with more offspring before they fled the pogroms and emigrated to Canada. They settled in Montreal in 1905, and there, in 1909, twins were born. A year later one son died of scarlet fever. The surviving son was Abraham Moses.

Kalman Klein was not a learned man, but he must have been a man of gracious intellect and imagination. In Poland he had been a pottery merchant travelling through the districts of Volhynia and Podolia. Palnick tells us that he was famous among the townspeople for the wonderful letters he sent home and that his postcards were read by the whole *Shtetl*.

He was also a very pious man. So pious was he, indeed, and so devoted to the letter of the Law, that once, in Montreal, he was out of work for a year because he could not find a job that would allow him to keep the Sabbath.[7] One may imagine the hardships of such a family in modest financial circumstances. But if orthodoxy wrought hardships, Klein's writings do not dwell on them. Instead, we are shown the portrait of a father who carries his son pick-a-back to bed, allows him to curl his beard, and tells him "tall tales about the Baal Shem Tov."

Orthodoxy, in this family, was not a burden but a treat. The young boy "Dreamed pavement into pleasant Bible-land"; in the synagogue he "followed, proud, the Torah-escorting band"; his mother, wearing the traditional perruque,[8] was a queen to him as she blessed the candles on the Sabbath table. Years later, these scenes are remembered still in "Autobiographical," and remembered with gratitude:

Oh memory of unsurpassing love,
Love leading a brave child
Through childhood's ogred corridors, unfear'd!

Klein had all the advantages, all the security, which loving parents and an orthodox education can provide, and he recognized that in their simplicity his parents had given him something that remained precious even when it was viewed later from the perspective of extended knowledge and greater sophistication. He retained a life-long affection for his parents' way of life and mode of thinking. In the poem "Heirloom" he later wrote:

My father bequeathed me no wide estates;
No keys and ledgers were my heritage.
Only some holy books with *yahrzeit* dates
Writ mournfully upon a blank front page—

Books of the Baal Shem Tov, and of his wonders;
Pamphlets upon the devil and his crew;
Prayers against road demons, witches, thunders;
And sundry other tomes for a good Jew.

For all their gentleness, there is irony in those words. Klein certainly did not think that the superstitions of the pale, the fear of demons and witches, made for good Judaism, but he respected the tradition that had given him the paradise of his childhood. Later in the poem, he speaks of his noble lineage, his proud ancestry. Irony again? Hardly. His parents had given him protected years; they had eliminated the ogres that threaten the sensitive young in homes less fortunate. They had been victorious in a battle that truly mattered. "The tallow stains of midnight liturgy," the evidence on the printed page of his father's untiring religious devotion, these, Klein explains in his poem, are his coat of arms. He writes in earnest. To have amassed knowledge and on the strength of it to have kept safe a child from fears and anxieties was not the fighting of a mean battle and not the winning of mean victory; certainly, it is not beyond comparison to the exploits of more bellicose ancestors who won their battles with weapons in hand.

Palnick's biography of Klein tells us that Kalman Klein took his son regularly to the synagogue and that he devoted Saturday afternoon to reviewing with him the week's *Sedra*, that is, the portion of the Torah that was read that week. He also saw to it that Abraham studied Talmud. He sent him to Kerem Yisroel Talmud Torah, a parochial school which opened its doors when Baron Byng High School had closed for the day. It was super-vized by Rabbi Simcha Garber, who took an active interest in Klein's education and for a while influenced his intellectual development. Young Klein, so the story goes, was a frequent visitor in the rabbi's house and at one point decided that he too wanted to become a rabbi.

The question is, what type of rabbi did he hope to become? The allusions to his father's books on the Baal Shem Tov indicate that the family was not unsympathetic to Chassidism, that highly emotional type of Judaism which the disciples of the Baal Shem Tov spread among the Jews of Poland and the Ukraine. But Klein attended Rabbi Garber's Talmud Torah school. Rabbi Garber, a Litvak from Vilna, a city known for its deprecation of Chassidic teachings, is described by Harriet Schneider, his grand-daughter,[9] as the very opposite to a Chassidic rabbi. He was a man who loved sober discussion, subtle scholarly debate. He was a man of reason. Very strict in his own orthodox observances, he was yet tolerant of people who could not follow his example. Klein enjoyed his intellectual prowess, his learning, his phenomenal memory. There is no doubt that there existed a bond of friendship between the rabbi and young Klein and that Klein's religious convictions at this time were mainly those of orthodox rabbinical Judaism. According to Harriet Schneider, the visits ended prior to 1922.

We cannot tell exactly when the peace of mind which Klein enjoyed as a child was finally lost. Family lore has it that in 1920, at the age of eleven, he "astonished a librarian by requesting, among other authors, Darwin."[10] He read a great deal. He was receiving the normal secular education of Canadian schools. When he reached the age of sixteen, he had already left behind his orthodox upbringing. We have his own word for it. In "Psalm II" (*Poems*, 1944), he speaks of himself as a free-thinker at sixteen; and David Lewis, who met Klein about that time, confirms that he was no longer following orthodox custom. Whether the awakening was painful—and if so, to what degree—we cannot tell. Only later do we find in the poetry traces of the upheaval in Klein's moral and intellectual life.

The early poetry, which he published at the age of eighteen, offers no evidence of great struggle. "Five Characters," a remarkable sequence which appeared in the *Menorah Journal* in 1927 shows, in fact, that no matter how his religious views had changed, his love for Jewish literature was not affected; his loyalty to his cultural heritage remained unimpaired. The poems indicate that Klein was at pains to bring the stories of the Bible closer to the modern imagination, to interpret them in a way that would kindle the interest of modern readers.

His approach is strongly reminiscent of cinematic techniques, particularly in the first poem, an impressive sonnet called "Ahasverus." We are first shown the King's crown. In it set, enticingly, is a cameo, a likeness of his empress, a "naked innuendo." Our eyes are guided from the crown to the figure of the cameo, and further, as in a cinematic close-up, to the face. When the light plays over it, we can see it smile, inscrutably, "as if it knew what was not known." The drunken king (reminiscent of Heine's Belsazer) calls for more wine. As he bends his crowned head over the cup, the inscrutable face greets him, his empress is "smiling from the wine." The king's unfulfilled desire and the maddening elusiveness of the woman are powerfully conveyed in these archetypes, and conveyed in what one may call visual terms. This is a poem which is designed to illustrate the constant relevance of the Bible tale.

The second poem shows even more clearly the desire to universalize what seems unique in the traditional story. The poem, "Vashti," opens with the chamberlain arriving to summon the queen to her husband. She refuses to come: the king shall not see her, "a naked swan." But the chamberlain realizes that the paleness of her skin is not the whiteness of a swan. She cannot come to the king because she is leprous. The universal truth implied in this interpretation of the tale is, of course, that human beings tend to refuse to do what in fact they cannot do. Caprice disguises inability.

Of the remaining three poems ("Esther," "Mordecai," and "Haman,") the most noteworthy is "Mordecai," which gives us the image of a man refusing to bow to an idol. When the people bow to Haman, only Mordecai and Haman remain erect, and thus one does not know for whom the people bow. The picture of the two men confronting each other across the cowed mass of the people remains strong in one's memory. There is a modernity of feeling here which makes one realize that Klein was not merely dreaming of Bible-land. He expended great skill in showing how inexhaustible are the inspirations of Bible literature.

A year later, in 1928, he published a minor composition, a group of ten couplets, mostly playful and uniformly naive, which bore the title, "Conjectures." Are snow-flakes feathers clipt from angel's wings? Are they furry hair trimmed from a Patriarch's beard? It is highly probable that these verses were composed for the entertainment of younger friends in the Young Judea organization which Klein (according to Palnick) had joined and of which he later became president. There is, however, one stanza which is of some interest here:

The snow-flaked crystal stars fall fast—
Age of miracles not past.

Here, for the first time, we see Klein gravitate to the point where religion and philosophy meet: he is intrigued with the idea that the miraculous need not be considered mythological; he delights in the thought that the miracle may be found in the intricacies of nature.

The same year, 1928, also saw the publication of a poem which superficially seems to reverse the trend. It is the "Ballad of Signs and Wonders," a clumsy, quasi-medieval ballad in which we are told of the miraculous rescue of the Jewish community of Prague. Klein here speaks of a miracle in the most primitive sense of the word. We hear of an apostate Jew who has turned traitor to his people. This monster tries to steal a beautiful princess, kills her accidentally in the ensuing struggle, and then accuses the Jewish community of the deed. The princess miraculously comes to life for just long enough to tell the world where the real murderer is to be found. All this is told in straightforward, deliberately naive language:

> She was tall and she was fair;
> She had long and golden hair;
> Lovely as the lilies are
> She was loveliest, by far,
> Of all virgins then or since;
> She was daughter of the prince . . .
> And in April she did seem
> Verily an April dream.

The villain is too preposterous to touch our emotions; he is a fairy-tale villain:

> Maledictions on his fame!
> May the earth forget his name![11]

This is not a poem in which one would expect to find evidence of philosophic speculation. It may be that it was written years before it was published, at a time of life when miracles of this sort, if not truly believed in, were perhaps accepted as part of the whole concept of tradition; it may be again that the poem was written chiefly for the entertainment of a younger audience; it may also be that it was written simply because Klein enjoyed trying his hand at the genre of the nineteenth-century literary ballad. There are, however, some more serious aspects to be considered.

First of all, there is the topic. If the poem was written about 1928, Klein's interest in the problems of apostasy assumes a certain amount of significance. At this time, Klein was already emancipated in his ideas. It is probable that he was anxious to clarify his own position. He knew that apostates were not always content with the mere change to another faith. Often they try to curry favour with their new co-religionists by turning against their original faith. As an infamous historical example of this, one may remember, for instance, the apostate Jew of Lombardy who betrayed Rabbi Meir of Rothenburg to Rudolph von Habsburg. To abandon one's faith, in previous times, meant inevitably that one abandoned one's community. He who turned his back on his religion turned his back also on his friends; and in the case of a Jew, this usually meant that he exchanged an existence full of difficulties and restrictions for a more comfortable one. This last aspect was still evident in North America in the 1920s and 1930s. One wonders, therefore, whether the "Ballad" is not a translation of feelings aroused by modern assimilationist Jews who showed themselves hostile to Judaism. The picture of the renegade, clearly, is deeply distasteful to Klein; and it may well be that he gave vent to his disgust by showing the renegade in the most primitive, most lurid form.

There is also another noteworthy aspect in this poem. Klein points out his feelings of friendship for the world of the Gentiles. As the poem opens, we are introduced to an idyllic scene: Prague is preparing for Easter. Christians are shown as friends and neighbours of the ghetto:

April arm in arm with Nisan
Doubles beauty of the season...
    And upon the market-curbs
    Lilies are sold, and bitter herbs...

One finds here the first indication of the oecumenism which becomes so pronounced in Klein's later writings.

Finally, there is the closing stanza which deserves consideration:

Israel, blow the shofar; Oyez!
Praise the Lord with hallelujahs!

Foes will ever seek to sunder
Life from Judah! God is wonder!
Miracles our way of living!
Raise your voices in thanksgiving!
    Let the sky and let the sod
    And all between now praise our God!...

It is as if a more personal feeling had suddenly forced its way to the surface of Klein's consciousness. "God is wonder! Miracles our way of living!" This does not contradict the old teachings, but it is also very much an expression of the philosophy towards which Klein seems to have been groping at the time.

But the first open admission that orthodox faith was no longer accepted appears in certain poems of 1929. It is most pronounced in the cycle "Portraits of a Minyan."[12] A *Minyan* is a quorum of ten men necessary before a Jewish service may take place. Klein drew a faintly humorous picture of each man, yet with serious undertones. There is Pintele Yid, who pretends to be emancipated but comes to say *Kaddish*, the prayer for the dead.

Agnostic, he would never tire
  To cauterize the orthodox;
But he is here, by paradox,
  To say the Kaddish for his sire.

Klein sneers at the man who enjoys the Scriptures for the wrong reasons:

For in a single breath to hiss
The ten outrageous names of those
Who on the Persian gallows rose—
Oh, this was pleasure, joyance this!...

We find here also the portrait of a man with definite Chassidic leanings, Reb Abraham, the jolly.

When God is served in revel
By all His joyous Jews,
(He says) the surly devil
Stands gloomy at the news.

Reb Abraham is the man who preaches enjoyment of life, of feasting, of food and drink and music. He is the playmate of little children.

And at Messiah's greeting
Reb Abraham's set plan
Is to make goodly eating
Of roast leviathan.

It is a sympathetic picture, and first proof of an increasing interest in Chassidism, its philosophy, its approach to life. We are shown the Chassid attacking evil, devouring it, making a meal of it, treating it as something which can be overcome by one's appetites, by one's hunger for life. It is an image which reveals deep attachment to this particular form of Judaism.

The most important poem in the cycle from the point of view of this inquiry, however, is "Sophist," a caricature which, astonishingly enough, is a portrait of Rabbi Simcha Garber, Klein's teacher.[13] Shockingly, Reb Simcha appears in a poem whose very title unequivocally proves that Klein, by now, had rejected his teachings. The old affection for the man, to be sure, is still there. The banter is gentle. One stanza makes much of the rabbi's phenomenal capacity to retain facts:

One placed a pin upon a page
Of Talmud print, whereat the sage
Declared what holy word was writ
Two hundred pages under it.

The last stanza pays playful tribute to his passion for clever exegesis:

But I think that in Paradise
Reb Simcha, with the twinkling eyes,

Interprets, in some song-spared nook,
To God the meaning of His book.

But there is a stanza, finally, that gives meaning to the title of
the poem:

That skull replete with pilpul tricks
Has long returned to its matrix,
Where worms split hair, where Death confutes
The hope the all-too-hopeful moots.

The security of childhood faith is gone. The ogres have free
play.

Thoughts of death were forced upon Klein when Sam Koslov
died. Koslov was the father of Bessie Koslov, Klein's high-
school sweetheart, the girl he was to marry in 1935.[14] The
cycle of poems "Five Weapons against Death," written for
Sam Koslov, was published in the *Menorah Journal* in 1929.
The poems, apparently, were offered for consolation; at least
one of them, "Club of Final Pain," is very moving. But a
critical attitude to the ritual pertaining to an orthodox funeral
intrudes in "Sword of the Righteous." Klein mentions customs
such as the tearing of garments or the turning of portraits to
the wall. Such gestures have become to him a sign, not of
piety, but of a lack of piety. He is differentiating between
custom and religious essence. He would dispense with gestures
which cannot comfort the dead. He would rather say: "He
who has given, He has snatched away."

Antidotes against the gloom of a lost faith, and paliatives
for a reality shorn of the reassuring routines of orthodoxy,
were love and art. At twenty, Klein was joyfully conscious of his
powers as a writer; he was also very much in love. The poem
"Business" speaks of both with exuberance. Its ending shows also
that Klein is rarely far from thoughts of religious significance.

And for the sake of you I am become
A trafficker in stars, and barter my
Knapsack of constellations for some high

Rare compliment for you; I am become
A hawker of the moon, who, never dumb,
Runs through the streets and shouts his wonders; I
Am certainly a magnate of the sky —
I lay before you all my glittering sum.
Yes, I would sell the flora of each clime
For price of metaphor; and I would dole
Out riches for the sake of one sweet rhyme
To sing its solo in a sweeter whole.
And I would buy a poem any time
And gladly pay it with my only soul.

A poet with orthodox leanings would hardly have written the last line. Neither could this line have been written by someone in religious torment. We may then ask ourselves whether Klein, by this time, had attained intellectual independence. A number of poems which appeared in 1929, under the heading "Sequence of Songs,"[15] are authentic expressions of youthful love and show that Klein, on the whole, was in a light-hearted mood, in excellent spirits.

But there is also a poem of that year which indicates that independence was not achieved easily, not, at any rate, without upheavals, and that it was indeed in love that Klein sought refuge. This is the poem "Haunted House." It is a little-known poem, overlooked by most critics presumably because it appeared in The Canadian Mercury, of which only a few scattered copies have survived.

The poem plunges one into a whirlpool of emotions. The technique, the very cadence, reveals more than a passing acquaintance with T. S. Eliot's "Rhapsody on a Windy Night"; but this does not diminish the impression that Klein is describing a strongly felt, personal experience.

Let the storm rage;
No better way is there
To ecstasize an autumn midnight
Than lavishly to stage
Fury climbing up a broken lightning stair . . .

The image, in its very hysteria, accurately sets the scene: chaos rages about a deserted house. Only a pair of lovers, seeking refuge from the turmoil, survey the scene from a window seat. Out there, noisy mourners are following a creaking hearse. "Are you not comfortable? Do you fear / The thunder storm as night is borne upon a bier?" The lovers are consoling each other while night, time of tranquillity, time of love, is murdered by the lightning storm:

> Draw you then closer to me—how it storms
> That tempest in your heart, and how your bosom warms!
> See you the sky—an oriflamme tattered,
>   A bowl of amethyst shattered,
>   An inky hieroglyph spattered
>   Against a parabolic wall. . . .
> This is too strong to last; this heavy fall
> Will weary as a madman pounding on a cell.

What kind of storm is this that slashes the sky? The word "oriflamme," with all its connotations, may provide the answer: the sky, oriflamme, becomes the sacred banner of Saint-Denis, the red silk on the lance of the French kings as they went to war, the sacred rallying point. It is in tatters now as the storm sweeps through the universe. The sky, too, becomes a shattered bowl of amethyst, and one may remember that the amethyst is named as one of the stones that adorned the breast plate of the High Priests of Jerusalem.[16] Again, the sky becomes "an inky hieroglyph spattered / Against a parabolic wall." Rugged clouds are seen as snatches of script blown across a dome, a wall of ether. But the word "parabolic" denotes not only the geometric curve of the dome. It refers also to the parable and the verity which the parable is trying to convey. The enduring truth looms majestically, impregnably beyond the fragmented words that have been written in its behalf. The old forms of Christianity and Judaism are torn asunder. The murdered night was not only the night of tranquillity and love; it seems it was also the darkness of

ignorance that is now lit up in a revolutionary storm. But the
wall, the parables, the verities beyond the word, beyond the
beclouding custom, will stand when the onslaught has ex-
hausted itself. The script may be torn, but the verities stand
unimpaired. It is madness to run against them or to attempt
to escape them.

The storm subsides. Klein gives us a sense of the calming
process in a beautiful descriptive passage. The moon comes out,
the wind grows calmer, "the poplar drips, sweating from his
great struggle"; the "vine-leaves rustle, catching their quiet
breath." One lover tells the other not to fear. There is silence,
except for something—something that seems to be going on in
the upper attic:

A bird-brained ghost moving with step erratic
Trying the door-knobs, pressing the wall's buttons. . . .
His slightest footstep threatens
Tranquility, until he too is static.

He is quiet. "Silence collects its broken pieces. . . ." Does
the bird-brained ghost represent memories of old custom, old
convention, old routines that were part of the old beliefs and
still haunt the mind? The buttons on the wall, are they door-
bells or devices that open doors? Does the ghost clamour for
readmittance to the land of the living?

The old ways cannot return. The noise in the attic ceases.
But what follows is by no means joyous liberation. The stormy
revolution is followed by silence and emptiness:

It is quiet in this house;
There is nothing else to do
But to listen to the mouse
That is listening to you.
There is nothing else to stage
But the spider in his hunger
Growing fat, and growing younger
In his age.

There is nothing here for thought.
Silence nullifies the sane.
And dust settles on the brain.
Here is naught.

In this nothingness, there is only love to cling to:

Nothing is here save you, my love and your
Flaming companionship consoling me
In this lone dust-infested house which we
Have entered, pushing on a latchless door.
Nothing is here, my love, except a poor,
A niggard modicum of empery
And four walls crumpling into meagre three
The fourth being exit. Here is nothing more.

Is the "niggard modicum of empery" the rationalist outlook; and the grey, joyless domain that of the "emperor Reason"?

If there is a consistent thought in this poem—and I think there is—then we can interpret the lines as a record of a struggle which is personal but which, at the same time, goes beyond the individual experience. As in Arnold's "Dover Beach," of which the poem is a strong reminder, the old religions have been swept away save for the unassailable verities that loom beyond the word like an impregnable wall. The custom, the ritual—all that made religion reach into daily life—has been discarded as meaningless; but the desire for it haunts the mind, and the imagination craves it even as it fears its restricting return. "Life is a haunted house, haunted by fictions," we are told. What else are these haunting fictions but long discarded belief reasserting itself?

In a world where human beings have a choice only between the night of ignorance, the storm of revolution, or grey and joyless lingering in a meaningless, rationalist existence, in such a world—as in Arnold's "Dover Beach"—consolation can be found only in human companionship and love. So we conclude that

Life is a haunted house through which two lovers
Holding warm hands are bravely sallying,
Ransacking cluttered bookshelves, lifting coffers,
Opening dusty cupboards, wandering,
Through rooms uncarpeted, up stairs unsteady,
Reaching at last the attic, and unclasping
The attic window, showing the full sky
With stars expectant of the frenzied grasping,
And splendour calling forth the heady
    Exclamation, and the single cry.

It is in the nature of love that those who feel it will again
reach out toward something beyond the graspable dust of
reality. They will again reach out toward beauty and wonder
and eternal values, and in this they will return to the domain
of the old religions. Again the revolutionary storm breaks
loose:

There goes the wind again, again the raindrops
Riddle the wet leaves. . . .

The lovers are not allowed to enjoy their happy state:

. . . once more the wind
Rides like a witch upon a broomstick,
Rides like a witch upon the poplar trees . . .
    Yet as I speak it is all over.

The storm again subsides. The "bird-brained ghost moves with
his step erratic; / His slightest footstep steps upon the mind."
Then he too grows silent, and here the poem breaks off. We
are left wondering whether the cycle will continue. Where are
the lovers now? Do they wander hopelessly through their
rationalist universe, a Porphyro and a Madeline who can never
escape into freedom but must forever grope their way through
cold ashes in an inhospitable mansion?

"Haunted House" is a poem of transition, and more than
anything else it convinces one that the upheavals in Klein's

RAY BAY

mind must have been considerable. Palnick, who has interviewed many of Klein's old friends, reports: "He respected his parents' views but for himself ceased to believe in all but the ethical verities. In a community where reform Judaism was anathema, this was to prove an irreplaceable loss for nothing satisfactory could fill the void."[17]

The writings which succeeded "Haunted House" seem to elaborate its message: we live in a distressful universe that offers no solutions, and love between human beings is the only thing that makes existence bearable. The flawed universe is the subject of a meditative short story which was printed in *The McGilliad*, a student journal of which Klein was an editor. Palnick mentions that one of the two courses in English Literature which Klein took at McGill University was a course on Chaucer given by Professor G. W. Latham; a faint echo of it may be detected in his story entitled "The Parliament of Fowls." It is a tale of King Solomon, written in a racy style. Its specific object is to let us know that the world is not as beautiful as it may seem. The king, who is about to write under the pseudonym of Koheleth a great work on vanity, is overcome by the beauty of a sunset as he listens to the birds who are debating its merits.

> Purple melted into carmine, carmine faded into scarlet, scarlet waned into crimson, and crimson disappeared into pink—the variations of the theme—Red. . . . The sunset was too beautiful even for Hebrew words, crisp words baked in the desert. . . . He thought of the Shunamite and the sunset, and of this glory about him, and he knew that all was not vanity. There remained a truth eternal;—and it was beauty.[18]

Moved to poetic creation, Solomon writes down words of exaltation. At this moment, one of the birds soils the paper on which he has been writing. Regarding this immediate evidence of how the world uses things of higher import, the king "spat royally." "Vanity," he said. "That isn't the word for it! Perfect beauty indeed!"[19]

The reference in this story to Koheleth reminds one that Klein on various occasions showed interest in the writer of Ecclesiastes, a fact which may be significant. This is how Hastings' *Dictionary of the Bible* sums up Koheleth's position concerning religious matters:

> God's work—the course of Nature—appears in the form of an endless cycle. . . . no amount of labour can produce anything new or of real profit—no one can add to, or subtract from, the unswerving chain of facts. . . . *Koheleth* gains no relief from expectation of Messianic peace and perfection, which animated the orthodox Jew of his day. There are left only the shreds of the convictions of his fathers, with a species of "natural religion" which has fatalism and altruism among its ingredients.[20]

Altruism is a kind of salvation. It becomes very important in Klein's work. The oecumenical tendency which made a timid appearance in "Ballad of Signs and Wonders" reappears with greatly increased vigour in the poetry of 1930. This time, too, his universality is concerned with real, contemporary issues. As president of the organization Young Judea, Klein was concerned with the political news from Palestine. The bloodshed during the Arab riots in 1929 appalled him, and his dismay was given voice in a series of poems under the title "Greetings on This Day." There is no doubt that he felt personally involved. His reaction was not merely that of a young man who held a leading position in the Zionist movement. He felt he knew and loved the places where violence was being perpetrated:

> O Safed, Safed,
> Though never have I left my northern snows,
> Nor ever boarded ship for Palestine,
> Your memory anoints my brain a shrine,
> Your white roofs poetize my prose,
> Your halidom is mine.

Nevertheless, in spite of his partisanship, he saw that the beloved land would yield fulfilment only when those who were "breaking the soil, as hard as the heart of Pharaoh" would live in harmony with their neighbours. Love, which in "Haunted House" extended only to the personal love between man and woman, reaches further here: "Izak and Ishmael are cousins met." Klein offers a conciliatory hand, and he does so with a flourish:

> Though blood was spattered, it has left no stain;
> The greeting on this day is loud Shalom!
> The white doves settle on the roofs again. . . .

The first poem in the series "Greetings on This Day" is directed against grief. This would be in keeping with Koheleth's approach to life, but it suggests also that Klein continued to be interested in Chassidic philosophy and that he was trying to apply it to actual practical living. The Chassid believes that God can be served only in joy. "Prayer shall not take place in pain and repentance, but in great joy," Martin Buber writes in his essay on the Chassidim. "Joy alone is true service to God."[21] A knowledge of this doctrine illuminates Klein's poem "Sorrow is a Leper." Grief is to be suppressed. The last poem in "Greetings on This Day" ends on a happy, forgiving note, and thus the entire series is in keeping with the teachings of the Baal Shem Tov.

Another poem of 1930, "Christian Poet and Hebrew Maid," combines elements of the preceding two. It is, by implication, a plea for personal love, but far stronger in it is the plea for general human understanding:

> The vulgate and the scroll are twin;
> The spire and dome advance their call;
> Mary and Miriam are kin.

The world can be beautiful. It should be greeted with joy: "Blow ram's horns; make a joyful noise." Love is to know no factions:

The nightingale proclaims no creed;
  The urgent thrush reiterates
No catechism: and the freed
  Canary holds no dark debates.
These sing; their exhalations cede
  The homage that the sky awaits.

   .   .   .   .   .

Even as does the turtle-dove
  And even as the skylark's tongue
Praises the permanence above,
  So can you pour from your full lung
Your vassalage to him of love,
  Your worship to the throne in song.

The poem shows the universalist tendency and consciously cheerful approach to life which we have already mentioned. But something new has entered here. Suddenly, there is religious exaltation. This is not theory put into verse but delight in a new and liberating thought. This is a call to prayer. All creation, each thing in its own way, praises the Deity. All men, regardless of creed, can pray to Him. "Ballad of Signs and Wonders" (in the last two lines)[22] also suggested this thought. But here the lines have the ring of fresh, authentic emotion. For a moment one may be tempted to see this as a return to the theology of previous years. But no: the set dogma has been discarded. It cannot be resurrected. What one finds in this poem is the belief in a great natural process that in itself is holy:

The rose is pollened by no themes
  Spiritual: the lily pales
Before the import of her dreams.
  The lilac blossoms, and then fails.
They spread their fragrance: the Lord deems
  Such cups so many hallowed grails . . .

Vegetation prospers and fades. The cycles of nature proceed without the influence of the supernatural spirit. That "the lily pales / before the import of her dreams'' suggests that Klein is awed, conscious of the temerity of this thought. But immediately there follows a reconciling idea: the denial of the supernatural is not blasphemous because nature itself is holy; life, the divine energy, is manifest in the cup of the flower. The word "grail," referring to the sacred vessel of Christian legend, may have been employed here not merely because the poem celebrates harmony between Christians and Jews; Klein may have used it specifically to bring to mind Robert Borron's version of the Grail legend. In *Joseph d'Arimathie* (*Estoire du Graal*), the Grail, the sacred vessel of the Last Supper, is used to catch blood from the body of Jesus. Thus, Christians seek within the Grail actual divine presence. This brings to mind also the idea of transubstantiation. In the Christian ritual, the presence of the divine is sought in a sacred chalice: physical nature, in the form of wine and bread, becomes divine. When Klein refers to the flowers as "hallowed grails," he equates natural, life-engendering energies within the cup of the plant with the actual presence of God; and he may feel also that the plant, physical nature itself, partakes of the divine. The poem seems to indicate that Klein by now was probing one of the great intellectual experiences of his life: he had discovered Spinoza.

Spinoza, Enthusiasm, and Disillusionment in the 1930s

Klein's interest in Spinoza appeared in 1931, when he published in *The Canadian Forum* the sequence "Out of the Pulver and the Polished Lens."[1] It is a cycle of poems sparkling with the excitement of fresh discovery, but the lines show also that a great deal of thought had already been expended on Spinoza's fundamental idea that God and creation are one, and that some time must have elapsed between the moment of first enthusiasm and the publication of the poems. The cycle consists of nine short, individual poems with widely differing techniques and great variations in sentiment. Together they form one urgent plea in defence of the great Jewish heretic.

That Klein felt drawn to Spinoza's philosophy is not surprising; for here worship could be directed toward observable reality. Worship here was not merely a ritual in a system of unsubstantiated speculation. Scientific knowledge, which was destroying reliance on the old beliefs, could not mar a faith which identified the natural forces themselves with the creative energy of the Deity.

More complex are the reasons why Klein accepted Spinoza's ideas in preference to other religious philosophies. His enthusiasm might have been kindled by other pantheistic systems. Among the eighteenth- and nineteenth-century writers, there were lesser-known men, some of whose ideas perhaps appealed to Klein if he was aware of them. In the pantheism of Karl Christian Friedrich Krause, which conceives of a universe existing within God and eventually merging with Him, Klein might have found congenial trends of thought; the optimism of Constantin François Chasse-Boeuf Volney, his theories concerning the pleasure–pain mechanism which leads mankind ultimately to universal happiness, might have appealed to him; Rudolf Hermann Lotze's teleology certainly would have struck kindred chords in Klein's consciousness. But these men and similar writers, even if Klein knew of them, could not rival Spinoza in his esteem. They were refining ideas which in Spinoza had received their great impetus.

The special fascination which Spinoza exercised upon Klein may be ascribed to at least three considerations:

Spinoza was an intellectual hero, a great original thinker. He was the innovator, the martyr who suffered for his convictions. His appeal to Klein's romantic imagination on this count was irresistible.

Spinoza was a Jew and convinced that he had remained true to his faith even though he introduced new and revolutionary ideas. Klein could identify his own doubts and yearnings with the intellectual struggle of Spinoza. In Spinozan teaching, he saw the creed he loved revitalized: because of its deeply Jewish insistence on the unity of the divine being and the many other instances of harmonization with the Pentateuch, Spinozan philosophy could, in a sense, be looked upon as a variation in Judaic thought rather than as a heresy.

The Spinozan system—and this, probably, was the most important consideration—was eminently rational. Equating reality with the Deity, it offered a concept which eliminated the tortuous question of the existence of God. Visible nature, as well as the invisible, also undeniable forces of nature, was here considered worthy of adoration. God's existence is manifest. He may not be exhausted in perceivable nature, but what is perceived is at least a part of Him. Spinoza thus provided Klein with an escape from religious doubt.

In its most basic essentials, the Spinozan system presented a creed of magnificent simplicity, and Klein's Spinozan poetry does not seem to give any indication that he was familiar with the complexities which emerge from a more detailed study of Spinozan philosophy. At this early stage, Klein also chose to ignore, or was unaware of, certain facets of this philosophy which, to a Jew and modern humanist who is concerned with the worth of the individual, must be singularly unattractive. The neutrality of the Spinozan universe, its unconcern with the destiny of the individual,[2] at this stage remained unnoted.

What we do find is immense relief and elation. The doubts have been resolved. A new religion has been discovered, one that enables Klein to retain some of his old creed in rejuvenated form. He is anxious to share his new knowledge. The cycle "Out of the Pulver and the Polished Lens" was obviously written to answer a personal need; but it was composed also because Klein wanted his contemporaries to rediscover Spinoza. He wanted them to acknowledge his relevance, his modernity. The elaborate care expended on the planning of the cycle was, no doubt, intended to help spread the message; the artistic level itself was to make certain that the message would not be overlooked.

The poems in "Out of the Pulver and the Polished Lens" are arranged in an interesting symmetry.[3] The first and the last of the poems are biographical. In the first, we are introduced to Spinoza, the lost son of the Amsterdam ghetto, the persecuted heretic. At the end, in the last poem, we see him redeemed, serene in the conviction of his righteousness.

The opening lines in Poem 1 set before us the hostile environment in which Spinoza's creed was judged and condemned. Klein casts an ironic glance at seventeenth-century Amsterdam, where a stronghold of orthodoxy opposed new currents of thought, not with logical counter-thrusts of argument, but with invective and dogmatism. The lines, painfully rough in places and not without obscurities, make clear the object of Klein's attack: it is aimed at those who believe that hostility and noisy affirmation of traditional views will bring back to the fold a straying intellect.

What better than ram's horn blown,
And candles blown out by maledictory breath,
Can bring the wanderer back to his very own
The infidel to his faith?

Orthodoxy of religion cannot be re-instilled once it has been abandoned. Only physical extinction, Klein suggests sardonically, will make a man of free intellect submit. The lost son cannot be brought back

... unless it be that from the ghetto
A soldier of God advance to teach the creed,
using as rod the irrefutable stiletto.

When one reads the poems in this cycle, one feels that the issues touched upon were very much Klein's personal concern, that the spiritual development described had a parallel in his own experience. The bitterness projected into the lines of this first poem probably stems from emotions that were directed against fossilized elements in Klein's own community.

The last poem, which shows us Spinoza triumphant, has corresponding autobiographical overtones. In Poem 9, we see Spinoza serenely happy, forgetting his enemies and an adverse fate, "Dutchmen and Rabbins, and consumptive fretting," while he is "Plucking his tulips in the Holland sun," gleaning whatever beauty he can from creation as far as it is within his reach. This picture of Spinoza may well give us an accurate enough idea of Spinoza's frame of mind during the late 1670s when the *Tractatus Theologico-Politicus* was complete and he had clarified for himself some of his most important ideas. But Spinoza's life, to the very end, was full of painful disappointments, and it is questionable how far, in fact, the strength of his theological convictions helped him to forget the immediate difficulties "Dutchmen and Rabbins" presented to him. The quietude of mind which is the dominant note at the end of Poem 9, therefore, suggests the mood of the poet rather than that of Spinoza. Klein offered us this vision of tranquil existence because for him, at this particular point, Spinoza's teachings provided tranquility: they made it possible for him to worship in spite of his acceptance of modern scientific knowledge.

The quiet ending of the sequence is significant also for another reason. It reminds one that there is something of the epic in this work. The journey from the persecutions of the Amsterdam ghetto to spiritual tranquility in "the garden of Mynherr" was heroic. The ogres of doubt that blocked the way had been vanquished by a heroic intellect. In his quest for truth, Spinoza had fought a victorious battle. For Klein, he was a figure of epic stature. Baruch Spinoza had rescued him from spiritual limbo, from the cold dust of his "haunted house." The struggle is over now, and an air of sobriety settles upon the scene, as it always does in epic poetry when the moments of greatness, of sacrifice and ecstasy are past and problems of daily living assume their normal dimensions.

Poem 9 places great emphasis on the righteousness of Spinoza's position. He is shown "gathering flowers for the One." In other words, he is living in accordance with the divine will. There are many episodes in Spinoza's life that could be looked upon as flowers in the garland of a good life. Klein calls him "The ever-unwedded lover of the Lord," and, by contrast, reminds us that Shabbathai Zwi

> ... for a time of life
> Took to himself the Torah for a wife,
> And underneath the silken canopy
> Made public: Thou art hallowed unto me.

Shabbathai Zwi, the Jewish religious leader of the seventeenth century, promised to lead his disciples into the Messianic age but plunged them into despair when in a turnabout as dramatic as it was erratic he decided to embrace Islam. Klein sees in him the prototype of one who obeys the formalities of religion without being truly committed. Spinoza, by contrast, proves that man may be alive to the divine principle without formalized creed, without adhering to prescribed ritual. "The ever-unwedded lover of the Lord," without compulsion, remains unshakable in his loyalty.

This loyalty, this *amor intellectualis* of God, is born from a philosophical system. The essential idea of this system, the climax in Spinoza's spiritual Odyssey, is the subject of Poem 5, the central poem in Klein's sequence. Here, in a most important passage, Klein abandoned all ostentations of poetic technique. He set the poem up in the form of two short prose paragraphs and thereby lent it the peculiar dignity of an understatement, of contained passion. Only closer examination reveals that there is iambic pentameter in these lines, and rime; and metaphor can be found in them—some of the finest Klein ever produced:

> Reducing providence to theorems, the horrible
> atheist compiled such lore that proved, like prov-
> ing two and two make four, that in the crown of
> God we all are gems. From glass and dust of
> glass he brought to light, out of the pulver and
> the polished lens, the prism and the flying mote,
> and hence the infinitesimal and infinite.

The "crown of God" here can only be understood as nature in its most comprehensive sense; and the word "we" as the sum of all individual parts of nature so far as their identity is discernible. The metaphor is traditional; it may fail to impress one with originality; but it is hauntingly appropriate. Gems in a crown are discernible in their peculiar texture and outline, but they are also an integral part of the whole. The individual— whether it be a star, an electron, a human being, a fly, or a flower, or the momentary shape of a snow flake or of a crested wave—is always an integral part of nature, and, as the word "gem" implies, precious and important. The worth of each part of creation is infinite because, in Spinoza's theology, creation itself is divine, a manifestation of God. Its workings, whether they appear in physical, chemical, or biological energies, are expressions of the will of God. Divine providence shows itself in the laws of nature, laws that can be grasped by reason and expressed in theorems; laws that are part of actuality, not mere belief. Frank Sewall, a commentator, explains Spinoza's approach thus: "Willing to regard the universe, including man, as a system of pure mechanics, his contention is that mechanics itself is spiritual and all is divine."[4]

As in music, where complex variation follows a comparatively simple theme, the traditional metaphor in Poem 5 is followed by intricate modern symbolism. Spinoza was by trade a maker of optical lenses. By the work of his hands, "from glass and dust of glass," there came then into being a device by means of which the prism, a phenomenon of great beauty, could be apprehended. With the help of the lens, too, it was possible to perceive "the flying mote," objects so minute and elusive that they could not be seen with the naked eye. By refracting rays of light, the lens brings into focus that which otherwise would have remained shrouded in obscurity. Spinoza's philosophy, on the spiritual plane, performs a parallel function. It seems to direct rays of thought and to clarify what was vague, blurred, lost in ignorance, so that truth becomes apparent. It answers questions concerning the nature of God and the nature of His individual creatures. The lens brought before man's eyes the circular, multifaceted prism in its spectral magnificence; Spinoza's philosophy opens man's eyes to the idea that the infinite, multifaceted, myriad-hued manifestations of nature are divine. The lens allows the human eye to contemplate the characteristics of a mote; Spinoza's philosophy answers questions concerning the individual parts of creation: the minutest particle is worthy of attention because it is an integral part of the whole of the universe; because it is of its substance; because it is part of the Deity. The pulver, the dust of glass, insignificant, opaque, unbeautiful to human sight, is of the same substance as the lens in which light is gathered and given direction.

In the second of the two paragraphs which make up Poem 5,

Klein rejects "the abracadabra of the synagogue," referring, no doubt, to the self-righteous claims of traditional religious teaching that presents mythology as fact. The meaning of this passage becomes clear when it is read in conjunction with Poem 4, which will be discussed later.

Poem 5 is preceded by three poems that speak of doubt and disaffection, of the struggles and dangers in store for the intellect that aspires to the free apprehension of truth. In these poems, we see reflected some of Klein's own scruples. We find here some of the argument that led to acceptance of the Spinozan creed.

In the corresponding three poems which follow Poem 5, one can discern Klein's sense of liberation. He has discovered a creed that allows him to worship while his intellect remains free, or rather, while his intellect is subject only to laws of logic to which it can without qualms submit. The poems are hymns, passionate prayers. Some of the lines belong to the finest Klein has written.

Klein evidently felt that there were significant differences of quality in the various types of alienation from religion. Dissatisfaction with the traditional creed could produce harmful, blighting activity; but it could also produce innovation, the great step forward. Poems 2 and 6 are concerned with these two aspects. They are what one may call "public" poetry. Even the metres chosen are of a popular kind.

In the rumbling quatrains of Poem 2, an unhappy doubter of the seventeenth century is put in the stocks, a warning to those who scurry from creed to creed in a futile search for certainty. Uriel da Costa was unable to choose between Catholicism and Judaism, eventually turned against both, and in 1647 committed suicide.

Uriel da Costa
Flightily ranted
Heresies one day,
Next day recanted.

.   .   .   .

What is the end of
This catechism?
Bullet brings dogma
That suffers no schism.

From the uncertainties of living, from the responsibility of having to make choices, he fled into the realm of the absolute. Certainty, Klein seems to say, will not be found in any of the old forms of religion; oscillating between the established creeds will not help.

By contrast, Poem 6, in heavily latinized couplets, remembers the sages who deviated from the prescribed path, but who, far from weakening the old creed, enriched and developed it. Koheleth is hailed, who spoke of the unchangeability in the laws of nature[5] and the oneness of creation.[6] The Cabalists are called upon with joy and with awe. Klein is evidently aware that in the Cabala a form of pantheism is accepted as part of Judaic teachings.[7] Spinoza's theories, we are told by implication, confirmed pantheistic ideas which had long been nascent in Jewish tradition. His mind represents a step forward, another stage in the development of the human intellect. He does not destroy Judaism; he carries its work further. Poem 6 is a Te Deum in praise of divine creation. Here are some of the lines:

Unto the crown of bone cry Suzerain!
Do genuflect before the jewelled brain!
Lavish the homage of the vassal; let
The blood grow heady with strong epithet;
O cirque of the Cabbalist! O proud skull!

   .   .   .   .   .   .

O golden bowl of Koheleth!

   .   .   .   .   .   .

Yea, and having uttered this loud Te Deum
Ye have been singularly dumb. . . .

Before the grandeur of creation, words, no matter how potent, remain inadequate. The words in Poem 6 are, of course, illustrating this inadequacy, and Klein was probably acutely aware of it. The grandiloquence of the lines stifles their emotional content.

Verses of public scorn and public homage are followed by poetry that speaks with intensity of personal experience. After the brashness of the ballad, Klein shifts to subtle free rhythm, and instead of the somewhat pounding incantations of the hymn, he now uses lyricism of exceptional beauty.

In Poem 3, we witness the torments of the emerging dissenter. The poem is to be read as a biographical fantasy. The thoughts expressed are meant to be those of Spinoza. But the disgust and fear in these lines speak of authentic knowledge. Klein here seems to have reached a feeling of complete identification with the heretic in his initial struggles.

> Malevolent scorpions befoul thy chambers,
> O my heart; they scurry across its floors,
> Leaving the slimy vestiges of doubt.

The task of reaching out for the truth brings with it distasteful, frightening doubts. Some blindly tear at the fabric of the old faith, destroying without being capable of reshaping it. Will he be one of those?

A menacing procession passes before his mind. The dissenter has to ask himself whether, after all, his doubts may be unjustified, whether punishment will overtake him even as it overtook the king of Babylon who would not believe when he saw the writing on the wall. There is the archetypal da Costa who exchanged one deficient dogma for another and was doomed to endless disappointment. There are the cowards who will meekly retain or abandon their creed when threatened; and there is the ignominious tribe of opportunists who will change religion for a bribe. If the dissenter desires truly to reach out toward independence, toward objectivity, toward a state of mind in which clarity may come to him, he must overcome fear of punishment or intellectual defeat:

Banish memento of the vermin; let
No scripture on the wall affright you; no
Ghost of da Costa, no, nor any threat.
Ignore, O heart, even as didst ignore
The bribe of florins jingling in the purse.

Klein perceives two things clearly: to abandon one's creed for
material advantage is unthinkable; but there are other dangers
which may beset even the most serious thinker once his faith
is weakened. He who would probe the nature of reality must
proceed in spite of dangers, in spite of the possibility that he
may be prompted by what Spinoza might call "inadequate
ideas."

The musings of Poem 3 are those of a man who does not
know whether his spiritual torture will ever cease. In Poem 7
we find him transformed. He has found certainty. He is secure
in his new creed. The two quatrains of this poem have the
quality of a love-lyric, spontaneity and personal fervour:

I am weak before the wind; before the sun
  I faint; I lose my strength;
I am utterly vanquished by a star,
  I go to my knees at length

Before the song of a bird; before
  The breath of spring or fall
I am lost; before these miracles
  I am nothing at all.

A lover who believed himself exiled has discovered that he will
always be part of the beloved. An intellect who thought himself
separated from the strength and beauty of the universe has
found himself absorbed in it.

There is no contradiction in the praise of the human intellect
which appeared in the hymn of Poem 6 and the concluding line
of Poem 7 "I am nothing at all." The juxtaposition merely

strengthens the central idea of the lyric: the human being, although a most stupendous part of creation, denies its individuality, its separateness. In ecstatic worship of each individual divine manifestation, it finds a union with creation as a whole. The words "I am lost" and "I am nothing at all" indicate not forlornness and annihilation, but a lover's sacrifice of selfhood, a melting of the individual into all-encompassing nature. This is perhaps as close as Klein ever came to an experience of ecstatic mysticism.

Poems 4 and 8 are concerned with theological argument. How does the theology of traditional religion compare with that of Spinozan philosophy? In the corrosive, satirical lines of Poem 4, the aspiring philosopher bids his followers to abandon the established forms of religion which employ imagination rather than reason to determine the nature of the divine, and which treat mythologies as actual truth or else reject them arbitrarily without valid argument. "Synods tell God to be or not to be...." In their divergence of opinion and in their pretence to exclusive and often disconcertingly detailed knowledge of the nature of God, the spirit of the divine eludes them. God, the all-embracing, becomes, in the eyes of the faithful, the protector of their own particular set of dogmas. They feel capable only of finding Him within the confines of their own house. "Polyglot God is exiled to the Churches." While the various established creeds claim special, definite knowledge of His being, the spirit of the divine is exiled from the realm of free intellect through which a more profound understanding of God might be reached.

Spinoza forsakes organized religion and its churches whose claims are without adequate foundation, and whose god, as Klein puts it, is "suspended in mid-air."[8] He leaves them to their belief in a supernatural existence that would deprive the divine principle of full contact with a living universe. Theirs is the naive concept of a remote deity who resides in a sphere to which the air of the natural sky has not access and who formulates arbitrary directions for the conduct of mankind:

The Lord within his vacuum of heaven
Discourses his domestic policies,
With angels who break off their loud hosannas
To help him phrase infallible decrees.

Spinoza, Klein says, bids us seek "that other Law," the law of
actuality. Poem 4, which precedes the definition of Spinoza's
philosophy (contained in Poem 5), expresses the derisive mood
of the malcontent who has broken with tradition but who is
still groping to define his own position.

The mood changes in Poem 8. This is the voice of a biblical
prophet: fervent, poetic, full of conviction. The dissenter's
spirit is at peace. Instead of attack on traditional religion, we
now find a defence of the new creed. Scorn gives way to a
spirit of conciliation. Poem 8 is the jubilant prayer of a man
who is somewhat in the position of a surgeon who has per-
formed a difficult operation and finds to his relief that he has
not destroyed life, as he had feared, but renewed it. The
philosopher realizes that his new ideas, far from being heretical,
have merely cleared away the encumbrances which hitherto
made it difficult or impossible for an inquiring spirit to
worship with true conviction. The new philosophy, he feels,
has liberated the essence of the old creed. Prayer now is no
longer a formula; it rises from the depth of man's being:

> Lord, accept my hallelujahs; look not askance
> at these my petty words; unto perfection a frag-
> ment makes its prayer.

Spinoza devoted a considerable part of his writings to prove
that scripture and natural reason did not essentially contradict
each other,[9] and it is this aspect of his work that is reflected
in Poem 8. Klein makes numerous liturgical references,
mingling words from the Bible with Spinozan thought. They
seem to merge without effort, and from the amalgam, there
rise majestic lines:

> Thy glory fills the earth; it is the earth; the
> noise of the deep, the moving of many waters, is

it not thy voice aloud, O Lord, aloud that all may
hear?

"The voice of the Lord is upon the waters," sings the Psalmist,
"the God of glory thundereth: the Lord is upon many waters."[10]
When Klein makes these words echo in his poem, he seems to
ask: Do they not anticipate the Spinozan idea that the glory of
the earth and the waters themselves are part of the Deity? And
again the Psalmist says: "Thou visitest the earth, and waterest
it: thou greatly enrichest it with the river of God, which is full
of water: thou preparest them corn, when thou hast so pro-
vided for it."[11] Klein seems to ask: Why should there be a
division between the divine power and the natural forces
through whose action the earth is watered and made fruitful
and glorious?

In some of Klein's words, Solomon's Song may be heard, its
special timbre of love, the voice that paints the landscape of
the Holy Land:

> The wind through the almond-trees spreads
> the fragrance of thy robes; the turtle-dove twit-
> tering utters diminutives of thy love; at the rising
> of the sun I behold thy countenance.

This is obviously written by a poet in whom the sentiments of
the Bible are very much alive. The ghost of *Sartor Resartus* may
hover about the opening phrases in this passage; but there is
in it also an indication that Klein's mind is receptive to ideas
such as those of the Lurianic Cabala, where the physical world
is nothing but a garment of the Deity.[12] This, to some extent,
implies a form of dualism: the physical part of the universe is
so far removed from the source of the divine that it acts merely
as a shell enclosing the divine essence. At the same time, we
hear Spinoza speak: in the Spinozan world, the almond tree,
like all vegetation, is part of the actual outer manifestation of
God; all consciousness—whether expressed in the voice of a
dove or in the emotions of a human being—is evidence of
divine love; the sun, like all sources of energy, may be con-

sidered part of the very countenance of the Deity, or that aspect by which the Deity is most recognizable.

In jubilation, Klein quotes from Psalm 139: "If I ascend up into heaven, thou art there; if I make my bed in hell, behold thou art there." These words, which King David addressed to the chief musician, contain the very key of Spinozan philosophy. They are, in their concept of God's omnipresence, paradigm of Spinozan pantheism. The quotation is followed by two lines which complement it:

> Thou art everywhere; a pillar to thy sanctuary
> is every blade of grass.

The Deity, in the Spinozan universe, is present in each atom, is at once sanctuary and essence. But again, it would be possible to give the words a dualistic interpretation: the sanctuary, the physical part of the blade of grass, could be seen as garment, as shell, for the life within, for the divine essence. Whether Klein is aware of the ambiguity in his metaphor is a moot question. He was probably less interested in fine points of theology than in the basic idea of immanence. It was a revelation to him that God could be sought in the totality of the universe, and he rejoiced because he could see the germ of such an approach to theology in earlier Judaic writings. "Go to the ant, thou sluggard," Klein reiterates from the Bible, "seek thou an audience with God. . . ." The divine principle, according to Spinoza, may be found in the humblest being. Klein, no doubt, sees in this a development of earlier sentiments: the Proverbs of King Solomon marvel at the wisdom that permeates creation. "Go to the ant, thou sluggard; consider her ways, and be wise."[13]

In Poem 8, Klein also takes the opportunity to make clear the basis on which his oecumenism rests. His declaration of brotherly love is all-embracing, and it is surely not by chance that there are in his statement of principle strong Christian connotations:

> I am thy son, O Lord, and brother to all that
> lives am I.

The echo of Leviticus merges with a Spinozan point of view: Moses was told, " . . . thou shalt love thy neighbour as thyself."[14] Spinoza says: "It cannot . . . be denied that he who by God's command loves his neighbour as himself is truly obedient and blessed according to the law, whereas he who hates his neighbour or neglects him is rebellious and obstinate."[15] In part four of the *Ethica*, Spinoza explains that man has a built-in desire to promote what he deems to be good and that, if he perceives reality adequately, he will know that his own good is best served when he lives in harmony with other human beings. Klein feels that in loving his fellow-beings, he loves part of creation, part of God. The rose, Klein says, is his own "blood and flesh." He appears to interpret Spinoza's idea concerning the oneness of the universe thus: since all individuals are essentially of one substance, to promote someone else's well-being means that one also promotes the true well-being of one's extended self.

The idea of the oneness of all existence is also at the centre of the final lines in Poem 8. Here too, for the first time, Klein makes a pronouncement that appears to offer a philosophical basis for the commandment "Thou shalt not kill."

> . . . thou art the world, and I am part thereof;
> he who does violence to me, verily sins against
> the light of day; he is made a deicide.

> Howbeit, even in dust I am resurrected, and
> even in decay I live again. . . .

An analysis of this passage shows that Klein was a thorough-going Spinozan as far as basic pantheism was concerned: in the Spinozan universe, all things, the light of day, the human being and the dust, are part of the Deity. It may then be asked why, in this case, a transformation of matter from one form of divine manifestation to another should be considered deicide. I think that Klein's words concerning deicide can be explained only if one concedes that he introduced here a concept of evolution. Clearly, in a pantheistic universe, one can look upon an action which turns a human being to dust as murder of the divine only if one is convinced that such a change is counteracting a divine progress; that is, if one believes that the essence of the divine resides especially in the life-producing energies that constantly strive toward a more highly developed form of existence, toward more and more consciousness. The most potent energies known within living creatures are working toward prolongation of life and the evolution of more highly conscious life. Klein seems to say that to reduce to dust a human being, the most highly developed organism on earth, affronts this progress. It is "deicide" because it brings an organism which is part of the Deity from a condition in which there is more consciousness, more life, to one in which there is less.

Deicide, as Klein later put it, is "the unspeakable nefas" which is "possible only in its attempt, not in its perpetration."[16] Divine energy cannot be stifled completely. Even the dust, to some extent, partakes of it. In Spinoza's concept, the entire universe is, in a sense, alive. Klein may have been aware also of other theories. According to Leibnitz, for instance, the dust itself is endowed with a certain amount of the *vis viva*, and modern science confirms that energy resides in all matter. When Klein says "Even in the dust I am resurrected," he echoes this thought, and he seems to imply also that the atoms of the dust can reassemble into higher organisms; the building activity of the divine, the life-producing energy continues.

To reverse the action of this power, by an act of will to put oneself outside its design is the unspeakable sin. Once Klein's meaning in this is understood, there can be little doubt concerning his ideas on the role of evil: that which is considered contrary to the essential activity of God, of the life-producing energy, cannot, at the same time, be ordained by Him. For Klein, the act of destruction which is directed against the individual part of creation affronts its entirety, its very essence: "He who does violence to me, verily sins against the light of day."

The sequence "Out of the Pulver and the Polished Lens" was reprinted in the anthology *New Provinces* (1936) and in Klein's collection of poems *Hath not a Jew . . .* (1940). Marshall pointed out that in the latter book the sentence concerning deicide was omitted, but that the idea reappeared later in *The Second Scroll*.[17] This raises two questions: what prompted Klein to delete the sentence in 1940, and why did he reinstate the idea in 1949? One cannot exclude the possibility that the change is merely aesthetic; perhaps Klein felt the poem would read better without this line. Then, it is also possible that, by 1940, he had rejected Spinozan philosophy; he may have felt the intensity of evil in the world precluded the belief that mankind partook of the divine. Against this, however, speaks the fact that the rest of the poem which clearly expresses Spinozan outlook was left intact. Another possibility suggests itself. The collection of poems, unlike *The Canadian Forum* and *New Provinces*, was designed to reach a wide public. Many of the readers were likely to be orthodox Jews. The sentence

> he who does violence to me, verily sins against
> the light of day; he is made a deicide.

could very easily be misunderstood as blasphemy. In 1949, when Klein voiced the same idea, he did so in a prose work which gave him the opportunity to elaborate his thoughts. At that time, he added a remark which, as we shall see, made it possible for orthodox readers to interpret the idea to their own satisfaction. I believe that the third explanation carries most weight.

In 1931, Klein published in *The McGilliad* an interesting short poem, "Exorcism Vain." The framework of this poem is the old Cabalistic belief that the Tetragrammaton may be used to exorcise inimical demons, but the thought conveyed here is modern and in accord with Klein's intellectual development. "The tongue has faltered," we are told. The holy name has been mispronounced. Because of this, the magic circle in which the demons could be isolated is broken and "The ghouls return to fructify their lemans."

It seems fairly certain that Klein equated the mispronouncing of the Tetragrammaton with man's attitude to religion and to life in general: the incorrect "pronouncement" of the Name makes it impossible for the Cabalist to banish the demons; it is because human beings falter, are unable to spell out correctly in their deeds and style of life a comprehension of the divine principle, that all kinds of horror are loose among the nations, that evil breeds and multiplies. Klein uses an image as hideous as it is powerful to drive home this point. Ghouls, in Mohammedan lore, are evil spirits that prey on corpses. In Klein's poem they come to fructify their lemans, their paramours, presumably the dead. In other words, those who are dead—spiritually dead (one may hear in this an echo of T. S. Eliot's thunder)—become a breeding ground for evil.

When this poem is read in conjunction with the Spinoza poems, it becomes clear enough what Klein meant. The spiritually dead are those who are unable to understand the divine nature of creation and thus cannot express adequate respect for the dignity of other creatures. Their attempts to worship in accordance with old custom, to live the good life in accordance with traditional attitudes, will remain futile. They can only come to life, and the selfishness and pride that prey upon their hearts will only be banished, when they will find enough courage to acknowledge unequivocally the true nature of the divine Law, when the Name of God will no longer be "mispronounced." Meanwhile, we are told, there is terror; there is tragedy in spite of all efforts.

The mispronouncement of the syllable
Conclusive renders the good deed undone—
Alas, the hesitancy in the call,
The stutter in the tetragrammaton. . . .

"Design for Mediaeval Tapestry," another sequence poem, was published in the same year in the *American Caravan*.[18] In each of the poems we find an example of life as it is lived in conditions where, as Klein might put it, the Tetragrammaton is being mispronounced. We are shown a panorama of medieval scenes. Men waste their lives steeped in gloom, in an atmosphere of futility from which there seems no escape. They either debase their lives with acts of hostility against their fellow men, or, incapable of asserting their dignity, they allow their lives to wither.

The despondency which speaks from these pages seems to indicate that Klein had, by this point, taken cognizance of Spinoza's view that the divine universe is not concerned with the fate of the individual.

According to Spinoza, all appetites are natural and justified. In the state of nature, wrong-doing is impossible; or, if anyone does wrong, it is to himself, not to another. Good and evil, in this philosophy, are relevant only to the self and are not absolute.[19] In other words, the individual is important only to himself and cannot hope to be loved as an entity by the divine of which he is a part. This idea, which Spinoza expounded in the *Tractatus Politicus*, comes dangerously close to the most ruthless of later relativist theories, such as, for instance, that of the logical positivists. These declared meaningless the metaphysical propositions which traditionally had furnished reliable standards of moral conduct. Spinozan philosophy appears, however, to differ from such theories when it is viewed in conjunction with ideas he had voiced previously in the *Tractatus Theologico-politicus*, for instance, where a concept of absolute ethics is implied: it is man's duty to honour God. To honour Him is to obey Him.[20] In order to obey, a knowledge of His Law is required. He who acquires this knowledge, acquires adequate ideas of reality and thus knows that his true well-being is best promoted if he lives in harmony with his fellow-man. Spinoza felt that the idea of Godhood was inscribed in the human heart, that is, in the human mind,[21] and that in this he was in accord with prophecies in Deuteronomy and in Jeremiah and with the Psalmist who sings,

I delight to do thy will, O my God:
Yea, thy law is within my heart.[22]

If a man fulfilled his duty to love God, he furthered not only his own welfare; he was bound to lead a socially acceptable life. Spinoza did not think that beyond this the individual was protected by Providence. The welfare of the individual, in Spinoza's view, was not of specific importance to the Deity.

With the discovery of Spinoza's basic premise, Klein had experienced ecstatic joy: he had found that the existence of the Deity was no longer a matter of faith and conjecture. It was a reality. But he found himself also in a world that seemed orphaned, deprived of that Providence to which the individual could turn for aid. Here, Spinoza's philosophy offered no solace. Though the natural laws continued their work, man in his longing for justice and comfort seemed as much alone as the inhabitant of a deist universe from which the Prime Mover had withdrawn. Klein's desolate view of the world is reflected in his writings.

We have no certain date for this sequence of poems. Whether Klein wrote "Design for Mediaeval Tapestry" before he became acquainted with Spinoza's ideas, or somewhat later, in a time of disillusionment, is uncertain. The picture he sketches at the opening of this sequence is one of creatures preying one upon the other. The weak, as Klein perceives them here, are without hope.

Somewhere a hungry muzzle rooted.
The frogs among the sedges croaked,
Into the night a screech-owl hooted.

A clawed mouse squeaked and struggled, choked.
The wind pushed antlers through the bushes.
Terror stalked through the forest, cloaked.

Was it a robber broke the bushes?
Was it a knight in armoured thews,
Walking in mud, and bending rushes?

Was it a provost seeking Jews?

No help is promised or expected. For human beings, a melioration of conditions would be possible if the divine covenant inscribed in their hearts were heeded. But the persecutors seem oblivious of the covenant's existence, or attempt to destroy it by burning books which spread its principle. We are shown

The market-place and faggot-fire—
A hangman burning God's true word.

Whether pagan or Christian, the persecutors are unable to read the natural law, the divine Law inscribed in the heart, and they follow narrow doctrines which teach them to hate.

The second poem in the series, "Reb Zadoc has Memories," catalogues the various humiliations to which mediaeval Jewry was subjected. We are introduced to

The Judengasse and its stench
Rising from dark and guarded alleys
Where Jew is neighbour to harlot wench

Perforce ecclesiastic malice.

There are, of course, always a few men whose intellect can decipher the divine message and who are able to formulate it. Such, for instance, is the poet, the troubadour, who dreams of the superior human being, the "parfait knight." But his word is perverted in the actions of the real knights, the crusaders who ravage Europe, who plunder, burn, and rape as they traverse the towns. A short poem in this series, "Judith Makes Comparisons," shows us this contrast most effectively. The divinely inspired word is being "mispronounced" in the actions of men.

The sardonic humour of these lines seems Heine-inspired.

Judith had heard a troubadour
Singing beneath a castle-turret
Of truth, chivalry, and honour,
Of virtue, and of gallant merit,—
Judith had heard a troubadour
Lauding the parfait knightly spirit,
Singing beneath the ivied wall.
The cross-marked varlet Judith wrestled
Was not like these at all, at all. . . .

Ignorance of the law of nature, the Law of God, exists, however, also among the Jews in Klein's "Mediaeval Tapestry." Deluded by their teachers, they mistake the iniquity of their fellow-men who cannot read the divine message for the will of the Deity, and they suffer silently and without resistance. The Hebrews Klein describes here moved their lips "in pious anguish. / They made no sound. They never stirred."

The poems explore different attitudes found among Jews who faced persecution. Some, like the "clean-shaved traitor-Jew" in "Reb Zadoc has Memories," simply ran away and joined their enemies. Like the apostate in "Simeon Takes Hints from His Environs," they came to the conclusion that, living in a Christian world, the prudent thing to do was to join the majority. Most Jews, however, kept their faith and suffered: the stoic in "Nahum-this-also-is-for-the-good Ponders" is convinced that

The wrath of God is just: His punishment
Is most desirable.

He tries to rationalize his misfortunes because punishment from a loving father is more bearable than indifference. The more pragmatic man in "Isaiah Epicure Avers" knows

That pain does render flesh most sore and hectic
That lance-points prick; that scorched bones hiss;
That thumb screws agonize, and that a martyr
Is mad if he considers these things bliss.

But he, too, though he cannot understand the reason why calamities should come upon men, seems to believe that they are ordained by the Deity:

> Seek reasons; rifle your theology;
> Philosophize, expend your dialectic;
> Decipher and translate God's diary;
>
> Discover causes primal and eclectic;
> I cannot.

There are those, like Ezekiel the Simple, who believe that a set formula and superstitious practices will summon God's intervention; and there are the more sophisticated, like Solomon Talmudi, who hope through untiring study and subtle exegesis of the old texts "to move the soul with sacred lever / and lift the heart to God in very deed." They hope that relief will come when individual Jews gain deeper insight. But Solomon Talmudi's efforts, Klein tells us, come to nought. He may have gleaned the "essence and quintessence of the book"; but his knowledge is dispersed by the winds as his manuscripts go up in flames. God helps neither those who misunderstand His Law nor those who understand and spread His word. Neither have those who live indeed a blameless life any assurance of divine help. Esther, in the poem "Esther Hears Echoes of His Voice," mourns a man of innocence and excellence.

> Whether he lulled a child or crooned the laws,
> And sacred as the eighteen prayers, so even
> His voice. His voice was so. His voice that was . . .

The good life offered no security: "His blood is spilled like wine."

It would be a mistake to assume that Klein here is giving us no more than examples of emotion and thoughts that have stirred individual Jews throughout the Middle Ages and since.

"Mediaeval Tapestry" reflects Klein's own pessimism, his own sombre speculations. There is divinity. Nature is divine. But strangely, strength is lacking in individual creatures. They "mispronounce" the Tetragrammaton, and no spark of divine energy helps to enlighten them. God ignores the lamentations of men. "How long, O Lord, will Israel's heart be riven?" cries Job in Klein's poem "Job Reviles." He receives no answer. Prayers may ring out toward Heaven:

The moon has left her vigil; Lucifer fades.
Whither shall we betake ourselves, O Father?
Whither to flee? And where to find our aids?

The wrath of people is like foam and lather,
Risen against us. Wherefore, Lord, and why?
The winds assemble; the cold and hot winds gather

To scatter us. They do not heed our cry.
The sun rises and leaps the red horizon,
And like a bloodhound swoops across the sky.

The processes of nature take their course, inexorable, undisturbed by the anguished questionings of the human soul.

"Design for Mediaeval Tapestry" was published in 1931, the year in which appeared "Out of the Pulver and the Polished Lens." Its central theme, the indifference of the Deity toward individual creatures and the unconcerned progress of nature, suggests disillusionment with Spinozan philosophy. But, of course, other influences could have produced a mood of despondency in Klein. He was well informed. The rise of national socialism in Germany could not be ignored by anyone concerned with Jewish affairs.

In spite of the image of the Christian which we find in "Design for Mediaeval Tapestry," Klein was certainly not specifically anti-Christian. In the year in which this sequence appeared, Klein also published a poem "Calvary," in which Christian imagery and symbolism are used with great effect.

The martyrdom of Jesus is a process to which the entire world is subject:

> Upon these trees was Autumn crucified . . .
> Do you not see the thorns, the ready bier
> Of leaves, the stains of blood? . . . Do you not hear
> His *Eli Eli* echo? . . . It has died.

Klein is always aware of suffering. He sees it diffused throughout nature; and Spinoza's teachings that in an ecstatic moment had made everything appear simple and joyful offer no explanation and no solution. The universe is divine; it is glorious; but it is impersonal and unconcerned; and it suffers. If, as Spinoza says, God comprises all substance, then He is a suffering God.

Klein feels no more secure at the mercy of natural laws that take no cognizance of the individual than Hardy did when he saw himself at the mercy of inscrutable chance. Spinoza, at this point, seems to give no more spiritual support than one may expect from crudest atheism. In 1932, yet another cycle of poems appeared, entitled "Talisman in Seven Shreds,"[23] consisting of seven Petrarchan sonnets. In it one finds ample evidence of anguish and questionings without hope. Klein had become extremely bitter.

The poems in "Talisman in Seven Shreds" are conceived with the golem legend in mind. Without actually relating it, they dwell on some of its possible philosophical implications. To some extent, this is a weakness in the poems, for the golem

legend is not sufficiently well known, and Klein writes as if
he took it for granted that his readers were familiar with it.

"Golem" is a Hebrew word that means "lifeless matter."
The idea that a creature, a golem, could be formed from clay
and then be brought to life goes back in Jewish folklore to
Talmudic times. In the Middle Ages it assumed importance
among the mystics who studied Cabala and, in particular, were
interested in the alphabet combinations in *The Book of Creation*,
which, they felt, could help them reach out toward God's
infinity. Since God makes himself known through creation,
they tried to seek Him through creative acts. Sometimes they
formed golems which, in moments of mystic ecstasy, ceased to
be lifeless. "It was only later that the popular legend attributed
to the golem an existence outside the ecstatic consciousness,"
writes Gershom G. Scholem. "It would appear as though in
the original conception the golem came to life only while the
ecstasy of his creator lasted."[24]

Great names in Jewish history are connected with some
forms of the golem legends:

> The Eleventh Century Bible exegesist Rashi, being thoroughly
> saturated with Jewish Cabala and with the supernaturalism of
> the mediaeval Christian world, even tried to give the account
> a dubious religious sanction:

> "They, Hanina and Oshaga [two rabbis, mentioned in the
> Talmud, who, with the help of a mystic formula, could produce
> a living calf], used to combine the letters of the name by which
> the universe was created. This is not considered to be forbidden
> magic, for the words of God were brought into being through
> His Holy Name."

> Jewish legend even has Rashi's great contemporary, the
> poet–philosopher of Valencia, Solomon ibn Gabirol, create a
> maid-servant golem. When the king heard of it he wished to
> put the Jewish poet to death for practising black magic, but
> Gabirol demonstrated to the king's royal satisfaction that the
> creature he made was not human, and forthwith he returned
> her to dust.[25]

Ausubel tells us that, by the time of the late Renaissance, golem legends were widespread. One of the best known was that of the golem of Chelm, which was said to have been created by the sixteenth-century Cabalist Elijah. He, too, it was said, had brought the creature to life by means of God's "Ineffable Name" which was written on parchment and placed on the golem's forehead. The creature turned out to be destructive and was returned to dust when the rabbi took from it the mystic parchment.

A comparatively well known story is that of the golem of Prague. It is connected with the historical Rabbi Yehuda Loew, the "Maharal," who came to Prague in A.D. 1572. Together with other Cabalists, he is said to have made a golem on the bank of the river Vltava and with magic circles and incantations and a quotation from Genesis to have brought him to life.

This golem had enormous strength, could understand human speech, and was absolutely obedient. But he could not speak, and thus the townsfolk thought him an idiot. He served the rabbi well in his fight against the enemies of the Jews. In particular, he rendered harmless and exposed a man who was about to fabricate one of the many blood accusations which were levelled against the Jewish community of Prague. When King Rudolf II issued decrees protecting the Jews against calumny, Rabbi Loew decided that the golem was no longer needed, and, reversing the magic formulae, returned the creature to its former state of lifeless clay.

The legend that Rabbi Loew's golem lies buried under pages of old prayerbooks in the attic of the most famous of European synagogues, the Altneuschul of Prague, has persisted into the twentieth century and is the subject of "Dem Golem auf der Spur," an exceptionally interesting essay by Egon Erwin Kisch.[26] In part, this essay appears to relate Kisch's personal experience as he tried to unravel some of the mysteries surrounding the golem story; in part it consists of historical and bibliographical information. Kisch also offers a modern political interpretation of the golem legend, an approach which Klein adopted in an article in the *Canadian Jewish Chronicle* of January 1939.

Among the literature referred to in Kisch's essay is a story about the golem which was published by Clemens Brentano in the *Dramaturgischer Beobachter* (Vienna) of 1814. It is clear, therefore, that the German Romantics were aware of the golem legend and that Mary Shelley too may well have known of it when she wrote her *Frankenstein*. Kisch believes that the golem legend is of importance in Goethe's Faust and in his "Zauberlehrling," and he sees parallels between the golem story and Hugo's *Notre-Dame de Paris*.

It is the tale of the golem of Prague that Klein had chiefly in mind when he wrote his sonnets. But his speculations go beyond the framework of the legend. The first poem, "Syllogism," compares the golem to fate, to Ananke, the Corinthian deity who represented necessity. He becomes the symbol of unfeeling mechanisms which govern the workings of the universe. The lines reverberate with intense fear. If the universe is an automation, alive, yet like a golem, obeying laws of necessity without regard to the welfare of man, and if, as Spinoza teaches, this universe is divine, what hope is there for man?

The second poem, "Embryo of Dusts," makes direct reference to the Rabbi Loew legend. He had raised a golem from "embryo dusts" that he might help the beleaguered Jewish community. Klein muses on the activities of historical anti-semites.[27] What champions, he reflects, has Israel had to counteract them? A mere golem it was that gave it help; help that was only temporary and ineffective in the long run. The idea which the poem leaves in the reader's mind is this: Whatever protection there is for mankind in general, and Jews in particular, rests in golem-like blind mechanisms.

The third poem, "Tetragrammaton," refers to those versions of the golem legend where the sages administered life by placing into the golem's mouth a parchment on which was written the name of God, the Tetragrammaton. In Klein's poem, however, the Tetragrammaton is placed into the creature's mouth not only to lend life; it is also the golem's ward, his responsibility. Thus, Klein sees the golem in all physical creation. The divine power that imbues it with life also places upon it a responsibility. In the poem, the parchment with the holy name is desecrated as soon as it touches the golem's mouth.[28] "A golem held the Lord's name, even as spit." Unequal to his task of guarding the parchment, the golem swallows it. It is gone, marred, desecrated. By analogy, one may say that creation is somehow unable to exist in accordance with the divine covenant. Man's greed is such that he arrogates to himself, "swallows" powers which he is intended to hold only in trust. As a result, the essentially divine aspect of his existence is violated.

This poem represents a low point in Klein's spiritual development. He has reached bottom in an abyss of disillusionment. If Spinoza is right, if the physical is indeed part of the divine, then, somehow, this physical part of creation manages to desecrate the higher aspect of itself; the golem part seems to triumph over the enlivening spiritualizing power. Obviously, this is no longer truly Spinozan philosophy.

In the following sonnet, "*Fons Vitae*," doubts concerning the divinity of matter are openly pronounced. Is the secret of vitality truly hidden in the physical part of creation? Klein wonders whether there is "life sanguine behind the scabrous epiderm." The golems which Ibn Gabirol and Maimonides fashioned seemed to indicate that such men knew the germ of life was hidden in physical substance (or, at any rate, that they imagined they had such knowledge). Klein searches for their secret, but of course he wants more than Ibn Gabirol and Maimonides ever knew.

> ...These men, then knew the pristine germ.
> *Sanctum sanctorum!* how can I ever pry
> behind the mystic chromosome? Grasp you,
> even as Tycho Brahe, by raking the sky?

What he wants to grasp is "the pristine germ," the *vis viva* of the dust, proof of the divine nature of the universe. His reference to Tycho de Brahe may give us a clue to the meaning of these lines.

Tycho de Brahe, the sixteenth-century astronomer, lived in Prague at the time of Rabbi Loew. Max Brod wrote a historical novel which is based on Tycho's life. This book, *Tycho Brahes Weg zu Gott*, was published in 1916, and its English translation, *The Redemption of Tycho Brahe*,[29] in 1928, four years before Klein published his "Talisman in Seven Shreds." It is probable that Klein knew the novel when he wrote his poems, for among his handwritten notes on the golem (notes which appear to have been collected for a projected and partly written novel), there is the entry "Max Brod's book." In this book, a portentous meeting takes place between de Brahe and Rabbi Loew.

Max Brod shows de Brahe as a kind of spiritual ancestor of Spinoza, a man who finds God in all creation. For Tycho the astronomer the real course of the stars was "a clear presentation of the divine law in the ordering of the world, a most exalted harmony, an apprehended unity of Creation, inscribed in characters of fire."[30] If Klein knew these lines, Tycho de Brahe must have become for him a Spinoza figure. When he asks whether the pristine germ, the secret of life, the true reality, can be grasped even as Tycho grasped it, or tried to grasp it, "by raking the sky," he is then asking whether, after all, it is possible for man to grasp it with speculation, by philosophical and scientific means, through logic; and he is doubtful:

> Can grace after meat in terms of x and y
> suggest the dark formula, the vital cue?

Can philosophy, after all, replace religion? Can it find the answers which religion failed to provide?

Klein begins to doubt the entire system. The physical world, with all its obvious deficiencies, seems too far removed from his concept of the divine. He can no longer accept that unity between them which would allow man to approach the divine through logic, through scientific investigation. He has, at this moment, come to look upon the theory of such a unity as just another of many religious ideas, one that is to be studied and doubted like any of the traditional sets of dogma. In the next sonnet, "Enigma," Klein questions whether pantheist theory can validly replace the tenets of the old faith. Jews, he reasons, have withstood calumny and persecutions of the most virulent kind. Is there not, perhaps, a sign in this that the faith for which they suffered gave them a higher purpose? Did they outlive their trials because, after all, "the finger of the Lord's right hand" made them a symbol of divine intent? Or is their survival the result of forces innate; did material, golem-like nature contain the mechanisms which allowed the Jewish people to survive?

In the sonnet "Guide to the Perplexed," pantheism is put on the same level as other sets of ideas, other religious dogmas, which are questioned and doubted; only its harsh mechanistic aspects seem to be accepted as a dreaded certainty.

do you your genuflexions to the Rose.

     .   .   .   .   .   .

Voices: He is the Anvil and the Smith
He is comminglement of yeas and noes.
He died and then trisected he arose.
The Rock of Ages is a monolith.
The kennels of the hounds of God are full—
Aye, what a baying at the moon is there!

Adoration of the rose, of divine nature, has become an alternative among other systems of theology. But the fear that the universe consists of matter unconcerned with human values is overwhelming:

What, then, is good and true and beautiful?
The tongue is bitter when it must declare:
matter is chaos, mind is chasm, fool,
the work of golems stalking in nightmare...

Philosophy led Klein on the road to atheism. He had gone as far as he could go.

The despair that speaks in these last lines becomes even more poignant when one considers the ironic title of the poem, "Guide to the Perplexed." Maimonides, in his famous *Moreh*, his *Guide of the Perplexed*, combined Aristotle's theory of the universe with Jewish theology. According to Isaac Broydé, Maimonides shows "that there is nothing in Scripture or rabbinical literature, if properly explained, that contradicts true philosophy."[31] To Maimonides, as to Aristotle, "the whole universe of existing things is like one organism in which everything hangs together."[32] To this organism, Maimonides then adds Jewish theology. Philosophy did not taint Maimonides' understanding of what was "good and true and beautiful." Aristotle thought that man's good lay in his being happy, and that happiness came about when a man preferred above everything else to be "engaged in virtuous action and contemplation."[33] Maimonides accepted this axiom; and he pointed out that such action and such contemplation were the natural consequence when a man followed the teachings of Judaism.

> Whoever serves God out of love, occupies himself with the study of the Law and the fulfilment of commandments and walks in the path of wisdom, impelled by no external motive whatever, moved neither by fear of calamity nor by the desire to obtain material benefits; such a man does what is truly right because it is truly right, and ultimately, happiness comes to him as a result of his conduct.[34]

Affinities between Aristotle's philosophy and Jewish faith helped Maimonides to function as a guide of those whose minds were perplexed with questions. When Klein had first contemplated Spinozan theory, he had felt that its ethics were reconcilable with faith. But here, the mechanistic aspect of philosophic teachings was looming into view and it overwhelmed him. By guiding men to philosophy, he now realized, he was guiding them into the nightmare of the perplexed.

In the final sonnet of the sequence, "Immortal Yearnings," we see Klein determined to escape the nightmare: no one can be certain that the nightmare is reality. In "Out of the Pulver and the Polished Lens," he had shown that acceptance of Spinoza spelled liberation, joy, peace. The poems in that cycle were an expression of certainty. Here, there is no certainty, no joy; neither is there peace of mind; philosophy has unleashed terror. There is only one way in which its doctrines can be made less menacing: philosophy must be placed on the same level as the doctrines of traditional faith. It must be questioned and doubted. Is there, truly, only unconcerned nature, or is there a separate spirit, a deity interested in individual human souls? Who, after all, can tell what is reality? Klein, at this point, seems to find solace in uncertainty.

> But I will take a prong in hand, and go
> over old graves and test their hollowness:
> be it the spirit or the dust I hoe
> only at doomsday's sunrise will I know.

A talisman is a charm which is expected to benefit its owner. The talisman offered here is torn and has lost this efficacy. "Talisman in Seven Shreds" can only serve to deprive the reader of such peace of mind as he may have, agnosticism being offered as the only relief.

It may be suggested that the comfortless theories of Spinoza were not alone in shaping Klein's frame of mind as it appeared in the poetry of 1932. Klein was studying law at the University of Montreal and it is possible—disillusionment being almost always a fashionable sentiment in the university—that he was influenced by the perennial issues of his immediate environment. At this time, however, the discontent of young intellectuals had especially serious, global problems to feed upon, and Marxism professed to have the cures. It may be argued that Klein's agnosticism was actually the result of Marxist influences which were gathering strength throughout the world. The depression, at this time, was causing unemployment with all its attendant suffering, and no sensitive individual could remain unscathed by the problems of a tottering economy, by the lethargy, the wastefulness and corruption, by the great hopelessness that became so characteristic of the nineteen-thirties. Klein does not appear to have suffered personal want, but it could hardly be supposed that he did not regard with interest any faction that proclaimed as its aim the betterment of social and economic conditions.

The new decade, crisis-ridden, cynical, morally and economically bankrupt, furnished ample argument for materialist philosophies. Klein's agnosticism blended with current atheist ideologies, of which Marxism was the most prominent. They confirmed his fears. Spinoza had taught him to worship creation as a whole. What was he to do when he perceived that, all around him, creation maintained a neutrality which, in effect, allowed iniquities to flourish? At this point, Klein certainly found himself in sympathy with Marxist teachings concerning the nature of reality. It does not follow, however, that he had arrived at his conclusions on the basis of Marxist theories. His approach to social ills and the imagery in the poetry of 1932 lack the stamp of Marxist doctrine.

Thoughts of revolution were undoubtedly in Klein's mind when he wrote the short poem "Earthquake"; but the symbolism used is Judaeo-Christian, and the revolution, one feels, is to take place in the heart rather than in the streets:

> "I think I hear a trumpet overhead.
>   A thumping on the lid—a white ass ride ..."
> The corpses murmured, stirred, "We are not dead!"
>   And turned and slept upon their other side.

Men cannot be resurrected into a more meaningful existence because they refuse to believe that a change, a resurrection is necessary. There is the dissonance of Yeats's "Second Coming" in this and a great deal of Eliot's irony. The dead referred to here are very much those of "The Waste Land." The Messianic trumpet seems to be calling them to an effective utterance of the Tetragrammaton rather than to the class struggle.

Another short poem, which was published with "Earthquake," is "Philosopher's Stone."

> "So have I spent a life-time in my search
>   To make, as it is said,
> Noble from base. Life left me in the lurch,
>   And dropt me with the dead;
> And now I find it, buried in the church:
>   It stands right overhead. . . ."

If the persona here is the capitalist whose entire life has been squandered in a search for the "philosopher's stone," that is, for means whereby to produce riches, the portrait drawn is certainly not a reproachful, Marxist one. The situation is seen sympathetically from the speaker's point of view. The philosopher's stone that was to produce gold (noble from base), has turned out to be a tombstone. The way of life that was geared to a search for wealth has proved futile, has led to spiritual deadness. Since the philosopher's stone of the alchemists was also connected with a search for the elixir of life, one may, perhaps, interpret the lines also more accurately in this sense: the man who sought a fuller life through accumulation of wealth finds that his philosophy results in a denial of life. The poem, read in this way, is certainly expressive of socialist thinking, if we use the term "socialist" in a very wide sense. The speaker's irony, used so effectively against himself, rouses one's compassion rather than one's antagonism.

In the philosopher's stone, Klein has created one of his most successful compressed metaphors, and an interpretation of the poem cannot, of course, overlook the fact that it may be understood also in a quite different way. The philosopher's stone could be a symbol of idealism and supreme achievement. The man who tries to lift himself from a base existence to a more noble one finds his efforts frustrated. The philosopher's stone turns into a tombstone: the idealist's work is turned into failure. The Church, which here may stand for society, for authority, for spiritual leadership in general, seals off the ambitions and hopes of the individual.

The poem which shows more clearly than any other that, in 1932, Klein's agnosticism and sense of disillusionment were not rooted in Marxist atheism is the "Soirée of Velvel Kleinburger." Among the poems that were not included in Klein's published collections, the "Soirée" is one of the best known. There is in this poem striking evidence of T. S. Eliot's influence; and this, in itself, gives some indication how Klein viewed the malaise of his environment.

Velvel Kleinburger is the little man who allows circumstances to blight his life. Klein introduces him in the person of a Jewish tailor, whose "soirée" takes place in dingy, fly-infested back-room dens of delicatessen stores and barber shops, where he eats from unwashed plates, perhaps meets a whore, and dreams of gaining Hollywood-style successes via a deck of dirty cards. His taste runs to diamond rings, a chauffeur-driven Rolls-Royce, and a woman in ultra-fashionable apparel boasting "jewels as large as wondrous eyes / The eyes of Og, the giant-king of Bashan." When the last game is over and Velvel leaves the smokey back-room parlour, he remains in a stupor:

... dreaming, he rises, and
Buttons his coat, coughs in his raised lapel,
Gropes his way home; he rings a raucous bell.

Social conditions, like a huge swamp, seem to suck humanity into the depth, and men like Velvel allow it to happen, continue to flounder in that strange somnambulist state.

The poem diagnoses the fundamental ills of the time: emotional deadness and greed, two conditions of the mind which are not mutually exclusive, as might be supposed, but, on the contrary, seem to intensify each other. A remedy is suggested, and it is made very clear that it does not lie in social revolution. While Velvel lingers at the gaming table, he may dream of violent change, but he knows that, in the end, it will not better his lot:

(Ho! Ho! the social revolutions on a table of roulette!)
.   .   .   .

When the deck is opened
The pauper once more gave
His foes the kings and aces
And took himself the knave.

Klein obviously felt that revolutionary change was likely to betray the people; that the condition of the poor would not be improved. The remedy lay within man himself.

Perhaps a clue may be found in Klein's comparison of the jewels, which Velvel desires in his dreams, with the eyes of Og. The significance of this comparison reaches beyond the obvious reference to size. Og, the giant king, was one of the Amorite rulers who had to be defeated before the Israelites could settle in the Promised Land.[35] Thus the jewels denote barbaric splendour, luxuries which bring danger. The desire for them has to be conquered before the promised land of a more dignified existence may be entered.

The solution for Velvel's problems is stated also more overtly when a phantom appears and points to the holy script. Velvel, of course, cannot be roused.

O good my brother, should one come to you
And knock upon the door at mid of night

And show you, writ in scripture, black on white,
That this is no way for a man to do?—
What a pale laughter from these ghosts; and "Who
Are you, my saint, to show us what is right?

Make a fifth hand, and we will be contrite;
Shuffle the cards, be sociable, Reb Jew!"

The men around the gaming table, more ghostly, more dead than the apparition that comes to draw them back into life, cannot be reached. The ethics of traditional religion remain unheeded. One realizes that, no matter how skeptical Klein may have become in theological matters, he continues to look to Judaism for spiritual guidance, and his ethics are formed there rather than in any modern system of thought. The impression that Klein looks at the world from a religious rather than from a political point of view is strengthened when one contemplates how close, at this point, he was to T. S. Eliot. In "The Fire Sermon," Eliot showed us the public bar in Lower Thames Street

> Where fishermen lounge at noon: where the walls
> Of Magnus Martyr hold
> Inexplicable splendour of Ionian white and gold.

The edifice of the Church of Magnus Martyr towers silently above the idle, indolent crowds. In Klein's "Soirée" too, we find this silent pleading, a message which cannot penetrate the consciousness of the emotionally dead.

Religion had assured Klein that man was in the care of Providence. It held the key to the good life, the ethical life. In philosophy, Klein sought theological truth, and the concept of an immanent Deity gave him the certainty of God's existence. A synthesis was not easy. Thoughts of the unconcerned universe, that in a sense negates the value of virtue, plagued him. One can discern them behind the short poem "Divine Titillation," which sardonically dwells on the futility of human attempts to make offerings, to reach out toward the divine.

> O, what human chaff!
> Trying to tickle my feet
> With spires! . . . What conceit!
> Indeed you make me laugh!

"Anguish," in a playful way, sees all creation shaped into an expression of distress:

> The moon
> Is sudden grief
> Across a star-pricked sky . . .
> It is an interjection crying
> O! . . .

Perhaps these poems are too lighthearted in tone to be taken as an indication of any significance. Their humour may be considered proof that Klein, at the time of writing, was not seriously concerned with metaphysical speculation. One may assume that Klein, a young man passionately interested in many contemporary problems, was not always capable of expending his emotions on esoteric questions.

In 1933, he published "Murals For a House of God," a sequence of poems which contains good lines and resembles "Design for Mediaeval Tapestry" in that here, too, he is concerned with the persecution of Jews in the Middle Ages, and here, too, is the implication that the innocent suffer. But, on the whole, Klein was in these poems concerned with history rather than with metaphysics. Exceptions, perhaps, may be seen in the main poem, "Rabbi Yom Tob Harrangues His God" (which, under the title "Rabbi Yom-Tob of Mayence Petitions His God," appeared in *Poems* (1944) and will be discussed later) and in the poem "A Young Man Moans Alarm Before the Kiss of Death," which contains these remarkable lines:

Beneath disastrous stars we live. And yet
The Lord Omnipotent, Omniscient, He—
Blasphemy! Blasphemy! Let me choke it! Let
No sacrilege foam at my mouth, no plea
Assault the sky, assail the heavens no vain threat!

Critics may hold that the words are merely those of an invented character and that they do not represent Klein's own feeling. To me, however, they sound authentic, personal, the cry of one who cannot bear the thought that evil may come from or be tolerated willingly by God. The words are much opposed to traditional teachings, and this may be one reason why Klein would prefer to let a *persona* speak. His sentiments show a vague affinity with Spinoza's Proposition XXXIII in Part One of the *Ethica*, where it is said that "Things could not have been brought into being by God in any manner or in any order different from that which has in fact obtained," but the poem reflects in no way the complexity and subtlety of Spinoza's arguments, and thus accords neither with traditional Judaism nor with Spinozan philosophy.

The Spinozan concept still occupied a prominent position in Klein's mind; but it was no longer looked up to as a gospel to be spread with enthusiasm. When it was viewed in its entirety, it had, no doubt, proved too formidable, too devoid of hope, to be adopted wholeheartedly. Its sombre doctrine, however, still haunted Klein in 1936, as becomes evident in a short story, "Friends, Romans, Hungrymen." This is a satire in which an unemployed workman meets God, asks for help, but is ignored. The symbolism is obvious: the universe is not interested in the fate of the individual. Clearly, the Spinozan view was still before Klein's mind, but Spinoza is no longer considered a peerless hero.

Klein concentrated his attention on concrete issues, carried on campaigns on behalf of causes that were consistent (albeit not always to the same degree) with both religion and philosophy. The preservation of Jewish culture, a religious duty, was the object of undiminished zeal. This is fully within the spirit of Spinoza's *Ethica* which holds that self-preservation is the essence of the individual. Oecumenism, to some extent foreshadowed in the Messianic idea, seems to have been strengthened in Klein's mind by the pantheist theory of the oneness of the universe. Socialism, firmly rooted in Talmudic precepts, is justifiable on that same philosophical basis.

Thus Klein had no difficulty in shaping his social and political life. As far as practical issues were concerned, religion and philosophy bade him do the same things, and he followed their guidance with fervour. Only sometimes did he remember the unsolved riddles and fears, the question why Providence would not come to the rescue of innocent victims, the nightmare of mankind wandering its "solitary way," exiled from an Eden where God's voice was heard and understood.

The Influence of the Chassidim and the Cabala

3

That Klein was drawn to Chassidism is obvious, for his writings contain many direct references which leave no doubt as to his sympathies. But he was not a Chassid in the strict sense of the word. There are important aspects of the Chassidic movement which were as alien to Klein as they are to any emancipated Jew. For one thing, Klein seems to have craved a rational faith, one that an educated American of the twentieth century could accept, and the Chassids of Eastern Europe often thrived on superstitions.

A most important institution in the Chassidic community was the trust the individual placed in the zaddik, the holy man (often a descendant of the Baal Shem Tov), who was supposed to have mystical insight that allowed him to act as intermediary between the Deity and the common people. The Rebbes never promised miracles. But their followers believed they had superior powers.[1] This trait of Chassidism had no attraction for Klein. On the contrary: when he reviewed Martin Buber's *Tales of the Chassidim*,[2] he spoke deprecatingly of its "zaddicolatry." Klein felt that Buber's sympathy for the movement had led him to an idealization of the zaddiks, and this, apparently, he could not accept.

A basic trait of the Chassidim is their pronounced reliance on the emotions. Their worship is a reaching out toward God through experience, through total involvement; and great emphasis is placed on the emotional state of the individual.

Such an attitude is atypical of Klein. He can feel strongly, but he does not abandon the intellectual approach.

Klein is, nevertheless, close to the Chassidic movement, and he is in this by no means an isolated American writer. The revival of Chassidism has become a well-known phenomenon. Meyer Waxman, for instance, in his *History of Jewish Literature* (1960), says that "During recent decades, Hassidism has become a favorite subject with Jewish writers, scholars and thinkers. . . . In fact, as far as Jewish literature is concerned, we can say that there is a definite trend or current in it which we may call Neo-Hassidism, and Martin Buber is to be considered a leading interpreter of this current."[3] Klein is very much of this Chassidic revival. He seems to be interested in the Chassid's love of nature, in the determination to worship joyfully, and, ultimately, in the theology which gives rise to this love and determination.

Some of Klein's Chassidic poems were published in the early thirties. According to Palnick and Rome,[4] "Dance Chassidic," like "Out of the Pulver and the Polished Lens," appeared in 1931. It may have been composed at a time when Klein's admiration of Spinoza was at its height. But this need not surprise us. Both Spinoza and the Chassid believe that the Deity is ever present in creation. The Chassid, like Spinoza, who considers all substance divine, stands worshipping before nature. Unlike Spinoza, he does not think that nature is God; but he feels that God is in nature, and therefore he considers closeness to nature a state which affords man special closeness to God. Klein's mind seems always receptive to the basic concept of immanence. It is understandable that he felt attracted to the Chassidic tradition while intellectually he accepted Spinozan theory.

In 1932, he published "The Ballad of the Dancing Bear,"[5] the tale of a Chassid who draws to himself and his people the favour of God. This was the year which saw also the publication of "Talisman in Seven Shreds," in which lines of unrelieved pessimism glaringly contradict the story we find in the "Ballad."

Explanations of this discrepancy may vary. It is possible that the "Ballad" was written much earlier and that publication was delayed. It may also be that the "Ballad," like other early Chassidic poems, was written not so much as a statement of religious affinity than as a poem of folkloric, poetic content.

Klein's attitude toward Chassidism at the time of the early poems is not completely clear. It is, however, certain that considerable sympathy with Chassidism existed, and that it was again strongly in evidence toward the end of the decade. This development seems logical. In Chassidism, Klein found a faith in the immanence of God which did not leave the individual bereft of divine love. Here, as in Spinozan philosophy, there was a feeling of brotherhood that linked man to all creation; but here, too, was a special destiny vouchsafed to man, a messianic condition which he could attain eventually if he devoted sufficient effort. In other words, Chassidism had much of the attraction of Spinozan pantheism and none of its austerity. It fell short only in one important aspect: like other forms of traditional Judaism, it had to be accepted on trust. It rested on faith, not on logical speculation. What proof was there that the Divine within nature was actually concerned with the ultimate fate of the human species or the human individual?

In the thirties, Chassidic theology probably appealed to Klein as an ideal rather than as a faith which could take the place of philosophy. At the same time, Klein evidently found that certain aspects of Chassidic thinking were relevant to the predicaments of the Depression and the increasing uneasiness among Jews throughout the world. The Chassidic movement had first gained momentum because, in the early eighteenth century, the Jewish communities in Eastern Europe were emotionally and economically exhausted.[6] Chassidism taught them that through nature they could approach the restoring power of God; it also taught them that it was man's duty in spite of calamity to worship God in joy and to enjoy life. Traces of both ideas can be found in Klein's writings of the thirties.

The well-known "Diary of Abraham Segal, Poet," published in 1932, suggests most clearly that Klein turned to nature for its healing influence.[7] Although in theme and setting it does not belong to Klein's Chassidic poetry, we may discern in it an echo of Chassidic teaching, especially as it was enunciated by Rabbi Nachman, the Bratzlaver, the great-grandson of the Baal Shem Tov.

The poem gives an account of a day in the life of a young Montrealer. The time is that of the Depression. The place is a city blighted by the denaturalizing forces of urbanization and mechanization. This is a world in which

> They clipped the wings
> Of fiery seraphim
> And made of them—ye angels, weep!—
> Dusters.

Elemental forces, elemental passions are degraded, pressed into the service of petty routines. Abraham Segal, the poet, is caught in a round of dehumanizing activities. His day is spent in a bleak factory office among other low paid workers. His only diversion—the prattling of the boss's would-be cultured wife who comes to visit. At noon, his spirit is starved, eager to reach beyond its confines. He would worship. But where can he go? In these surroundings the soul's cry for comfort turns into a plea for food. At the North-Eastern, a cheap cafeteria, we hear it bleat: "Waiter, a plate of beans."

A pocket edition of Shakespeare brings temporary solace. But Abraham Segal soon returns to the sombre realities of his world, where priests promise salvation in the hereafter while their flocks wallow in drink and prostitution. A passage composed largely of Shakespearean quotations tells us of the populace and its "immortal longings," and we remember the Egyptian queen who had such longings when she too was on the brink of suicide.

Traditional religion, philosophy, politics, and economic success cannot be counted on to bring relief. Wherever Abraham

Segal turns, he finds blight. There is no communication between him and his kin. He flees, seeks escape and relief in the cinemas, the poolrooms, the dance halls, the lecture rooms, the political meetings. All—all turn out to be empty, vulgar, or platitudinous and boring. It is only when, at last, he finds his way into an oasis of nature, that he experiences joy and contentment, a restoration of his spirit. Abe Segal meets his girl on Mount Royal:

> Within the meadow on the mountain top
> Abe Segal and his sweetheart, lie. Lover,
> Sweet is the comradeship of grass, the crop
> Being mown, the hay dry, dry the clover;
> And sweet the fiddling of the crickets, dear
> The bird-song for a prothalamium.
> They see again, his eyes which once were blear.
> His heart gets speech, and is no longer dumb,
> Before the glass o' the moon, no longer high,
> Abe Segal nattily adjusts his tie.
> Gone the insistence of inveterate clocks;
> The heart at last can flutter from its bars.
> Upon the mountain top, Abe Segal walks,
> Hums old-time songs, of old-time poets talks,
> Brilliant his shoes with dew, his hair with stars . . .

It may be interesting, in this context, to recall how Rabbi Nachman, the Bratzlaver, whom Klein so much admired, extolled the healing influence of nature. In a biographical note, Martin Buber tells us that Rabbi Nachman "was married and settled in the village where his father-in-law dwelt. Here for the first time he came near to nature, and it gripped him in his innermost heart."[8] Later, as a teacher, Nachman said:

> When man becomes worthy . . . to hear the songs of the plants, how each plant speaks its song to God, how beautiful and sweet it is to hear their singing! And, therefore, it is good indeed to serve God in their midst in solitary wandering over the fields between the growing things and to pour out one's

speech before God in truthfulness. All the speech of the fields enters then into your own and intensifies its strength. With every breath you drink in the air of paradise, and when you return home, the world is renewed in your eyes.⁹

A similar sentiment is expressed also in one of the Bratzlaver's tales, "The King's Son and the Son of the Maid," where a cruel king goes hunting and lies down to rest under a tree: "The tree stood in blossom and bent its branches above clear water. There the king was overcome by pangs of conscience that he had committed an injustice and driven away an innocent man."¹⁰

Klein has, upon occasion, been called "a romantic poet,"¹¹ and one cannot discount the influence of nineteenth-century Romantics, notably of Wordsworth, on Klein's thinking concerning the restorative power of nature. But neither can one overlook the guidance he received from Chassidism, especially as later poems show Klein's specific interest in Rabbi Nachman, the Bratzlaver. The title of the poem "Diary of Abraham Segal, Poet," which seems to combine Klein's name with that of his friend, the Yiddish Montreal poet J. I. Segal, may also be significant, for Segal was closely connected with the Chassidic tradition.¹²

In the late thirties, at a time when Klein seemed preoccupied with immediate political problems, he not only remained interested in Chassidic thinking, but also showed an increased awareness of its applicability to contemporary issues. Proof of this may be seen in his verse play *Hershel of Ostropol*, published in 1939.¹³ The story of this play is set against a Chassidic background, and its hero is the epitome of the Baal Shem Tov's doctrine that God can be served only in joy. The Chassidic teachers reacted against the depressing circumstances in which their congregations had to live out their lives; they countered the gloom that was generated through the tradition of the Lurianic Cabala, full of lamentations, which forebade rejoicing while Jews dwelled in exile,¹⁴ a gloom intensified by the hostility of political and economic conditions. It is in the spirit of the early Chassidic teachers that Hershel of Ostropol, the eternal jester, shows his fellow Chassidim how to live. He is aware of his people's martyrdom; he himself is smarting with personal disappointment and humiliation; but he knows only one answer: one must be happy. ". . . Never let melancholy / Again perch on our brows and caw our folly," he says. Even in the greatest extremity his mind dwells on past bliss and the certainty of future salvation.

The play may have been written long before 1939, but even if this is the case, Klein's decision to publish it in that year suggests that he still endorsed its message. The Chassid believes that the essence of the universe is joyous, and that creation responds when man shows he understands and appreciates its magnificence. Klein took a traditional Chassidic folk-hero of the Eulenspiegel and Nasreddin variety and subtly turned him into a spokesman for this doctrine. He who lived by this truth triumphed over disaster, accepted whatever goodness was granted him, and trusted in ultimate salvation. The reward is inherent in the service the Chassid renders the Deity: in his effort to feel joy he does, of course, increase immensely the chance that he will live a joyful life.

In 1939, Klein wrote a poem in which he unequivocally declares himself a prophetic believer. The poem, dated through internal evidence, was probably written too late for inclusion in the collection *Hath Not a Jew . . .* (1940); it later appeared as "Psalm II" in *Poems* (1944). The headnote reads, "Maschil of Abraham: A prayer when he was in the cave."[15] We are to think, presumably, of Plato's cave and the famous metaphor. Here, Abraham (Abraham Klein, like his Biblical ancestor) is the one who has knowledge of the substance. His problem is to communicate this knowledge to those who believe that the shadow alone constitutes total reality.

O Lord, in this my thirtieth year
What clever answer shall I bear
To those slick persons amongst whom
I sat, but was not in their room.

Klein emerges as a prophet of faith, one who feels that it is his responsibility to communicate what he knows to be true.

> O could I for a moment spare
> My eyes to them, or let them hear
> The music that about me sings,
> Then might they cease their twitterings.
>
> Then might they also know, as I,
> The undebatable verity,
> The truth unsoiled by epigram,
> The simple *I am that I am.*

Klein feels that he must proclaim the truth; but he faces the difficulty of Eliot's Prufrock: no matter how great his effort—even if, like Lazarus, he returned from the dead and spoke with knowledge of the beyond—no one would listen, or accept his offering. There is, however, a marked difference between Klein's and Prufrock's position. Prufrock is resigned. Klein, it seems to me, is still reaching out with all his strength. If he himself cannot gain the power to show others the truth, he says in this poem, he begs God to convince them. At this point, Klein's pessimism seems to have vanished. He simply rejoices once more in the knowledge that God *is.* We are not told what led to this renewal of joyful religious emotions, but an analysis of *Hath Not a Jew . . .* , the collection which must have been in preparation in 1939, may suggest the answer.

Klein included in this collection poems which covered all the most important aspects of his thinking as far as it pertained to matters of Judaism; and the arrangement of the poems seems to indicate a definite plan. It gives the impression that Klein was endeavouring to make a statement concerning the development of his religious thought. Poems concerned with theological questions form a prominent part of the collection. They include, in this order, "Out of the Pulver and the Polished Lens," the enthusiastic affirmation of Spinoza's philosophy; the "Talisman in Seven Shreds," which gives an account of

his disillusionment in terms of symbolic legends and proto-
types of Jewish folklore; and "Design for Mediaeval Tapestry,"
which shows, in terms of individual experience of misery and
human helplessness, what had caused him to become dis-
illusioned. Klein seems to say to his readers: we have this great
thinker, Spinoza; he beckons us to follow him; but beware—
his philosophy offers no comfort, and the evil that has been
rampant in the world and which torments us still is, according
to this philosophy, of no moment to the power that makes the
universe.

Then, as if to console the reader and to afford him a glimpse
beyond despair, come the Chassidic poems. The sequence in
which they are arranged suggests increasing optimism. They
are interspersed among other poems which appear to have no
direct relevance to them, and it can only be conjectured that
the pattern which emerges was consciously intended by Klein.
There is, at any rate, a progression in the poems of Chassidic
theology which it would be difficult to ignore.

The first of these is "Reb Levi Yitschok Talks to God." It
is based on an old Yiddish folksong, "Levi Yitzchok's
Kaddish,"[16] in which the renowned rabbi pleads his case
before the Heavenly Judge. It opens with these words:

Good morning, Lord of the Universe!
I, Levi Yitzchok, son of Sarah, of Berditchev,
Have come to you in a law-suit
On behalf of your people Israel.
What have you against your people Israel?
And why do you oppress
Your people Israel?
No matter what happens, it is:
   "Command the children of Israel!"

Like Spinoza, the rabbi acknowledges his ignorance of the
causes of evil; and, like Spinoza, he assumes that evil must
have a purpose which is hidden from his understanding.
Spinoza believed that what is considered evil may be part of

a wider, not comprehended scheme.[17] The rabbi believes evil may be a punishment, though he does not know in what way punishment was incurred. Both accept the idea that evil may have a purpose, but, unlike Spinoza, the rabbi in the folksong is determined to do something about it. Unlike Spinoza, he believes that the individual can, somehow, be in direct communication with the divine power, that he can influence the Deity, that he can make himself heard like a child pleading with a parent. "I will not stir from here!" he says. He will continue his pleading and his praise, hoping to wrest a response from the Divine even as Jacob wrestled with the angel until he was blessed. There was in the rabbi's attitude nothing audacious, Klein explained many years later; for the rabbis considered themselves "familiars in heaven."[18] In other words, they were convinced that the individual could count on being loved by the divine spirit.

Like the rabbi in the folksong, Levi Yitschok of Klein's poem pleads the case of his people. Why is there suffering? However, while the rabbi in the folksong is confident and keeps on struggling, Klein's Reb Levi Yitschok humbly accepts the fact that he will remain ignorant. Like Spinoza, he acknowledges that the ways of the universe are unfathomable.

He has come to the synagogue of Berditchev. He pleads his case:

> How long wilt thou ordain it, Lord, how long
> Will Satan fill his mickle-mouth with mirth
> Beholding him free, the knave who earned the thong,
> And Israel made the buttocks of the earth?

Around him, everything takes its course. Remote, relentless, disinterested, nature proceeds in the usual way:

> *Somewhere a loud mouse nibbled at a board,*
> *A spider wove a niche in the House of the Lord.*

There are echoes here of "Haunted House," of some of its hopelessness. The rabbi pleads; he is not answered.

The candles flicker,
And peeping through the windows, the winds snicker,
The mice digest some holy rune,
And gossip of the cheeses of the moon. . . .

Such lack of concern for the individual very much suggests
Spinoza's universe.

Good men groaned: Hunger; bad men belched of food;
Wherefore? And why? Reb Levi Yitschok talked . . .
Vociferous was he in his monologue.
He raged, he wept. He suddenly went mild
Begging the Lord to lead him through the fog;
Reb Levi Yitschok, an ever-querulous child,
Sitting on God's knees in the synagogue,
Unanswered even when the sunrise smiled.

Like Spinoza, he finally accepts his intellectual frailty: evil
cannot be explained. Yet, unlike the philosopher, he seems to
feel that he is personally in the care of Providence. The image
of the child begging for guidance suggests trust, optimism, the
conviction that man may commend his cares to infinite
benevolence. In this poem, Klein combines an objective,
philosophical point of view with Chassidic, subjective fervour,
with a trusting religiosity. Although the framework of the
poem is derived from a folksong, and there may also be some
parallel with George Herbert's "The Collar," the content does
not depend wholly on literary antecedents. It seems to rest on
a substratum of personal experience. Klein may look wryly at
the rabbi's futile mutterings; he may smile as he recounts the
rabbi's attempts to make himself heard; yet, his sympathy, as
he describes him when he is reaching out for help, is genuine
enough, so genuine that one cannot help feeling a deep,
personal significance in this poem.

The intensely emotional ending of the next Chassidic poem,
"Dance Chassidic," testifies to Klein's attachment to the
Chassidic tradition. Unfortunately, most of the preceding

lines are very awkward, and the poem as a whole, therefore, does not succeed. It describes the Chassid, who combines his worship with music and dancing, with strange ritual gestures, that to the uninitiated onlooker may seem odd, even bizarre. S. A. Horodecky, in *Leaders of the Hassidim*, tells us that Rabbi Nachman found joy prevailing in "spheres of liberty." He "discovered melody in the whole universe, in every man's soul."[19] Rhythm was important to him, we are told, and he responded by dancing. One understands then that the Chassid, in his dance, finds a level of existence where the oppression of the pale vanishes. The dance becomes a symbol of certain essential ingredients of life. While he dances, the Chassid reaches out toward the divine power, not only with his mind, but also with his body, with his entire being.

In "Dance Chassidic," Klein explains some of the specific gestures:

> Let this be humility;
> Back bent in the pious reel,
> Head inclined imploringly,
> And palms upward in appeal.
>
> Let this be pride;
> Beard pointed upward, eyes aflame like *yahrzeit* lamps,
> And right hand stretched as if it held God's left hand
> in it,
> Marching as into Paradise, while each foot stamps,
> Crushing Eternity into a dusty minute . . .

Klein sees in the Chassidic dance the symbol of a philosophy, the symbol of a way of life. The Chassidim dance

> Until above the Jews, above the Scroll, above the
> Cherubim,
> There broods the Immanence of Him . . .

The dance is a response to something that beckons from the universe. Veiled, barely formulated, there is in the ending of

Klein's poem the suggestion that the divine powers immanent in the universe respond in turn to the fervour of the dance and enter the consciousness of the dancer.

In the third poem, the "Ballad of the Dancing Bear," divine response is more than merely implied. Unequivocally, it becomes the central theme of the poem: man's efforts to reach out toward divine power are not in vain. Success can be magnificent. It must be noted, of course, that the setting in "Ballad of the Dancing Bear" is that of the folk tale where the miraculous becomes part of everyday existence and that Klein placed the poem in a section of his collection, *Hath Not a Jew...*, which consists mainly of verse intended for children. But I do not think that this means Klein wanted to belittle Chassidic mysticism and to imply that it was valid only in the context of fantasy intended for the young. I believe that he considered immediate, complete success an ideal which could be realized only in an archetypal myth, but that he felt such myths had to be kept alive and kept before the eyes of the young. There is much evidence in *Hath Not a Jew...* that Klein thought Chassidism a good tradition in which to bring up a child. He repeatedly refers to it in the verses intended for children.[20]

"Ballad of the Dancing Bear" is interesting on many accounts and has been rated as one of Klein's most successful poems.[21] Much of what Klein has written presupposes a knowledge of Jewish legends, stories or anecdotes. The reader who lacks this knowledge often has no access to the deeper meaning of his writings. In "Ballad of a Dancing Bear," however, Klein develops a traditional motif in full. The story is told in its entirety, thus making for a more satisfying experience for most readers.

We have here the tale of the poor Jew who is forced to dance for a despotic overlord, and who dances so well that the tyrant and all other onlookers are won over to his side. In essence, this motif can be traced to the very roots of Jewish history. We hear the Psalmist's complaint: "they that carried us away captive required of us a song; and they that wasted us required of us mirth, saying, Sing us one of the songs of Zion.''[22] In Canadian literature, the motif appears also in *Healer of All Flesh*, a novel by the Montreal surgeon Abraham Stilman. Here it is the Ukranian policeman, Vassilii, who tries to make young David dance to humiliate him in public. Avrum, David's father, steps in and dances in the market square: "The primitive Gopek melody sounded to him like an angel chant of *Kedusha*. . . . A sense of unalloyed happiness suffused his entire being and he seemed to soar in a realm of religious exaltation."[23] Avrum prays as he dances. The spectators are electrified and awed.

In Klein's poem, the action is set in Poland. Pan Stanislaus, a landowner in whose domain there is a sizable pale, habitat of many poor Jews, waxes rich by levying oppressive taxes. He is attended by Thaddeus, an anti-semitic priest who persuades him to impose new and yet heavier taxes which Jews are to pay on penalty of expulsion from their homes.

Meanwhile, a princess, Paulinka, languishes in the castle-tower. Her body is ailing under an evil spell.

> From her couch she sadly watches
> Days that amble by on crutches.

Her mind is bruised with sorrow:

> Upon her couch she sits and sings
> Of the Lord's unfavoured things.

Among the Jews, there is great perplexity when they hear of the new trial in store for them. Only Motka, the water carrier, does not seem to be touched by the general discomfiture.

> It was rumoured he was one
> For whom God preserved the sun.

In other words, he is supposed to be a *Lamed-vav*, one of the thirty-six hidden saints of Jewish legend who are said to appear in every generation, "on whose virtue the foundations of the world are supposed to rest . . . unlettered and insignificant men who work at the most humble trades and therefore pass unnoticed among their fellow-men."[24] While the Jewish population, unable to raise enough money, dejectedly prepares to leave,

> Motka peddles joy; no worries
> Come to mar his witty stories.

He trusts

> That the Lord could not reject,
> Nay, nor scorn His Hebrew sect.

Stanislaus, who all the while is carousing at his banquet table, has had too much beer and suddenly conceives "A thought torturesomely droll." He sends for a Jew to come to the castle and dance for his amusement. Motka tells his distraught fellow-Jews to cease lamentation; he will volunteer; he will go and dance for Stanislaus. Tall and awkward, Motka rises, seemingly oblivious of his jeering spectators,

> Dancing, waving paws in air,
> A pathetic Hebrew bear
>
> .   .   .   .   .
>
> *Drummers, drum; and fiddlers, fiddle!*
> *Make a music for the Zhid'l!*
>
> Happy as a bloated louse,
> The fat baron Stanislaus
>
> Swills his beer, and munches pork
> While he keeps time with his fork.

Stanislaus, at this point, is not so much a symbol of evil. He is stupid, selfish, crude; brutish rather than satanic.

Motka's dance becomes more and more animated. While he dances, he prays. Slowly the spectators are drawn to imitate him:

> Even servants drop their plates,
> Drop the ducal delicates;
>
> Guardian-varlets leave their stances
> And leap into Mottel's dances.
>
> Yea, the butler breaks his bottle
> As he strives to out-do Mottel.
>
> Lo! the Pan, sucking a bone,
> Suddenly forsakes his throne,
>
> With him in the circle hop
> All the lords; they cannot stop.

The compulsive dance is a motif not unknown in European literature. We find it in Robert Mannyng's *Handlyng Synne*, in the story of the Dancers of Colbeck. Those who have willed a dance with sinful intent are condemned to dance and to go on dancing. But it is typical for Chassidism and for Klein that in his ballad the compulsion turns out to be beneficial in the end. Dancing, in the Chassidic tradition, is an act of service, and the compulsive dance becomes a symbol of inspiration. Those who are brutish are forced to join in their victim's exaltation and thereby become more sensitive to the music, to life; they become humanized. As a Chassid, Motka accompanies his dancing with prayer, and the dance itself becomes a form of prayer. He imposes a feeling of harmony upon his fellow-men because, fundamentally, he is striving to be in harmony with all the universe.

His prayer is heard. As the dance reaches its climax with everybody compelled to join in, the princess, Paulinka, appears. She is healed,

Rises, trips toward him, halts,
And takes Motka for a waltz!

Henceforth

Paulinka the princess sings
Of God's unforsaken things.

Gentle, innocent, suffering Paulinka is liberated. Obviously,
she stands for that aspect of humanity which is enslaved and
crippled by the evil spells of a brutish, blundering, and sense-
less part of mankind. In Klein's poem, Paulinka seems to be
of Stanislaus's household. It is because he is humanized that
she regains her health.

There is general conciliation. Only the wicked Thaddeus is
unhappy, as was to be expected. But, significantly, no harm
comes to him. He is unhappy only to the extent that he
regrets seeing his evil schemes come to nought. Everybody else
goes happily about his business.

Motka sells his crystal waters
Earning dowries for his daughters.

He spreads well-being, happiness, love; his crystal waters come
from the springs of life.

The dance becomes symbolic of a life-style. But one cannot,
of course, pretend that Klein was concerned with something
uniquely Chassidic. It is true that the religious dance in
Europe is rare, except among the Chassidim, but sometimes we
come upon reminders that the deeply serious significance of
dancing is not altogether forgotten in other cultures. In eastern
and southern Europe, in particular, the dance is expressive of
an attitude to life. We may recall the episode in Tolstoy's
War and Peace, where Natasha begins to dance and everybody is
in dread that she may not do it well and disgrace herself. Those
who watch her are relieved when they find that the old peasant
dance is in her blood. She danced so perfectly that in her dance
she showed she understood all that was "in her father and her

mother, and her aunt and every Russian soul."[25] When Motka dances, and dances well, he strikes kindred chords in the hearts of his Slavonic spectators, perhaps rouses in their hearts something like a recognition of our common humanity. In this sense, the miraculous effect of Motka's dance may be explained in psychological terms.

The Chassidim have not been the only Europeans in modern times who regarded the dance as a means whereby man could assert his dignity as a human being. The Greeks, for instance, proved with a dramatic gesture that they still knew the power of Terpsychore when they danced on Mount Heroon before hurling themselves from its cliffs to escape the invading Turks;[26] and their spirit lives in Kazantzakis's vision of Zorba, who sees his hopes and ambitions disintegrate, but at the moment of his greatest humiliation, frustration, and disappointment gets up and dances. Zorba, the Greek, like Motka of the Chassidim, affirms in his dance the invincibility of the divine spark in man.[27]

The symbolism in "Ballad of the Dancing Bear" reveals the kinship between Chassidism and other, seemingly remote cultures. At the same time, it emphasizes the traits usually considered typical of the Chassidic movement: the belief in the beneficial influence of a joyful heart, the resort to emotional prayer, and the trust that man may draw upon himself the favour of God.

Klein may have felt that, through his writings, he was continuing the work of Chassidic teachers, that he continued where men like Rabbi Nachman had left off. Consider, for instance, the rather interesting possibilities in the genesis of "Ballad of the Dancing Bear." It is my belief that this poem was conceived specifically with the tales of Rabbi Nachman, the Bratzlaver, in mind and that, in a way, it was to supply the last in a series of Rabbi Nachman's tales, the story Rabbi Nachman would not tell. In the story "The Seven Beggars," a boy and a girl, two destitute children who are lost in the forest, are befriended by seven beggars. The children grow up and marry. At their wedding feast, the seven beggars appear and each offers a story and a special gift. The first story is told by a blind beggar whose mind can see into the deepest mystery of things. Then a deaf beggar speaks. His ears are closed to the desires of the world; therefore he is able to preserve the simple ways that make for a good life. On the third day of the wedding, another beggar, a stutterer, tells his story. He speaks of the eternal word and song that fill his soul. The fourth beggar has a crooked neck. His own form may be misshapen, but he is the master of empathy: he can project himself into the nature of others and can generate compassion and helping strength. The fifth beggar is a hunchback whose back, in fact, is strong and straight and who carries the burden of the world. The last beggar to tell his tale is a man with crippled hands. He recalls how the gates of prisons have sprung open at the touch of his finger and how from wounds he can draw forth the poisoned arrows, nullifying their effects. He tells of a king's daughter whose heart had been pierced by the poisoned arrow of a prince who was enamoured with her and pursued her ruthlessly. The waves of great waters bore her into a castle and made a bed for her, and there she remained until he, the man with the crippled hands, came and healed her. There can be little doubt that the king's daughter of this tale is a close parallel to Klein's Princess Paulinka.

In the introductory part of Rabbi Nachman's tale, it is said that the seventh beggar is a man with lame feet. But his tale is never told. So far we have found that each beggar was able to serve the Good of mankind with that part of his body which, to a superficial observer, seemed defective. We anticipate then, naturally, that the seventh beggar will somehow serve mankind with his feet. It is left to our imagination to determine how this may be achieved; and Klein, I suggest, has supplied the answer with a thoroughly Chassidic motif: Good is wrought by means of the dance. It is true, Motka is not a beggar; but, as a water carrier, he follows a humble trade. He is not lame, but he is by no means a born dancer; at the beginning, we are told, he is awkward like a bear. Like the men in Rabbi Nachman's tale, he overcomes his disability in his eagerness to achieve, to serve, and he spreads a healing, conciliatory influence.

Even if "The Ballad of the Dancing Bear" is in some sense Klein's version of the missing tale, however, this in itself would not, of course, prove that Klein had come to regard himself as one who followed the early Chassidim. The fascination with the mystery of an untold tale could have been purely artistic. It is not by chance, as Roy Daniells has pointed out,[28] that Il Penseroso chooses the Cambuscan tale to brighten his night. The romantic mind is always attracted by what is unfinished.

A more definite proof of Klein's persistent allegiance to Cabalist and Chassidic ideas can be found in the last section of the collection *Hath Not a Jew. . . .* This section, strangely, consists of only one short poem which, according to Caplan, was first published in 1930 under the title "Orders." It consists of only eight lines; and from an artistic point of view, it does not seem to merit the position of special importance Klein assigned to it in his collection.

> Muffle the wind;
> Silence the clock;
> Muzzle the mice;
> Curb the small talk;
> Cure the hinge-squeak;
> Banish the thunder.
> Let me sit silent,
> Let me wonder.

In *Hath Not a Jew . . .* , the poem retains the original title. But, in addition, it is given the rather puzzling section heading "Of Nothing at All." This seemingly unintelligible heading gives us an important clue. The significance of the word "nothing" becomes clear when one recalls a passage in the *Zohar*. In its mystical interpretations of the Pentateuch, it speaks of "the Ancient One, the All-Hidden One, the Transcendent, whose designation is Ayin (Nought) because He is above comprehension."[29] Gerschom G. Scholem discusses the concept of the "nought" that is found in the *Zohar*, and he has this to say: "When . . . the *Zohar* speaks expressly of . . . nothing, it is always taken as God's innermost mode of being, which becomes creative in the emanation of the *sefiroth* [divine potencies and modes of action]. 'Nothing' is itself the first and highest of the *sefiroth*. It is the 'root of all roots.' "[30] Agus explains the mystic's concept of "nought" in this way:

> The mystical ecstasy of "adherence" to the divine will, and the "putting off of materiality," is achieved through love and joy, but these feelings are in turn based upon total self-abnegation, humility and the cultivation of the capacity to look to the "inwardness of things." . . . This is the basic rule: the essential distinction between the domain of holiness and "the other side" is the category of self-dissolution in holiness, which is expressed in the statement, "there is no I at all." . . . To learn to unsay "I," man must learn to realize that all his perception and conceptions are not ultimate realities, but only the sheen of the outer façade of existence. We approach reality to the extent to which we recognize the "nonbeing" of the sensed universe. What is "naught" to our sense-bound understanding is in truth reality. To sense this truth, we must acquire the capacity to transmute our consciousness of self into an awareness of "non-existence." For it is only when we sink back into the universal silence of the "naught" that we enter the "inwardness" of things that constitutes their divine, vital spark.[31]

Agus draws attention to similar ideas in the writings of medieval Christian mystics, notably those of Meister Eckhardt, and in Buddhist philosophy, but he points out that Jewish mystics avoided reducing consciousness to a vanishing point. They lived by two seemingly contradictory maxims, "I am but dust and ashes" and "It is for me that the world was created." As Agus puts it: man is nothing, but the realization of it is of cosmic importance. The Chassidim, he says, created a vast folk literature extolling humility and "the consciousness of being 'naught.' " One may, in this context, recall the last line of Poem 7 in Klein's "Out of the Pulver and the Polished Lens": "I am nothing at all."

This is not to suggest that Klein accepted all the tenets of Chassidic metaphysics. What the section heading "Of Nothing at All" makes clear, however, is that he was exploring Cabalist and Chassidic thought with sympathetic interest. Further proof of this came in the years following the publication of *Hath Not a Jew*. . . . In 1941, there appeared, for instance, the "Psalms of Abraham." In one of them, "Psalm 172," Klein prays for a green old age, close to nature. He who has "expiated life in cities" wants to melt slowly into the greenness of nature. The Chassidic overtones here cannot be ignored.

Klein, one realizes, is trying very hard to serve God in joy. But, in 1941, this task is exceedingly difficult. In "The Psalter of A. M. Klein," he acknowledges that reality rudely contradicts his vision of a benevolent universe. The world is created beautiful.

> From pastures green, whereon I lie,
> Beside still waters far from crowds
> I lift hosannas to the sky
> And hallelujahs to the clouds.

But something is intruding to mar the lovely image. Where the cloud should be, he finds "the fierce carnivorous Messerschmitt."[32] The Chassidic creed is put to a cruel test. So is the Spinozan doctrine of the perfect universe. 1941 is one of the darkest years in the entire history of the Jewish people. Klein feels guilty because in the face of that unbelievable horror, he recoiled. Included in the "Psalms of Abraham" is "A Prayer of Abraham that He Be Forgiven for Blasphemy":

> Consider my speech, O Lord, not too severely;
> It does not mean what it does seem to say.
> With strangers I must see my tongue says merely
> The hollow naught, the vacuous cliché!

It is not so when he tries to communicate with his God. Here
he is honest, as honest as he was when he addressed his father
whom he loved.

> Surely, Lord, You would have it this way rather.
> I speak to you this day
> Even as once I spoke to my sire now with You.
> And I never loved one more than I did my father.

With his entire being he would worship. In the "Psalm for
Five Holy Pilgrims," the five senses are brought as offerings.
But to serve thus is insufficient. The essential man must be
involved.[33]

> Not sight, sound, smell, taste, touch, his freight,
> One brings his heart for pawning with his fate:
> He, surely, he shall come within the Gate!

Klein is constantly struggling to create within himself the
correct attitude; an indication that he now feels man's attitude
is of transcendent importance. In 1941, he publishes two
remarkable poems, each showing how firmly he tries to come
to terms with what he considers his intellectual duty. They
are the "Psalm of Resignation,"[34] and the psalm "To the
Chief Musician Upon Shoshannim. A Song of Loves."[35]

The "Psalm of Resignation" shows Klein as a man infinitely
tired:

> I shall no more complain; I shall not ask
> The question that betrays the doubting soul.
> Tactful my words, my face shall be a mask.
> I shall but say the flaws are part of the perfect whole.

No pious Jew, no Spinozan could have expressed a more
complete acceptance of the world as he finds it than Klein did
in the last line of this stanza. It is a chilling thought that a
Jew, or indeed any thinking human being, could have written
thus in 1941. But the line has to be considered in conjunction
with what goes before and what follows. In the concluding

lines Klein, very much like his Rabbi Yitschok, appears exhausted with crying out for help:

> Can it be otherwise?
> For I am weary of the quarrel with my God,
> Weary of cavilling at the works of the Lord;
> For who indeed can keep his quarrel hot
> And vigorous his cries,
> When He who is blasphemed, He answers not,
> Replies no word, not even a small sharp word?

Klein seemed to have come to the conclusion that man, facing the enigma of evil, had to accept suffering with resignation, had to adopt what traditional Judaism and Spinoza agreed upon was the right attitude in the face of disaster.

The poem does not sound like a literary exercise. It seems to be an authentic record of emotional experience. In the face of what was happening in 1941, questions as to why such ordeals should befall the Jewish people seemed fruitless. No explanation acceptable to reason can be imagined. Klein then was confronted with two possibilities: negation of the religious and philosophical ideas that had hitherto sustained him, or complete acceptance of their most difficult tenets. He chose the latter; and yet, even so, he acknowledged that in the depths of his mind he could not truly accept them: "My face shall be a mask," he says. Before whom, we ask in bewilderment, was he willing to pretend? Was he trying to put on an act before the eternal energies that are the universe? Or was this a jest? Was this, perhaps, one of the instances that would prove John Sutherland's allegation that Klein was "not the poet to express a serious idea or even a serious emotion?"[36] Was he, at this point, trying his hand at some wry humour? I do not think so. I believe the poem, in this very confusion, conveys Klein's state of mind. It is proof of a desperate desire to do the right thing, to follow the dicta on which religion and philosophy agreed, and at the same time, it is proof also of awareness that in the very depth of the heart rebellion could not be quenched.

The psalm "To the Chief Musician Upon Shoshannim. A Song of Loves" is gentler. It is as if Klein were persuading himself that acceptance in a bleak mood is not enough, that the world must be viewed not only with meekness but also with gratitude and joy.

> But this day into thy great temple have I come
> To praise thee for the poisons thou has brayed,
> To thank thee for the pollens venomous, the fatal gum,
> The banes that bless, the multifarious herbs arrayed
> In all the potency of that first week
> Thou didst compose the sextet of Earth spoken made!
> Behold them everywhere, the unuttered syllables of thy breath,
> Heavy with life, and big with death!
> The flowering codicils to thy great fiat!

From these lines speaks infinite love of nature. Each created thing is viewed with tenderness and with readiness to see its potential for Good:

> The hemp of India—and paradise!
> The monk's hood, cooling against fever;
> And nightshade: death unpetalled before widened eyes;
> The blossom of the heart, the purple foxglove!
>
> The spotted hemlock, punishment and prize,
> And those exhilarators of the brain—
> Cocaine;
> Blood of the grape; and marrow of the grain!
> And sweet white flower of thy breath, O Lord,
> Juice of the poppy, conjurer of timeless twilights,
> Eternities of peace in which the fretful world
> Like a tame tiger at the feet lies curled.

The lines are strongly pantheistic. The breath of the eternal is manifest as a flower, or it is a force within the potent influences of vegetation.

The poem was reprinted in *The Second Scroll* under the title "Grace Before Poison" and probably contributed more than anything else Klein had written to the idea that he was ready to accept evil complacently as something out of which can come good. There is, however, an important aspect which contradicts this view. There are indications that the evils Klein had in mind when he wrote this poem were limited and specific. When he thanks God for His creations, he speaks categorically of "The banes that bless," and even they are considered somewhat outside the divine intent: they are the "unuttered syllables" of the divine Word. Klein acknowledges that there are evils which ultimately are productive of good. These he considers as part of the divine order, and he is grateful for them; but this order excludes evil which is intrinsically destructive. We have here the marked difference between the pain inflicted by the scalpel and the pain inflicted by the murderer's knife.

Related ideas may be found in one of Klein's short stories, "No Traveller Returns . . . ," which was published in 1944. Here, a Dr. Necrovivos, who prescribes potions that kill and potions that bring eternal life, is executed by electrocution. His grave is struck by lightning. Soon afterward he appears as a mysterious herbalist who looks as if he were part of the soil and tells of the great wisdom he has unearthed. He says he has found the formula for life: "Poison fought with poison; bane with bane battled; electricity shocked by electricity." He mentions the refreshing massage he once enjoyed from a lightning bolt.

This is a complex allegory; perhaps too involved to make a truly successful story. I interpret it thus: Nature (the doctor) kills, but also produces eternal life. (In the cycles of nature, decline is a bane which men deplore but which is part of a process which brings more life.) When man kills, he is misusing his natural energies and acts *contra naturam*. (The doctor is electrocuted.) The natural energies, misdirected by man, are, however, essentially beneficent. (The doctor is restored to life by lightning.) The *vis viva* reasserts itself in the very dust. Nature counteracts the misuse of its energies.

That questions of religion and philosophy, faith and

rationalism, continued to occupy Klein can be seen in an article in 1942, on the occasion of the thousandth anniversary of the death of Saadyah Gaon, the famous Talmudist of the Academy of Sura, who worked to achieve a synthesis of religion and metaphysics. "Saadyah," writes Klein, "is the father of rationalism in Jewish theology. The problem which faced him has faced sincere men of all religions in all ages."[37] Later in the article, Klein adds: "Again there was established the dictum of Sir Francis Bacon: 'A little philosophy turneth a man's heart away from religion, but depth of philosophy bringeth him back again.' " Klein, too, was struggling along the path that led from philosophy back to religion. Spinozan pantheism, in which rationalism and faith in the Deity are reconciled, had pointed the way. In Chassidism, a Spinozan philosopher lost in the desolation of an unconcerned universe could renew his hope. But both Spinoza and Chassidism affirmed the perfection of a world which, in 1942, revealed itself as one of unprecedented horror. The will to love was contradicted by the manifestations of reality; the desire to adopt the noble attitude, the position of resignation long approved by philosophy and religion, was mocked by the hideousness of events. The incompatibility of what man was supposed to think and feel and what his mind and emotions made him experience thrust the sensitive intellect into the clutches of madness.

The mind cannot grasp the full horror confronting it, cannot truly believe that it exists. In 1942, Klein wrote his "Sennet from Gheel."[38] It sounds like the wild, mad, desperate laughter of one who has let his mind seek refuge in a fog of insanity. Diction and syntax mirror the fragmented, mutilated condition of warring mankind and are re-welded with crazy ingeniousness. Klein seems to have found a technique suitable to his purpose in *Finnegans Wake*:

And these touched thunders, this delyredrum
Outbrasting boom from shekels of cracked steel
Arrave the whirled goon dapht, as zany in Gheel!

Bedlam and hundemonium[39] are sane compared to "these wild-bats that frap in belfrydom."

> Or are these horrorbingers we are guerred,
> And hale in Gheel, and lucid like the rest,
> As good and woad as other humus merde?
> If so, sweet Lord of Hosts, kind exorcist,
> Fling us, un-levined, back to whence we erred,
> Zuruck[40] to our lunasylum of the blest!

How could ideas, systems, truth, be quarried from something that seemed to disintegrate into chaos? The burden, at that moment, was great. The cruelty of what he saw, its incongruity with what he felt he ought to believe, all this must have suggested the thoughts of madness which haunted Klein at this stage. His moving "Psalm XXII," which appeared in *Poems*, 1944, speaks of his fear of mental affliction. Klein was obviously concerned at this time with the problem of alienation.

Indubitably, he also reached out toward other knowledge, new solutions; but he found them wanting. "Come Two, Like Shadows" is basically a rejection of belief that relies on the preternatural and yet a rejection of the purely science-oriented approach. Plato and Freud are phantoms lacking the potency to rescue man from the labyrinth into which he has strayed: the former belittles concrete nature, preaches "Love that is fleshless, passion that is dry—"; the other seems to attach too great importance to the physical.

> That other shadow has a bedside manner.
> He holds my wrist; he bids me speak out Ah;
> Tell him about the dream of the crimson banner
> And of the carnivorous ladies that dream saw.

Salvation, Klein appears to say, must be sought in the one-ness of the spiritual and physical and in the recognition that both are integral parts of sacred nature. One of the poems which show that Klein always gravitated in this direction is

"Desideratum." It begins with an affirmation of Cabalistic ideas. One may distinguish between three elements of Cabala: the first is one of systematization of numbers and letters which are to yield esoteric knowledge; its principles and method cannot seriously appeal to the modern mind (notwithstanding the great interest W. B. Yeats took in them). There is a second level, that of mythology,[41] which abounds in deeply poetic visions. Thirdly, there appear in the Cabala the progressive, pantheistic ideas of an emanation theory. To Klein, therefore, the Cabalist is not a mythmaker to be put on the same level as astrologers and alchemists. Certain basic ideas of the Cabala exercised an important, respectable influence. "I am no contradictor of Cabbala," writes Klein,

> that there are nerves two hundred-forty-eight—
> couriers through the forest of the flesh—
> is sure arithmetic, and sacred.

The nerves bring knowledge of abstract notions to the organism of concrete matter. The spiritual and the physical are intertwined. Matter is permeated with spirit. Its "arithmetic," that is, the system according to which nature functions, is holy. What is needed is a mode of existence that would allow matter to exist purely in accordance with spiritual dictates. But in the following lines, Klein is conscious of a division between spirit and matter. At the end of the poem "Desideratum," he dreams of existence that is redeemed from all grossness.

> Instance this much desired case: the skull
> though severed from unbleeding shoulders, lives.
> Severed, it ambulates to some green knoll,
> its eyes upon the blessed sunshine thrives,
> its ears, they are two beings all of sound,
> its mouth, though throatless, speaks; its sheathed brain,
> a watch whose tickings were in heaven wound,
> unwinding Time . . .[42]
>   The severed body? Let

that body, headless, go about its business,
its grosser tasks, ejaculate, excrete,
digest, perspire, micturate. The head
knows no dependence, lives!

At this point, Klein's view is clearly dualist. Matter is imbued with spirit but not identical with it. Such a theory suggested more readily an explanation of the manifest ills of the world. Grossness resided in matter that somehow did not come under the immediate influence of the Spirit. The solution then is a mode of existence entirely regulated by the brain, by reason, by the spiritual. In such a state it was possible to focus attention on the essential goodness of the world. The image of the severed head, perhaps, suggests also that to live by reason alone necessitates a severing of connections with whatever interferes, and that this may be a painful, costly process.

Poems, the collection Klein published at the end of the war, in 1944, shows a conscious turning away from horror, a conscious attempt, in spite of all, to appreciate the essential goodness of creation. The theory of the entirely mechanistic, unconcerned universe is now definitely rejected. Klein identifies himself openly with Chassidic thought and with the Chassidic approach to life.

The opening poem in the first part of the collection, which Klein entitled "The Psalter of Avram Haktani" (The Psalter of Abraham Klein), is a psalm which shows the direction he had chosen. The poem actually has a double meaning. On one level, it may be understood as political comment, on another it may show us what Klein considered to be man's spiritual duty. All the seers, he says, have their eyes put out, and all the prophets are burned upon the lips.

There is noise only in the groves of Baal.
Only the painted heathen dance and sing,
With frenzied clamouring.
Among the holy ones, however, is no sound at all.

This may be the lament of one who, in the nineteen-thirties and early forties, saw how the forces of destruction scored one victory after another while men of good will were left intimidated, bemused, and impotent. In the light of other poems in this collection, however, one may understand this also as a statement concerning the contemporary attitude to religion. Men look at disaster, and they are blinded; they can no longer proclaim the magnificence of the universe. The atheist has his day, for those who have deeper insight are silenced. The implication, of course, is that they ought to speak out.

The next poem, "Psalm II" of 1939 (which has been discussed), affirms that Klein was concerned about the lack of faith among his contemporaries. As to himself, he admits that rebellion still lurks within, that the heart must be made to obey. In "Psalm III" he envies the unthinking beast:

For easier is the yoke than weight of thought,
Lighter the harness than the harnessed heart!

He cannot overlook evil; it is too oppressively present. It stifles joy. "No song today wells from the heart / That has no morrow!" cries Klein in "Psalm XIII." Grief makes it difficult to serve God joyfully; but to do so is not impossible. Klein is capable of it because he reaches the conclusion that evil is not from God. The horror is not sent by Him. In this, Klein takes a decisive step away from traditional teachings. In "Psalm VI," the Lord looks down and sees what is being perpetrated:

Scholars, he saw, sniffing their bottled wars,
And doctors who had geniuses unmanned.

The gentle violinist whose fingers played
Such godly music, washing a pavement, with lye,

And God, in anger, "Summoned the angels of Sodom down to earth." Bane is fought with bane. Only that part of destructive activity which eliminates aggression and makes for survival is part of the divine order. In essence His will is a constant building and becoming:

> A field in sunshine is a field
> On which God's signature is sealed.
> ("Psalm VIII")

Evil is the intruder. Essentially, creation is good. Within it resides infinite potential for goodness. Klein makes it his business to seek it out and to make others perceive it. The collection of 1944 contains many poems which seem to have been written for this purpose.

There are, for instance, the little portraits of men, real or imagined, whose life makes the potential a reality, in whom goodness becomes concrete, manifest. "Pslam X" speaks of the *Lamed-Vav*. Klein here appears to have had a real person in mind whom he thus honours. "Psalm XI" speaks of "a mighty hunter" who catches beasts, but only to look after them during the winter and to release them in the spring.

> Meanwhile the tiger
> Eats tiger-lilies
> And milk is fed to
> The wild colt's fillies.

Children's verse? Perhaps. But what could be more refreshing in times of intolerable stress than a song of innocence, more apt to remind one that somewhere, somehow, loveliness still exists?

There are a number of nuptial verses in this collection;[43] "serene lovesongs" one might call them, reminders that peace and happiness are possible. If their stylized solemnity fails to touch us, it is probably because in literature, longing and passion tend, on the whole, to be more interestingly portrayed than fulfilment. Tolstoy said in the opening passage of *Anna Karenina* that "All happy families resemble one another, every unhappy family is unhappy after its own fashion." Problems goad the imagination; but the nuances and variations of peace are comparatively limiting.

"Psalm XII" tells of men poor, blind, and crippled who dance in praise of whatever good they can find. The blind man has his dog, the crippled man his chair; and their gratefulness is expressed with all their strength: they dance. The vision is a thoroughly Chassidic one.

Avram Haktani at last merges his voice overtly with that of Rabbi Nachman, the Bratzlaver. "Psalm XXIX" bears the head-note "To the Chief Musician, a Psalm of the Bratzlaver, a Parable." In this poem, a dying king advises his son:

> Be of good cheer, of noble temper be;
> And never let the baneful wind blow dust
> Between yourself and your felicity . . .

Klein evidently felt called upon to continue in the wake of Rabbi Nachman, to teach as he had taught.

The head-note of "Psalm XXX" reads: "To the Chief Musician, a Psalm of the Bratzlaver, which He Wrote Down as the Stammerer Spoke." Here Klein makes direct reference to Rabbi Nachman's tale of "The Seven Beggars." The poem contains mystical, moral contemplations, very much in the spirit of Rabbi Nachman.

"Psalm XXXI," addressed "To the Chief Musician: a Psalm of the Bratzlaver, Touching a Good Gardener," was inspired by the tale of the deaf man in "The Seven Beggars." The deaf man enters a country which has been conquered by a cruel king and has fallen into corruption. With the help of others, he vanquishes the enemy and makes possible the return of the good gardener who spreads his blessings throughout the land. Klein retains much of the symbolism, the allegory, and the poetic mystery of the tale. But the poems of 1944 in which he identifies himself with the Bratzlaver ultimately lack the verve, the laconic directness, and the lustre of that last, "untold" tale which, I believe, we find in the "Ballad of the Dancing Bear." What is important here is that the Bratzlaver poems furnish proof of Klein's allegiance to the Chassidic tradition.

One of the most revealing and, I think, one of the most successful poems in the collection of 1944 is "Psalm XXIV," "Shiggaion of Abraham which He Sang Unto the Lord."[44] It is a longing, a seeking of "the mystic word" that shall evoke the Deity from infinity. The name of God is sought in the sound of the heart, in the sound of thunder. And in the end, there is a note of contentment:

> I have no title for your glorious throne
> and for your presence not a golden word,—
> only that wanting you, by that alone
> I do evoke you, knowing I am heard.

Pantheistic philosophy, which finds God in creation, here mingles with deeply Jewish faith: the individual can draw upon himself the divine response. The personal relationship of the individual with his God has, of course, always been a general Judaic tenet; but the emphasis, on the whole, rests on man's actions rather than his thoughts. To trust the power of one's emotions is mystical; it is Chassidic in character.

Mention must be made here of "Psalm XXIII," in which Klein proposes to break into heaven and to break the scales on which heavenly justice is being mis-weighed. Henceforth, justice shall be done. The poem evoked the wrath of Randall Jarrell. In his review of Klein's 1944 collection, he wrote: "That a religious poet should say it and not even notice that he has said it, not even attempt to mediate between it and the absolutely contradictory sayings that form the substance of his work, is more than extraordinary."[45] It must be admitted that an incongruence exists; but if one keeps in mind Klein's interest in the Cabala and in the Chassidim, his attitude may not appear quite so blasphemous as Randall Jarrell seems to suggest. In the Cabalistic, especially the Lurianic view, man does not wait meekly for evil to disappear. He has to act to help God's intent. It is easy to see how a poet steeped in the lore of the Cabala would consider himself far from blasphemous if he proposed, metaphorically, to take it upon himself to destroy a defective instrument, scales in which heavenly justice was misweighed and which, therefore, counteracted God's essential order. One must consider Klein's repeated portrayal of the relationship between God and man as one between father and child. If, in addition, one takes into account that the Chassidim felt they could achieve a very personal relationship with the Deity, and if one recalls Klein's remark that the rabbis considered themselves "familiars in heaven,"[46] one may well understand the spirit in which "Psalm XXIII" was written.

Chassidism continued to exercise its fascination. In 1947, Klein published another "Psalm of the Bratzlaver."[47] This poem is based on words spoken by the first beggar, the blind man, in "The Seven Beggars."[48] The mind retraces evolution, goes back to the very beginning of existence.

> The apple fallen from the apple tree
> O child remembering maternity!
>
> The candle flickering in a mysterious room:
> O foetus stirring in the luminous womb!

The seed is remembered, and the intent before conception; and the memory travels back into the time before creation.

> Recall the fruit's taste ere the fruit was fruit—
> Hail memory of essence absolute!

One senses the mystic's effort to reach out. With his will and emotions he seeks to make possible something like comprehension, to effect a merging of the part with the whole, of the physical with the ideal.

> Recall the odour of fruit when no fruit was,
> O Spirit untainted by corporeal flaws!

Recall the fruit's shape ere the fruit was seen,
O soul immortal that has always been!

Klein follows closely some of the lines in Rabbi Nachman's
story, where one man recalls "how the flavour of the fruit
entered into the seed," and another declares: "I still have
within me...how the shape of the fruit joined the bud."[49]
We see here the strongly Chassidic effort to penetrate the
mystery of creation poetically, with the emotions as well as
with the mind. Understanding is to lead the way, but poetic
intensity is to help bring about something like a more conscious
union with the Divine:

Said one, and he the keenest of them all:
No thing is what I vividly recall—
O happy man who would remember thus,
The mystery beyond the mysterious.

Here it is again, the Cabalist's term for ultimate reality: No
thing. To approach it, in some way to "adhere" to it, this is
what the mystic seeks to achieve through ecstatic devotion.
When Klein speaks of the "happy man" who can "remember,"
he is extolling the mystic whose efforts are crowned with
success.

The poem was reprinted in *The Second Scroll* under the title
"Of Remembrance." It occupies a place of honour among the
prayers in "Gloss Hai," giving eloquent proof of Klein's
continued sympathy with Cabalist and Chassidic theology.

Ethics   4

The Nurturing of Culture

It would be misleading if one pretended that Klein's constant preoccupation with Jewish culture was rooted wholly in his ideology. His devotion to Jewish tradition, basically, is the normal love of the values and mores one absorbs during one's formative years. When Klein began to write poetry, he naturally drew upon the material which was most vivid in his imagination. He invented variations on stories from the Bible and from Jewish history and legend.[1] When education, career, and politics drew him more and more into the mainstream of Canadian life, his attachment to Jewish culture seemed to become more conscious and deliberate. There are indications that to Klein the nurturing of culture is a religious duty.

It is true that he wrote lines deprecating the superstitions of orthodoxy, as, for instance, in "Five Weapons Against Death" or "Plumaged Proxy." He has always been aware of the dangers of petrification that exist when a culture is the ward of a minority and to a large extent separated from developments in the larger social experience. In *The Canadian Jewish Chronicle*, for instance, he published the sardonic tale of a learned Chassidic rabbi who taught his parakeet to say the Kaddish.[2] In the same vein—as if to show that the problem of mechanical and, therefore, worthless observance is by no means remote— he also wrote an amusing article, "The Value of Prayer," which concerns an actual Canadian court case involving a man who offered to say Kaddish on behalf of two brothers and then sued them for a hundred dollars. In Klein's work, the words drawing attention to the poetry of Jewish custom are, however, more prominent than his criticism. The branches of the menorah become for him "Eight blossoms breaking on a winter night";[3] he seeks new inspiration in the ancient ceremonial of the Seder, in its dignity and dreams.[4] His reproaches are less impressive than his praise.

One way of serving the cause of Jewish culture was to illustrate that the relevance of the Pentateuch transcended its religious and historical content. Klein published studies designed to prove that the Bible contained many ideas fundamental to later literary endeavour.[5] He argued that all basic plots are present in the Bible. Among the articles in a series entitled "Marginalia—Toward an Aesthetic," there is one in which he develops a theory of aesthetics based on quotations from Genesis.[6]

From the words "Now the earth was without form and void, and darkness was upon the face of the deep," he deduces that three things are requisite in the creation of art: "(a) form, (b) content, (c) light. By the last one must understand internal light-radiance; external light is already assumed in the concept of form." This idea is then further elaborated. The internal light must be of two kinds. Just as the heavens are brightened by the sun and the moon, so the work of art must have one light for day and one for night in order that it may be appreciated. It must be significant in two ways. If, "in a poem, everything is as clear as daylight, it might as well have been written in prose; if, on the other hand, its moonlight radiance shrouded in shadows threatens to remain so for ever, it is a light again unsatisfying; it thwarts the natural desire for clear and complete vision."

Again, quoting from Genesis, "Let the waters swarm with living creatures, and let the fowl fly above the earth," Klein expands his theory of ideal art: it must be dynamic, not static;

protean, not uniform; self-multiplying, not sterile. He refers to the creation of man in God's image and tells the artist to learn from Genesis. He sees the artist as a creator who is "completely surrounded by mirrors."

It is in the Bible that Klein finds the prototype of the poet. Many personages could be named, he says, but he chooses Joseph because Joseph is a dreamer; and yet, "it is not to things fanciful and fantastic that Joseph gives interpretation. . . . He never loses touch with things; he never loses touch with people."[7] Moreover, there appears to be room for some interesting elaborations of this symbolic view of Joseph as the archetypal poet.[8] The envious brothers, for instance, strip him of his coat. When lifted out of the dungeon, Joseph is ready to show humility, to shave himself and to change his raiment. Klein here points to an amusing parallel. We are reminded of the cruelties inherent in literary squabbles; of the writer who learns how to please after he has found himself isolated, neglected, and despised. Alternatively, we may, of course, spin this out also in another way. We may see in this an allegory of psychological truth: often an artist will accept the advice of critics only when he is "lifted out of the dungeon," when a measure of recognition is accorded him.

Another way in which Klein sought to further Jewish culture was through the dissemination of knowledge which normally is accessible only to those who receive a thorough parochial education. A somewhat clumsy early attempt to draw attention to sages of Talmudic fame can be seen in "Ave Atque Vale,"

the opening poem in *Hath Not a Jew.* . . . Klein here bids farewell to the Mermaid Tavern and its "goodly feres" and joins "that parfait jolly company," the sages of the Talmudic academies of Sura and Pumbeditha. He then catalogues names and events of Jewish history and legend, some of which, as Earl Birney remarked, are impenetrable even to orthodox Jews. "Who but a Talmudic scholar," asks Birney,[9] can enjoy a poem made up of references like the following:

> The smiling Kahana; Shammai in a mope;
> Hillel instructing an obtuse Ethiope;

Klein hoped—fondly, no doubt—that such verse would kindle the uninitiated reader's interest. The vague, yet pregnant, reference was to lead the reader to investigate further.

Those willing to do research might find out, for instance, that Shammai was an eminent scholar of the first century B.C., a man often in disagreement with his greater contemporary, Hillel. It was, presumably, because of this that Klein says he was "moping." Hillel, a descendant from the House of David, a native of Babylonia, a timber-cutter, a doctor learned in the Law at the time of Herod, the founder of a school and probably head of the Sanhedrin, is a figure of major importance in Jewish history, and the episode Klein refers to is one of the most cherished. When a heathen who wished to become a Jew asked for a summary of the Jewish religion in the most concise terms, Hillel said: "What is hateful to thee, do not unto thy fellow man: this is the whole Law; the rest is commentary."[10]

Many of Klein's allusions concern colourful personalities. There is "uncouth Akiva," the hero of many legends, who stood by his conviction that the authority of the Patriarch must be limited, and who was brave enough to oppose Gamaliel II in his own home. Akiva, eventually, was martyred because he transgressed Hadrian's edicts against the practice and teachings of Jewish religion. Another name Klein mentions is that of Johanan Ha-sandalar, the sandal-maker, or cobbler, one of

Akiva's disciples, who survived Hadrian's persecutions and transmitted the traditional Law. When Akiva was in prison, Johanan wanted to know whether the rite of Halizah (the rite of removing one's shoes before prayer, still of great importance to Moslems) was to be performed also in private. He passed the prison as a hawker, crying: "Who wants needles? Who wants books? What about private Halizah?" Akiva understood and, through an aperture, called: "Hast thou kosher?" thus smuggling into his response the word of approval, "kosher," which denotes validity.[11]

Klein's verse,

Finding for vermin dietetic uses,
Reb Meir and his se'en score ten excuses

refers, no doubt, to another disciple of Akiva, a second century Tanna, reputed to have descended from Nero and to have become a convert to Judaism. The name "Meir" denotes "the miracle worker." When Meir's sister-in-law was taken to a Roman brothel, he entered the place disguised as a Roman and rescued her. Tradition has it that he told the frightened keeper to say "Meir's God, help me" whenever he found himself in danger, and to prove his veracity approached the savage watchdogs which cringed at his feet. Meir introduced many arguments to prove a thing legally clean and as many more to prove it unclean;[12] hence Klein's amused reference to the dietetic uses of vermin.

Most of the names Klein mentions are famous enough. But Birney is right when he complains that some allusions defeat even those familiar with Jewish tradition. Who, for instance, is the "smiling Kahana"? The *Jewish Encyclopaedia* lists six men of that name, and which man and which episode Klein had in mind when he spoke of Kahana's smile remains a mystery. Klein's poem is intended to give zestful impetus to the curiosity of any reader willing to quarry the wealth of Jewish historical literature. But, in some cases, fairly extensive research is necessary to make scant phrases yield their store of history and anecdote, and a well-annotated edition of Klein's work is needed to help the uninitiated reader who wishes to appreciate its baroque richness of allusion.

More accessible are the poems Klein wrote to honour individual heroes of Jewish history. Here too he wants to keep alive knowledge which is in danger of being lost in the cultural amalgam of American cities. "Yehuda Halevi—His Pilgrimage," a poem of forty-two stanzas, most of them Spenserian, was published in the special Rosh Hashanah number of the *Canadian Jewish Chronicle* of 1941, in honour of the eight-hundredth anniversary of Halevi's death.[13] The Zionist Organization of America awarded the poem the first prize in an essay contest conducted by its Youth and Education Department. Otherwise, it received little critical attention. It was reprinted in *Poems* (1944). John Frederick Nims, reviewing it in *Poetry* (Chicago), thought it dull, "as if it were written more from a sense of duty than from impulse of mind or feeling."[14]

Klein tells us how Halevi, the poet, physician, and philosopher, spent his youth in security and happiness, renowned for his pious songs and his jousting with the wittiest of his contemporaries, until, one night, a dream began to trouble him. He sees an imprisoned lady whose home has been taken by enemies, and unable to forget this dream, leaves his native Toledo, staff in hand, to find her. After various adventures he reaches Jerusalem, where it becomes clear to him that the city itself is the princess for whom he has been searching. With his beautiful ode he addresses the holy city; and here, Klein uses a translation of Halevi's own words.[15] Halevi wants to fall upon his face and kiss the very stones. But he can only pour out his love. He cannot free the city. He is murdered, and only the memory of his song remains, a perpetual comfort in her misery.

It is true, of course, that few modern readers can find pleasure in the Spenserian vocabulary or this stanza form; it must be admitted also that the demands of this exacting form seem to have subdued much of the sparkle, the originality of imagination that distinguishes so much of Klein's verse; but the fusion of Spenserian elements with the story of the great medieval Hebrew poet assumes specific meaning. By employing Spenserian elements, Klein, in effect, furnished a comment on the story and a definition of his hero: Halevi, he seems to say, is comparable to the knights of the *Faerie Queene*. The knights joust with swords, the poet with his wit. Spenser's knights are personifications of Christian virtues; Halevi represents a Judaic virtue, loyalty to the city which is the symbol of faith. He follows the traditional calling of the knight errant. He sets out to rescue a distressed lady, risking his life (and, in his case, indeed losing it) in her service. Spenser's knights used to be much luckier in their adventures, but Klein, one must not forget, had historical facts to take into account.

It is fitting that Klein should have chosen to remind us of *The Faerie Queene* rather than of the many medieval romances of the knight errant in which the dragon, once conquered, is unquestionably dead. Spenser, as one critic remarked, was a realist: the Duessa is defeated, but she comes back.[16] In other words, the fight of the knights is continual. In Klein's poem, the situation, in this respect, is much the same. The distressful condition which Halevi sets out to remedy persists. But through his ode, Jerusalem will again and again be comforted. Halevi's poetry continues to raise a standard on her behalf.

A poem of more immediate appeal which Klein seems to have written with a very similar purpose in mind is his "Rabbi Yom-Tob of Mayence Petitions His God." It is strongly reminiscent of "Reb Levi Yitschok Talks to God," for here, too, a pious man prays to be heard, while all around him nature proceeds unconcerned: "Where the crow flew, there flies the crow." Like Levi Yitschok, Yom Tob realizes that his great questions will not be answered:

Who climbs upon the golden stair
Of the sun goes blinded by the glare.

Yom-Tob, like Levi Yitschok, eventually finds solace in a feeling of trust. God's sign comes to him not in the voice of the thunder, but "in the still small voice." Blessing the sun, the cellar floor, and the silent stones of his prison, Yom-Tob pronounces benedictions also on the "haloed knife / Which pries the door to the eternal life."[17]

While, however, the poem of Levi Yitschok gave one the impression that Klein was sublimating personal feelings, in "Rabbi Yom-Tob Petitions His God," he seems to be more concerned with Jewish history and Jewish lore. He seems to have fused here the stories of two personages, that of the historical Yom-Tob of Joigny, who, with his community, was burned in the synagogue of York in 1190, and that of the legendary martyr Amnon of Mayence, whose dying prayer (U-Nesanneh-Tokef) is recited on the Jewish New Year's day and contains the line: "The Great Trumpet is sounded: the still small voice is heard."[18] The knife, or sword, as a means of escape from one's enemies plays a role on other occasions in Jewish history, the most noted one being the mass suicide of the Zealots at Masada, described by Josephus Flavius in *The Jewish War*.

There were various ways in which Klein contributed to the perpetuation of Jewish tradition. He wrote the occasional short story in which the setting was deliberately Jewish.[19] He translated the writings of famous Jewish authors, such as Bialik and Agnon. Through his translations he made accessible to English readers the work of Yiddish-speaking Canadians, such as J. I. Segal, Moishe Dickstein, and Israel Rabinovitch.[20] He discussed in print and on radio Jewish writers of note[21] and helped to publicize the names of newcomers. As editor of the *Canadian Jewish Chronicle*, he had available an ideal forum where his extensive Judaic learning could be brought before an interested audience. Here he published not only leading articles, commentaries on current affairs, reviews, poems and short stories, but also scholarly essays, such as "The Yiddish Proverb," "Of Hebrew Humour," "Riddle Me This Riddle," and "Bible Manuscripts." On many occasions, he included in the pages of the *Canadian Jewish Chronicle* little-known excerpts from the Aggadah, the collection of legends and sayings of Jewish sages. In 1949, he combined his knowledge of law[22] and his Hebrew scholarship and wrote a series of commentaries on the draft constitution of Israel,[23] wherever possible pointing out in what particulars the proposed constitution was in accord with the Scripture and the spirit of the Tannaim. Klein thus made his journal an effective unifying agent in the cultural life of the Jewish community, constantly helping to keep alive the past and to improve knowledge of contemporary endeavours.

Obviously, such devotion to a cause cannot be explained solely on the basis of an emotional attachment to childhood memories. A man of Klein's manifold interests could continue to harness so much energy on behalf of Judaism only because he considered this cause a vital ingredient of his philosophy. No doubt, he worked to a large extent by instinct but this instinct was sanctioned by religion and philosophy, by all the main influences that had shaped his intellect.

In his *Ethica*, Spinoza stressed that "Everything, in so far as it is in itself, endeavours to persist in its own being."[24] To abandon the culture of his ancestors, an organism of which he was a part, Klein would consider an act *contra naturam*, and thus, in the Spinozan sense, an act counter to the divine Law. He considered himself a transmitter of culture and felt that generations were looking through his eyes.[25] It was up to him to help the culture into which he was born to realize its potential.

Instinct and a sense of duty, of course, would not have sufficed to keep alive Klein's enthusiasm. To give so much of oneself to the propagation of a culture, one has to be convinced that its perpetuation is immensely worthwhile. In emancipating himself from orthodoxy, Klein had shown that he was not accepting things blindly. Transmission did not mean simply the handing on of belief and mores that had lost their validity in the modern world. To Klein, Jewish culture is an organism in the process of becoming. The transmitter is responsible for its nourishment and improvement.

In this, Klein had the support of traditional religion, which teaches that the Jewish people will be instrumental in bringing about the Messianic age. He also had the backing of Ahad Ha-Am's and Mordecai Kaplan's modern nationalism. The father of cultural Zionism, Ahad Ha-Am, considered Judaism "the national creative power, which in the past expressed itself in a form of culture which was primarily religious," but which has a potential that can be realized in various forms.[26] Unlike Paul Valéry and Oswald Spengler, whose predictions held out little hope, Ahad Ha-Am did not believe in a natural decline of civilizations. While he resembled these writers in that he dealt with questions of culture as if he were concerned with biological organisms, he took a much more optimistic view: "He saw life as a continuous process of evolutionary change, in which the one unalterable law was that of the adaptation of beliefs and practices to ever-changing human needs; and, of course, Jewish life and Judaism were not exceptions. . . ."[27] The process of adaptation came about through the operation of an impersonal force, the "instinct of self-preservation." When there was no interference, this instinct worked out a people's cultural destiny gradually and without violence. Each culture had a potential for regeneration.[28] Individual cultures were looked upon as organisms with creative powers. They were entitled to existence, and to destroy a culture is, then, a crime.

Kaplan, who developed Ahad Ha-Am's philosophy further,[29] places greater emphasis on the responsibility of the individual in the evolutionary process of Jewish life and stresses the importance of the cultural influence to the well-being of the individual. Kaplan's religious-cultural program demands that "the Jew bend every possible effort to help his people become a factor for the good life";[30] but the people is the source of "spiritual self-realization of the individual Jew."[31] In other words, the ancient Messianic dream can be realized only if every member of the community adds his potential for making the good life a reality, and, conversely, it is in drawing upon the spiritual resources of his community that the individual's potential can best be developed.

This last principle has been questioned. Why should a man's activity for the betterment of the human condition be confined to the framework of a particular culture? Are there not many social groups striving to the same end? Why should he decide to identify himself with one in particular, especially when such identification is fraught with disadvantages of many kinds? Jean-Paul Sartre asked this question and proposed a solution in his pamphlet *Antisemitism and Jew*. Since the ideals of socialism accord in so many ways with the ideals of Judaism, would it not be best if emancipated Jews forgot about their Jewishness altogether and continued their philanthropic work in the socialist camp? In this way, they would remain true to their ethics and escape persecution. Such was Sartre's proposal.

Klein's opposition to it was unequivocal. Reviewing Sartre's pamphlet in the *Canadian Jewish Chronicle*, he wrote: "At a moment, in the penultimate chapter, it looks as if Sartre is insisting upon Jewish authenticity, an acceptance by the Jew of his lot and not flight from it, and a consequent self-development within a given situation. The espousal of such a solution, of course, would bring Sartre into the camp of Rabbi Mordecai Kaplan, and would make out of the *Partisan Review* but a supplement of *The Reconstructionist*." But Sartre's suggestion that Jews should divest themselves of their Jewish identity and use their energies within the socialist movement elicited Klein's satiric humour and his passion. "I do not intend an aspersion upon Socialism," he wrote, and he quipped, "some of my best trends are Socialistic, but Socialism," he continued, "it is clear from Sartre's exposition—involves assimilation, the loss of distinction, the unified amalgam, and thus the solution is, after all, but the dissolution one was seeking to avoid. Of such a solution, in which the Jewish is lost, lost not vainly but for the enhancement of the human, but lost none the less, of such an *existenz*, the authentic Jew can only ask: Do you call this living?"[32]

It is clear, then, that self-realization, for Klein, has intrinsic value. While the individual needs the culture to develop his talents, the culture in turn can flourish only when the individual is allowed self-fulfilment to the limits of his best capacities. This conviction seems to be at the core of Klein's widely praised "Portrait of the Poet as Landscape," the last poem in the *Rocking Chair* collection.

A society that allows talent to wither deprives itself of vitality. It is an ailing organism. In Klein's poem, the social fabric is weakened because the poet is ignored, he who "once unrolled our culture from his scroll" and made his world exist more intensely through his praise. Others, less clear-sighted and less sensitive than he, usurp his function. He will go on, of course; his native talent will send forth its light, but robbed of potency, ghostly, it will persist merely as an illusion of potency within decay: he will shine "like phosphorous. At the bottom of the sea."

Thomas Gray, in his "Elegy," sang of men who died poor villagers while perhaps they had the making of poets and kings. But Gray accepted that

> Full many a gem of purest ray serene,
> The dark unfathomed caves of ocean bear.

Klein's vigorous symbolism seems to cry out against waste of talent; waste of life. His poet becomes the prototype of all talent that continues unobserved, ignored, and rejected, be it the potential engineer who lingers untrained in the African bush or the unemployed Ph.D. in an American city. Klein's bitterness is directed against forces that prevent an organism, whether corporate or individual, from making the best use of its potential. Such interference, he seems to say, is an attack upon life.

It is in this sense that we have to judge Klein's intolerance of assimilationist tendencies in the Jewish community: the assimilationist, he felt, neglected his duty to further a heritage of immense capacity for good.

In the early days, when he lashed out against those who tried to merge with the majority, pride was, no doubt, an important factor: the pride of the disadvantaged minority. Antagonism to non-Anglo-Saxon elements was widespread in North America. In 1930, even so usually humane an individual as Stephen Leacock demanded that orientals should be barred from immigration and that, while "European foreigners" might be admitted, their coming should in no way be facilitated.[33] "It is unlikely that in the more recent period anyone in a responsible social role would express such illiberal views publicly," writes John Porter in 1965 with regard to Leacock's chauvinism.[34] In the early thirties, such racism was, however, a widely accepted social fact.

In 1930, Frederick Philip Grove published *The Yoke of Life* with its crude anti-semitism. The villain there has not even a name; he is merely referred to as "the Jew." The grotesquely sinister portrait in this book was certain to infect receptive minds with the plague of racial hatred. Nevertheless, Grove was four years later considered a worthy recipient of the Lorne Pierce Medal, an award given for distinguished service to Canadian literature. The disservice rendered on the sociological plane, on the level of human relationships, was evidently not taken into account.

"Canada as a whole does not accept Jews, for the simple reason that they are Jews," wrote Leon Edel in 1932,[35] and he quoted from Klein's sonnet which begins, "Now we shall suffer loss of memory."[36] In this poem, Klein ironically proclaims that Jews will give up their language and mores, and deny their ancestry. What results can they expect?

> Our recompense—emancipation day.
> We will have friend where once we had a foe.
> Impugning epithets will glance astray.
> To Gentile parties we will proudly go;
> And Christians, anecdoting us, will say:
> "Mr. and Mrs. Klein—the Jews, you know . . ."

In the thirties, a Jew who was eager to merge with the Gentile population of North America was likely to meet with subtle and, at times, not-so-subtle discrimination which remained operative even when a superficial rapport was established. It is understandable that Klein showed contempt for Jews who were so devoid of pride and common sense that they elected assimilation.

With the outbreak of war, however, important changes took place in the social consciousness. As the hallmark of National Socialism, racism lost its pretence to respectability. Its worst potentialities now became manifest. Many Canadians modified their views. In 1943, for instance, a pamphlet by Stephen Leacock, *Canada, The Foundation of Its Future*, was published in a limited and private edition by the House of Seagram with a preface by Samuel Bronfman. It was enthusiastically reviewed by Klein, who remarked that Leacock was not "one of those fastidious immigrant-inviters who want only the descendants of those who came over with William the Conqueror."[37] In 1944 Gwethalyn Graham published her *Earth and High Heaven*, a novel which somewhat idealizes its Jewish hero and eloquently pleads for social acceptance of intermarriage between Christians and Jews. The book was immensely popular and received the Governor General's Award. It "awakened Canadian readers to the horrid actuality that the nightmare of antisemitism which was haunting Europe was one of their own recurrent dreams," said Eli Mandel.[38] In an article published by the Canadian Jewish Congress in 1951, we find this remark: "In ever wider circles in Canada, antisemitism and other aspects of group prejudice were condemned as unacceptable and as foreign to the traditions of the country. The heritage from the past has not completely disappeared, but the acute danger which faced the Canadian people and the Jewish community of Canada in the late 1930s has certainly disappeared to the extent that it is difficult even to reconstruct it in our imagination."[39]

Within a decade, Canadians had done a great deal of rethinking as to the type of country they wanted to have. There was no fear of persecution and little of social discrimination. A Jew who wanted to be absorbed in the mainstream of society could no longer be accused of defecting into the enemy camp: the enemy, to a large extent, had disappeared. Opposition to assimilation, therefore, could no longer be explained as justifiable pride. Klein's attitude, however, did not change. He recognized that liberalism, acceptance of minorities, was as a rule a greater menace to their individuality than repressive attitudes; and his persistent argument against the Jew, and particularly the Jewish writer, who became assimilated sprang from his fear that the organism of Jewish culture might be lost and its unique mission frustrated.

In an article, primarily directed against a U.S. assimilationist, Jerome Frank, Klein wrote: "No responsible leader (Gentile) has ever declared that a man's Judaism was a handicap to his Americanism. On the contrary, a man's loyalty to his race and religion is an additional guarantee of his loyalty to his country."[40] Klein here makes clear that he regards the nurturing of the culture into which a man is born as a moral commitment.

Disloyalty is Klein's main concern in two articles on the American poet Karl Shapiro. In a review article on Shapiro's

Person, Place and Thing, Klein says: "There is not any indication anywhere that the poet is aware of the rich cultural heritage which should have been his." Klein does not believe that it is "the function of the creative artist to be a public relations counsel for his people, though it is no disgrace if he is," but he does feel that a man should not contribute to the prejudices and slanders that beset his race. He does not have to perpetuate group libel: "Obsequiousness is not a national, but a human vice," writes Klein, "concupiscence not a semitic but an international predilection. Shapiro need not circumcize these qualities into our rite. That is the path of self-hatred; and the more regrettable in that it is followed by a poet. . . ."[41] Shapiro's volume is referred to also in a later article. There are in this book, Klein says, "a half-dozen references to Jews, all, all self-denigratory to the point of masochism."[42] Similarly, when he discussed a symposium of Jewish writers in the United States in which all participants had declared that their Jewish origin had "only negative meaning to them," Klein found that concerning Judaism, they were "either singularly silent or, if outspoken, outspoken to the most self-denigratory degree."[43] Again referring to Shapiro, he deplores that a writer "who succeeds in glamorizing a soft drink emporium, can find nothing worthy of reference in a culture which has spanned the centuries and covered the continents."[44] What gave impetus to Shapiro's later interest in Judaism may be a matter for conjecture. Advancing age brought Wordsworth and Heine to renew their ties with the creed of their fathers. Today, a changing social climate and political developments seem to have induced rebels like Irving Layton and Mordecai Richler to modify their views. Personal and social circumstances may have influenced Shapiro. Yet, one wonders whether criticism such as Klein's may not have played a considerable part in the reshaping of Shapiro's attitude to Judaism.

Klein is convinced not only that the individual has the duty to help maintain his native culture; he also believes that the individual can best fulfil himself within the fold. In the case of artistic endeavour, he even goes so far as to deny that an individual can function properly when he ignores traditional influence.[45] In this, Klein seems to have been less than fair. The talented individual will draw upon whatever inspiration is at his disposal. If he is deprived of his original ethnicity, as, for instance, Joseph Conrad was, he will find some other framework for his ideas. Personal experience will, in any case, be one of the most important sources of inspiration. One can name Jewish writers who, in terms of their daily lives as well as in terms of subject matter, were assimilated, and yet their artistic achievements are magnificent. Arthur Schnitzler comes to mind, or Zweig, or Werfel, or Kafka. Heine, above all, showed that assimilation and artistic success are not mutually exclusive.

The idea that the individual will thrive best when he expresses his native cultural traits is, however, widespread in Canada. Ronald Sutherland, writing in *Canadian Literature*, said: "Thériault, Klein, Marlyn, and a number of other writers make clear, when an individual consciously sets out to become assimilated by another ethnic group, the consequences most likely will be isolation and demoralizing loss of self-respect."[46] With his zeal to perpetuate individual culture, Klein finds himself among those who contribute to the evolution of the present pattern in the Canadian social system, which favours cultural plurality. Yet, Klein has also been influenced by the social trends which make that system possible. While a liberal acceptance of minority groups endangers their existence because their members tend to merge with the majority, that very acceptance of minorities also produces the climate which strengthens the position of those who promote the cultural life of the group.

How passionately Klein feels that individual culture must survive, how convinced he is that even the most benevolent attempt to erase it is detrimental, may be seen in the short story "One More Utopia," written in 1945.[47] In this surrealistic tale, the narrator meditates upon universal love.

Suddenly, a visitor with a nondescript face walks into his mind, tells him he has found Utopia, and offers to conduct him there. He leads him across "a long stretch of indistinct and unidentified thought" into a city where everything is automated and antiseptic. They enter a kind of hospital where every person is eager to do something for the other fellow. "It was as if everybody were playing a game: illustrate the Golden Rule." But all persons here look exactly alike, and all look like the narrator's guide and host, who points out that the people in this place had all been war casualties with burned and scarred faces and that he had given them new faces by plastic surgery. The doctor explains that ordinary sutures and graftings had proved insufficient. Although the patients had been made to look more or less like other people, "the scars which their experience had left upon their minds remained, the memory of ordeals which they had suffered could not be banished. Something more was needed." Since the persistence of their difficulties lay in the fact that the patients *knew* their experience to be personal and different from that of other people, the doctor proceeded to change their outlook on life. He made them forget their own identity by giving them all exactly the same face, and, as a model, chose, of course, his own. The result seemed beneficial. "The ego which looked at its own face and saw that it was the face of its fellows lost its personal insistence." When a man looked at his neighbour, it was as if he looked in a mirror. "All about him he saw self." In this way, egotism became altruism.

The narrator spends some time in Utopia. Slowly it becomes clear to him that the inhabitants are far from happy. Eventually, the doctor confesses that all is not well. He loses members of his community: they commit suicide. Deprived of the possibility to express themselves, to fulfil themselves as individuals, they lose the will to live. People are driven out of their minds by monotony; the condition becomes unbearable. General rebellion finally erupts when a man begins to clamour for his own face. He wants it back—with the burns, with the scars. To him, the idea that he should be able to love only someone who looks like himself is an obscenity. "You killed me," he screams at the doctor, and the cry, elemental and desperate, is taken up by the rest: "Give us back ourselves."

Obviously, Klein here refers to the Jewish experience. But he is also making a case for individuality in general, individuality of cultures, of nations, of individual persons. The story is a parable of the individual's craving for self-perpetuation as an individual, an instinct which Spinoza considered a fundamental law of nature. It is in this light, I believe, that Klein's aversion to the idea of assimilation must be understood.

That Klein's tireless activities to serve the cause of Judaism and his opposition to assimilationist trends were not the result of chauvinistic egocentricity can be seen in his efforts to speak on behalf of cultures other than his own. A man who works on the assumption that his own culture is the only acceptable one rarely shows much tolerance for those of other persuasions. Klein's oecumenic tendencies prove that he had that respect for alien entities which befits one who seeks divinity in all creation.

His desire for harmony with other races, religions, and cultures, so evident in the early poems "Ballad of Signs and Wonders," "Greeting on This Day," "Christian Poet and Hebrew Maid," and "Calvary," reappears with conscious emphasis in the early war years. In the upsurge of brotherly feeling which then stirred the people of the United Nations, he held that liberty was indivisible.[48] At that time he wrote "Polish Village," a poem about a peasant who returns to his depopulated village and finds his father's mangled body hanged. Seeking refuge in a church, he sees there "Jesus recrucified into a swastika." The twisted, fractured statuary in the desecrated place of worship becomes the symbol of a maimed and broken population.

E. K. Brown, in his book *On Canadian Poetry* (1943), complained that Klein portrayed Christians as cruel oppressors, that he always sees them from the outside. He was, no doubt, thinking of poems such as those in the cycle "Design for Mediaeval Tapestry" and "Ballad of the Dancing Bear," where Klein is concerned with persecution and oppression. E. K. Brown seemed to have no knowledge of the conciliatory current in Klein's thought. Brown's criticism, however, showed Klein that he was not sufficiently understood, and it may have helped to spur him to clarify his position. In the 1940s, at any rate, Klein wrote poems which show that his universality extends to both the religious and the national sphere.

At this time, the new appearance in Canada of the little magazines of poetry provided an additional incentive for Klein to compose poetry which was of general interest to Canadians. Not that the pages of *Contemporary Verse, Preview, First Statement*, and, later, *The Northern Review* were filled with Klein's oecumenical statements. Far from it; the one significant poem of this kind appeared in *Preview* in 1944. This was the poem "Montreal." Altogether, the new little magazines printed eleven of Klein's poems between 1943 and 1947. They represented writers who were interested in ideas and techniques; and their new, vigorous activity had, necessarily, a stimulating effect on Klein. But it was not primarily in the magazines that his new secular poems appeared.

A great deal of his attention was now focused on the French-Canadian *milieu*, its religion, its mores, its problems. "This shift is not surprising," says Desmond Pacey in *Creative Writing in Canada*, "for French Canada has much in its life which would appeal to Klein's temperament."[49] The view that Klein's interest turned to the Quebec scene because of certain similarities between French Canadians and Jews is shared by other critics.[50] Yet, this factor, it seems to me, is a minor one, except in that the French culture of North America, like Jewish culture, is fighting for its existence and thus would be of special concern to Klein. I believe that, apart from this, Klein was drawn to write about French Canada not so much because he felt there was a kinship between French-Canadian and Jewish ways, but because, on the contrary, there were such pronounced differences. To him, as to the rebel in "One More Utopia," the idea that one can accept only those who are like oneself is repugnant. In his sympathetic approach to something so alien as Quebec Catholicism, he is deliberately seeking out the stranger and shows that he can have affection for him.

He would, no doubt, have shown greater interest in other cultures to which he was a stranger if he had had more contact with them. He wrote a sympathetic poem concerning Indians: "Indian Reservation: Caughnawaga." However, his knowledge of the Indian people was too scant to make him more productive in this area. Here he could only be the outsider, the observer.

It was a different case with French Canadians. Born in Montreal and a graduate of the University of Montreal's law school, Klein was sufficiently acquainted with the language, attitudes, and problems of his French fellow-citizens to be able to express his views in concrete terms. The new poetry brought him The Edward Bland Fellowship Prize, awarded by Black Americans for poems of quality and social importance,[51] and most of the relevant poems are included in the collection *The Rocking Chair and Other Poems*, for which Klein received the 1948 Governor General's Award. The volume greatly enhanced his reputation.[52] Klein's oecumenic tendency here appears in two ways. He aims at a linguistic fusion of English and French; and he writes from the French point of view.

Northrop Frye called Klein's linguistic experiments, "one of the liveliest poetic experiments yet made in the country."[53] In 1948, when Klein published the poem "Parade of St. Jean Baptiste" in the *Canadian Forum*, he explained: "This is one of a series of experimental poems making trial of what I flatter myself to believe is a 'bilingual language' since the vocabulary of the poem is mainly of Norman and Latin origin. There is no word in it (with the exception of articles and auxiliary words) which has not a relationship or similarity to a synonymous word in the French language."⁵⁴

A poem written in the same vein, but better known because it is included in *The Rocking Chair and Other Poems*, is "Montreal." In it the linguistic fusion helps to make vivid the atmosphere of a city in which two cultures are thriving side by side. Here is stanza 4:

> Grand port of navigations, multiple
> The lexicons uncargo'd at your quays,
> Sonnant though strange to me; but chiefest, I,
> Auditor of your music, cherish the
> Joined double-melodied vocabulaire
> Where English vocable and roll Ecossic,
> Mollified by the parle of French
> Bilinguefact your air!

Klein's linguistic experiments did not start a new trend in Canadian literature, and their impact was not very great. They prove, however, that Klein's oecumenism was quite conscious and deliberate.

Of greater social significance are the poems in which Klein assumes the psychological make-up of a Catholic French Canadian. Anglo-Canadian literature, of course, contains other works in which attention is focused on French Canada. In one of the most important of these, E. J. Pratt's "Brébeuf and his Brethren," the issues actually antedate the evolution of Quebec culture: the heroes are Frenchmen. Pratt here is writing as a Protestant Christian about the struggle of French Catholics who are Christianizing the new continent. The oecumenism in Pratt's work, therefore, pertains chiefly to the Christian churches. W. H. Drummond wrote with affection about the *habitants* who were his neighbours and patients, but, as Klein put it in his poem "Doctor Drummond," he did not know "the true pulsing of their blood." Klein shows that he can offer French-Canadian Catholics more than just sympathetic understanding: he is capable of a larger participation.

This does not entail enthusiastic acceptance of every facet of Quebec life. The tourist, the outsider, may praise everything that comes to his attention; the native son, though he will love more deeply, will see beyond the superficial glamour. Poems in *The Rocking Chair* show us that Klein views French-Canadian society as a liberal French Canadian might, a man who has emancipated himself from the orthodoxies of his own culture but who loves and respects its basic features. He is not afraid to be critical. In "The Spinning Wheel," for instance, he attacks the social wrong which, he feels, is inherent in the seigneury system of Quebec. In the poem "Political Meeting,"[55] he casts a cynical glance at politicians with fascist leanings, who stir the crowd to racial intolerance.

It is in regard to the Catholicism of French Canada that Klein demonstrates most impressively his oecumenical feelings. The often quoted poem "For the Sisters of the Hotel Dieu," which speaks eloquently of his gratitude to the nuns who nursed him after an accident, is an expression of tender admiration.[56] Klein here remains consciously the stranger, the observer. In "Cripples," another well-known poem in *The Rocking Chair*, his point of view is ambivalent. Here we find the envy and regret which the emancipated intellect experiences in the presence of complete, unquestioning trust in an orthodox faith. When Klein watches the crippled pilgrims, who ascend the stairs of the Oratoire de St. Joseph convinced of its efficacy, he cries out:

And I who in my own faith once had faith like this,
but have not now, am crippled more than they.

Very similar sentiments are found in "Parade of St. Jean Baptiste." But here Klein seems to go a step further. A Jew, like a Catholic, could envy those who put their trust in miracles; but no form of Judaism allows images to be connected with worship, and Klein's sympathetic glance at the procession in which the image of the Saint is carried through the streets of Montreal represents a gesture which he could not make *as a Jew*. A ceremony in which the veneration of an image plays a part is so alien to the Jewish approach to religion that sympathy with such a ritual by Jews is not even remotely feasible. Therefore, when Klein looks at the faithful who follow the image of the Saint and speaks of the potency of symbols that are murdering grief, relieving suffering, and sporting away anguish, when he concedes the therapeutic influence which the image exercises on the frustrated heart, he divests himself for an instant of his Jewish outlook and sees with the eyes of one for whom the image which is carried in procession cannot be anything but a "jewelled toy," yet who still considers this manifestation of Christian orthodoxy with affection and is anxious to explain and justify its survival.

Klein is not the only Jewish writer capable of assuming the Christian point of view. One may recall Asch and Werfel, and, of course, one will inevitably think of Heinrich Heine. It can be argued that Klein followed Heine, who proved in "Die Wallfahrt nach Kevlaar" that he could absorb something of the poetic genius of Catholicism without accepting its doctrines. But when Heine chose to write about Christian themes, his interest was focused on their poetic content or on historic and political aspects. When Klein writes about a nationality or religion which is not his own, one often senses an added dimension. He writes subjectively. His poems proclaim the essential oneness of mankind. In this he resembles Asch and Werfel. Yet, the position of Sholem Asch, after the publication of *The Nazarene*, was much in doubt. Klein called him "The Thirteenth Apostle" and remarked acidly that the story had been told much better in The New Testament.[57] Werfel had vowed that all his writings should celebrate the sacredness of man, and his devotion to the idea of universal brotherhood enabled him to declare himself a Jew even as he wrote the foreword to *The Song of Bernadette*. However, in his art, Werfel did not find it necessary to concentrate his efforts on his own heritage. On the whole, his writings are not concerned with Jewish themes. It is different with Klein, who is not only a Jew by race and social commitment[58] but a writer who shows in his work that a most resolute insistence on one's own cultural identity may be reconciled with immersion in another culture. He gives constant proof of an ardent sense of serving the Judaic tradition; yet, momentarily, he can assume a French-Canadian Catholic point of view.

Klein's oecumenic tendency is most impressively realized in "The Sugaring,"[59] where the maple trees become symbols of martyred saints. Sentiment, metaphor, and diction are so thoroughly Christian here that they would satisfy even the orthodox among Catholics.

Interestingly, "The Sugaring," so strongly Christian in content, is also an outstanding example of a technique which Klein probably acquired through his knowledge of Jewish literature. A Jewish writer who may have inspired him is Mendele Mokher Sefarim, the grandfather of modern Hebrew and Yiddish literature. Shloime Wiseman, in his review of Klein's *Hath Not a Jew...*,[60] explains that one of the distinguishing characteristics of Mendele's style is a tendency to Judaize nature, both animate and inanimate. The fir trees, for instance, recite the evening prayers that are traditionally recited on the evening of Rosh Hashonah; in winter, the trees are clad in prayer shawls. Wiseman believes that, consciously or otherwise, Klein returned to the manner of Mendele in poems like "Venerable Bee," in which the convoluted rose becomes a *"torah* scroll," or "Scholar," in which the small green mosses become a *"rashi* script." The Biblicizing of nature can be detected in such early poems as "Seasons," in which autumn is "the memory of Joseph's coat." An example of how Klein tends to Biblicize everyday life can be found also in his late poetry, for instance, in "Bread," where the bakers at their work appear as Levites in priestly robes. Combined with Christian metaphor, the technique appeared in the early poem "Calvary"; but it is in "The Sugaring" that its appearance becomes most significant; for here Klein is consciously reaching out toward another culture. This is possible because, to him, human beings are of one substance: like grains in a river of wheat that run through a prairie elevator and from time to time assume different hues in an observer's eye.[61]

Because he has been able to overcome the distance which separates men of different cultures, Klein's oecumenism is of special importance to the social philosophy of today's Canada. In some of his work, Klein goes beyond the widely accepted "Canadianism of the mosaic," a system in which units are sharply and permanently separated from each other, in which there is a common purpose but no fusion of identities. Perhaps the symbol of the mosaic, which at present is so prominent in the Canadian consciousness, is not a particularly happy one: in earthquakes a mosaic is likely to fall apart, and in a cold climate the binding cement is likely to crack. Klein seems to point to a much more vital form of co-existence, one which ultimately reaches beyond Canadian politics into the outer realm of international affairs and into the inner realm of personal relationships. His own identity is so strongly established that we are left in no doubt as to its nature, nor need we fear for its power to endure. Nevertheless, he can become, in emotion and comprehension, someone else. If we wanted to allegorize this mode of being, we might think of a spectrum. Its separate colours can never be destroyed. Again and again, they will emerge, each in its own individuality. Yet, it is in their fused state that we know them as the element which floods the earth with brightness and warmth.

That Klein's encompassing oecumenism is not simply a coincidental by-product of inborn kindness, but an important ingredient of his conscious philosophy, can best be seen in a brief essay, "Of Lowly Things," in which he said: "There is nothing—neither among things animate nor those inanimate which may be considered lowly, but . . . all things and all people stand equal in the great and universal design."[62] "Of

Lowly Things" was published in 1944. It was the year in which Klein also published *The Hitleriad*.

In the Defence of Life

Klein's instinct, upbringing, and conscious philosophy, all prompted him to love, and he found it difficult to adjust his approach when he came into contact with iniquity and hate. He felt he had to speak out when the quality of life was at stake or when life itself was threatened; but many times, particularly during the war, when his sense of justice was outraged, he found it difficult as an artist to harness his indignation. One may, perhaps, ask whether his emotions lacked strength or whether his religion and philosophy interfered with the natural desire to combat evil. But this is not likely. There can be no doubt of the vigour of his feelings, and Judaism and the philosophies which influenced him accept the necessity of struggle when life is threatened. Why, then, is Klein's power to translate anger into art flagging, particularly when he strains it to the utmost that his cause might be served? No single answer can be given, and no simple answer can suffice. Klein directed his pen against social injustice; he wrote against war; he indicted the persecutors of his people. If he failed to reach the vehemence which critics expected, the reasons must be sought in a variety of circumstances.

Judaic teaching, Spinozan philosophy, family tradition, and contemporary history combined in the development of Klein's

socialist views. Before he had reached the age of ten, he was
adept in *Baba Mezia*,[63] which is part of the Babylonian Talmud
and deals with laws relating to trade and industry. It contains,
among others, chapters on the relationship between employer
and employee, on the obligations of landlords, and on the
biblical injunctions against usury. It is a work which drives
home the truth that matters of economics are not secular
issues to be regulated arbitrarily, but are matters of sacred
ethical obligation. Klein's father saw to it that his son was
steeped in Torah and Talmudic learning. But he was not an
other-worldly man who venerated principles merely in theory.
As a presser in one of Montreal's sweat-shops, he was aware of
the problems, the needs, and the frustrations of industrial
workers, and he was not going to accept passively the miserable
conditions under which they laboured. He joined the Union-
Presser's Local 167 and became a member of the Amalgamated
Clothing Workers of America.[64] With this background, it is
natural that his son should have been moved to join in the
struggle for a more just society. The Spinozan theory of the
unity of creation provided a philosophical basis for principles that
were already firmly established. Contemporary conditions, the
denial of a dignified existence to vast numbers of people who had
lost their livelihood, made social questions a matter of urgency.

In a poem which was published in the series "Barricade
Smith: His Speeches," Klein tells us what he expects of the
poet in the nineteen-thirties. "Of Poesy" is not a particularly
good poem, but it is a proclamation, a kind of manifesto.

> Bard, paying your rental of the ivory tower,
> With the old coin of hoarded metaphor,
> Abandon now the turret where you cower;
> Descend the winding staircase; and let your
> Speech be, not of the thrush's note, long sour,
> But of the Real, alive upon the floor.

This is merely what Klein himself is trying to do at the time.
As late as 1934, he had still enjoyed the medieval ballad in the

manner of Heinrich Heine.[65] This kind of enjoyment he will now forgo for the serious task of alerting the ethical consciousness of his readers.

He raises his voice in protest in "Friends, Romans, Hungrymen," a fantasy which combines savage bitterness and gentle humour to create excellent satire. The story reads at times as if it were jointly written by Kafka and Leacock or Kafka and Sholom Aleichem. Another of Klein's prose pieces of the period is "Beggars I Have Known," an ironic essay which reveals subdued criticism of the establishment that forgets crippled veterans and the indigent old.

The 1930s dragged on and iniquity scored triumph after triumph, while inertia, impotence, stupidity, and, in some instances, callousness stifled the voices that demanded redress. There were, at last, moments when Klein, like so many of his contemporaries, felt that forcible change was the only solution. Thus, Klein wrote a number of poems in which a more militant form of socialism comes to the fore. We find these poems in the series "Barricade Smith: His Speeches." They are far from his best achievements, but they show something of his frame of mind at that tense and harassing time before the war. The two poems which, perhaps, show best the degree of his exasperation are "Of Violence," and "Of Dawn and Its Breaking." In the poem "Of Violence," he speaks to the rich, the smug, the emotionally obese. He wants them to know fear: their security is a sham; wages slither and rates soar; the rich see coupons fall like manna from their bonds (which, by implication, they regard as Heaven) while the poor know twelve months of Lent. The muscles of the workers throb menacingly in the engine of the Rolls-Royce, but the rich refuse to hear it. Violence must not be mentioned in their presence; it is a word too uncouth for polite ears. Through Barricade Smith, his persona, Klein tries to force the affluent to listen to the whisperings of reality.

At this time, violence presented itself to Klein as a possibility to be reckoned with. A great rallying of strength, some great concerted act that would liberate the people from unemployment and poverty, seemed the only remedy that could cure the inveterate social disease. "Of Dawn and Its Breaking" is a call to arms.

> Where will you be
> When the password is said and the news is extra'd abroad,
> And the placard is raised, and the billboard lifted on high,
> And the radio network announces its improvised decree:
> You are free?
> Where will it find you, that great genesis?

Will it find you in the barbershop, Klein asks, "Waiting for the call of next?" Will it find you "reading with de-trousered back / Hearst's tabloid, previously torn?"

> Or will you be—O would that you should be!—
> Among those valiant ones returning to their homes
> > To tell
> Their daughters and their sons to tell posterity
> How they did on that day,
> If not create new heaven, at least abolish hell.

The use of the word "genesis" in connection with revolution or radical social change indicates that, to Klein, social betterment, the devising of a "new deal," is something that bears strong religious connotations. To create better conditions for mankind means participating in the creation of the world. In creating better social conditions, man becomes an instrument of the divine.

When we look at the poem as a whole, we may feel that it sounds like revolutionary verse. But it is not without ambiguity. The words are not necessarily those of a revolutionary. Admittedly, Smith may be exhorting the people to man the barricades. But it may be noted that he would be using the same words if he wanted to recruit protest marchers and pickets before hurrying off to the conference table. In some of the lines, there is a great deal of strength, yet one does not feel that they carry the conviction of the true violent revolutionary. The poems have neither the verve nor the inexorable beat of propagandist poetry; it is impossible to imagine that they could rouse anyone to violent action.

It is not without significance that at the end of the Barricade Smith series we find a semi-humorous piece which may indicate a renunciation of force. This is "Of the Lily which Toils Not." It contains the portrait of a worthless socialite whom Barricade Smith loves from afar. He could gate-crash one of her fabulous parties, but he does not do it. How we are to interpret this is not altogether clear. Barricade Smith's nostalgic love for the rich and idle Lily may show, in ironic allegory, that the working classes are in fact infatuated with the type of life which, as socialists, they are expected to hold in contempt. Smith's inaction, his unwillingness or inability to force his way into the banquet room may signify that Klein, by implication, reproaches the working classes for their timidity, for their refusal to enforce their demands. But on the other hand, Smith's conduct may simply tell us that the working classes are in no mood to use force. It may be that Klein is saying merely that the people are watching the luxuries of the rich with longing, and that they are not resorting to un-constitutional means to get what they want; in other words that they ought to be legitimate, invited guests at the feast.

The revolutionary tendency in Klein is a faint and passing feature of the late thirties. It is not without ambiguities. Klein's personality is essentially that of a reformer. Violence, particularly violence generated in civil uprisings, requires the renunciation of certain ideals, and Klein was never really prepared to accept this alternative, bitter though he was, caustic though he could be. Revolutionary violence presupposes a hatred of persons; Klein can barely dislike any individual human being.

Ultimately, he sees members of the ruling classes as them-selves victims of the system, caught and helpless, like those

whom the system oppresses. This idea is faintly evident in a
very early poem, "Fixity," which Klein published in the
Canadian Mercury in 1929:

> Amber opaque are autumn skies—
> And autumn trees and autumn men
> Are as so many captured weeds
> And as so many fossiled flies.

During the thirties, when social injustice became flagrant and
was constant in his consciousness, he did turn against particular
individuals; but his weapon was satire, and satire always holds
a glimmer of hope that its victims may be capable of reforma-
tion.

Particularly amusing is the portrait of Milady Schwartz, the
employer's wife in "Diary of Abraham Segal, Poet," who
condescendingly comes to chat with the office staff.

> Are we all happy at our several jobs?
> Wages are low, but hope eternal bobs
> Upwards; and money, after all, is pelf.
> Moreover, so many poor people go
> Looking for work, tramping their both legs lame,
> It is a pity, a disgrace, a shame!
> Why only last week she was overjoyed
> To go to the Grand Ball, Chez Madame Lloyd,
> And dance all night for the poor unemployed.

Less successful are the portraits of various jaded characters in
and around the law courts. Klein produced a series of poems
under the significant title "Of Daumier a Portfolio," pointing
an accusing finger at such characters as the corrupt judge and
the corrupt policeman.

Satire is still the means by which Klein attacks social
injustice and corruption in the 1940s. We find it in poems
like "The White Old Lady," describing a house of ill fame;
in "Monsieur Gaston," which is the portrait of an underworld

character; in "The Spinning Wheel," the content of which has already been discussed; or in the rather unpoetic "O God! O Montreal," where Klein is concerned about the salaries of municipal employees. But in the late 1940s, his satire is no longer shrill. Margaret Avison speaks of Klein's "mature and acid tolerance." He seems to look at human failings with something like amused compassion. He has mellowed. Conditions may still cry out for change, but he sees them now less as consequences of human callousness than as examples of human weakness and vanity.

The employer is no longer treated with antipathy, as Milady Schwartz was in 1932. Instead, he is now seen as just another human being caught in an environment from which he cannot extricate himself. The poem "Dress Manufacturer: Fisherman" is a case in point.[66] It is the portrait of a man who is trying to "grow a moss" on the "granite of his effort." He has come from the city to spend a day fishing. Now he sits

> among the bulrushes his childhood only read,—
> over cool corridors
> pearled with bubbles, speckled with trout,
> beneath the little songs, the little wings,
> his city ardours all go out
> into the stipple and smooth of natural things.

As in the "Diary of Abraham Segal, Poet," nature affords respite. But Klein now realizes that the employer, too, is much in need of it. The manufacturer craves for a life away from the pressures of his working day; and we can guess, of course, that he will be forced back into the old groove, once the holiday is over. The exploited workers and the manufacturer who wastes his life on efforts which can bring him no true contentment are caught in a treadmill which is not of their making.

This idea, which in "Dress Manufacturer: Fisherman" is present only by implication, becomes explicit in "Pawnshop." Here, society is described in terms of a building in which the pawnshop is housed. Everything is second-hand and jaded. Everything has its price. People give up their prized possessions in order to survive. Each one is a debtor who cannot escape. The pawnshop "owns us" all. The clerk at the counter is himself a pawn. In other words, those who govern are themselves victims of the system. But destruction of the building—that is, of society—would not help. It becomes, when we are "free from it, our dialectic grave." Klein seems to say that revolution, liberation, is followed merely by dialectic, by the dehumanized, lethal argument of warring revolutionary factions.

In this poem, Klein looks at the social scene no longer with bitterness but with pity. Ingeniously, he likens the three globes, the traditional sign of the pawnshop, to three time-bombs. They are attached to the building and menace the entire structure. The globes are burnished, golden. The pawnshop's sign fakes a value which it does not possess. It symbolizes, at once, greed, empty glamour, and danger, all hallmarks of an ailing social system.

Adam Smith is referred to as the architect of the building. He and like-minded men have designed an economic system in which a "let-do hospitality," a laissez-faire attitude, plays a considerable part. Their intentions were excellent, no doubt, but what later generations have inherited is a system which has proved unsound and unjust, and with the dangers already built in:

> Whose lombard schemes, whose plotting kapital
> thrusts from this lintel its three burnished bombs
> set for a time, which ticks for almost all
> whether from fertile suburbs or parched slums?
> The architect is rusted from his plaque.
> Was his name Adam? Was his trade a smith
> Who thought a mansion to erect of wealth
> That houses now the bankrupt bricabrac,
> his pleasure-dome made myth
> his let-do hospitality made stealth?

Klein, indubitably, is pleading here for a more humanely planned economy. But this is not all. His reference to Adam is double-edged. The possible ambiguity of the name allows us to consider the biblical Adam as the protagonist.

Through the allusion to Adam, Klein may be saying that the inadequacies of modern society are rooted in the generations of distant history; and that they are rooted, ultimately, in human nature itself, in shortcomings that could be understood only if the concept of evil in general could be explained. To some extent, this seems to have been Klein's approach to social problems. It is not surprising that he lacked revolutionary zeal.

Klein's socialism is essentially religious. He envisages an ideal equalitarian society and prays "That wealth and poverty be known no more."[67] This is a paraphrase of words we find in Proverbs: "Remove far from me vanity and lies: give me neither poverty nor riches; feed me with food convenient for me."[68] Klein always mistrusts wealth. In one of his later poems, "Commercial Bank," he likens the banking house to an enchanted jungle where respite is found in the shade of "broad green leaves,"

> Yet it is jungle-quiet which deceives:
> toothless, with drawn nails, the beasts paw your ground—
> O, the fierce deaths expiring with no sound!

Of particular importance in Klein's writing is his contempt for a certain type of philanthropy, the "charity" which the wealthy show to their poor fellow-citizens. The ancient Judaic doctrine of the Golden Rule, certain Christian teachings, Spinozan ideas concerning the unity of the universe, and the thought of modern political philosophers, such as John Stuart Mill, combine here with modern socialism. "One buys moral credit by signing a cheque, which is easier than turning a prayer wheel," writes Bernard Shaw.[69] Klein's Milady Schwartz goes to a charity ball which, significantly, takes place "Chez Madame Lloyd." The name "Lloyd," with its inevitable connotation of an insurance empire, implies that the woman, by going to the Grand Ball, hopes to assure herself of blessings; she tries to buy moral credit.

The theme is recurrent. In "Beggars I Have Known," one of his indigent acquaintances tells Klein: "A rich man can't live without a beggar. He needs him to protect his conscience."[70] Barricade Smith speaks of "that smug lechery / Barren and sterile charity."[71] "Of the Lily that Toils Not," tells us sardonically of the debutante's charitable activities, of how she drives to the slums in her limousine.

Klein is seeking a form of socialism in which the economic order is a reflection of harmony in human relationships and social life is identical with religious life. Referring to the ideas of Mordecai M. Kaplan, and declaring that in this respect he allied himself with Kaplan's thought, he wrote in 1942: "The aspiration toward a better social order is an integral part of [Judaism],...Of philanthropy it conceives...love of man— not the Olympian love of the mighty man throwing sustenance to the mean, but the love of man which exists between equals, and which manifests itself in the thousand kindnesses to which human relationship gives scope."[72]

Klein hoped to make his influence felt also in terms of practical politics. He was active in the labour Zionist movement.[73] In 1948, he was a CCF candidate contesting a seat in the federal elections. He did not win.

To be against war, one does not need to be religious; and one does not need a philosophical basis for one's condemnation of bloodshed. Neither is there much need for metaphysical justification when men fight to preserve their very existence. The best war literature, in fact, has always been concerned, not so much with meditation, as with *reportage*. Klein, as Palnick reveals in his biography, was not qualified for active service during World War II. He had, therefore, no immediate experience of the war. His writings on the subject are the meditations of an observer who is far from the scene of action.

In the thirties, Klein opposed war. In the cause of peace, he wrote one rather remarkable poem, "Blueprint for a Monument of War." The subject was topical because, in 1937, the federal government was preparing to erect a monument to commemorate those killed in World War I.[74] At that time, new conflicts were already brewing, and the erection of such a monument seemed a mockery to many who felt that those who had died "in the war to end all wars" had died in vain. They objected to a monument which, in a sense, was to celebrate the great carnage. In this spirit, Klein wrote his sombre satire. It contains some strong lines. Like Wilfred Owen, he is debunking the absurdities of Horatian patriotism.

What makes the poem interesting in regard to Klein's religious thought is its *postscriptum* entitled "Appendix for the Pious—Isaiah, chapter sixty-seven." The Book of Isaiah has only sixty-six chapters. Here, perhaps, Klein gives us a hint that he regards himself a prophet in the modern age, a poet who continues where the voices of the Bible broke off.

When we look at the last verse of the Book of Isaiah, we find it foretold therein that the worshippers shall go forth and look upon the carcasses of men who have transgressed against the Lord; "for their worm shall not die, neither shall their fire be quenched; and they shall be an abhorring unto all flesh." By appending a passage called "Isaiah, chapter sixty-seven" to his poem, Klein seems to equate the main body of his poem with chapter sixty-six in the Book of Isaiah, and more especially, with the last verse of chapter sixty-six. It appears then that the monument of war is a modern equivalent of the carcasses of those who have transgressed against the Lord; for it is a perpetual reminder of those who have waged war, who have killed. The mysterious lines of Isaiah concerning the worm that shall not die and concerning the fire of the carcasses that shall not be quenched become meaningful here: the sight of the war memorial keeps the "worm" of old discords alive; the fires that were kindled in the war which the monument commemorates have barely subsided, and, in 1937, there was every indication that they might soon burst into another conflagration.

The postscript itself elaborates on the nature of the fires that are not quenched. We are reminded of how the flames of hate flicker and rekindle. In the final lines, we encounter a vision that has in it something of the terror of the atomic age, intimations of a fear that has not yet broken upon the world:

> Peace shall be heard in the land, but who shall hear it? Truce shall
> be called in the land, who shall hearken unto it?
> For your brothers shall lie in foreign fields, where the crow may
> bring them tiding, and the worm whisper the news.

The reference to the "foreign fields," echoing Rupert Brooke's "The Soldier," links the waste and heartbreak of the past with a picture of future devastation.

One year later, however, Klein was no longer a pacifist. Important victories had been won by the forces of aggression, racism, and political coercion: the Rhineland had been occupied; Abyssinia had fallen; Austria had given up the struggle. In Spain, the resistance of democratic forces was crumbling. A victory of the rebels meant a defeat of the working class. A rebel victory also meant that racist Germany would enlarge its sphere of influence. For Klein, there was then no choice; as a Jew and socialist, he supported the Republican cause. He was, in 1938, a practising lawyer; he had a wife and a baby son; he did not feel he could join the volunteers who set out from Canada to fight for the Spanish government;

but in one of his poems, "To One Gone to the Wars,"[75] he deplored the fact that he was prevented from doing so. When World War II broke out, Klein wrote: "The issue is clear . . . Jews of the lands of freedom must meet the enemy with a battle cry."[76]

In the early 1940s, he published a number of poems concerning the war: "Ballad of the Days of the Messiah," in which originality of vision is in sharp contrast with the deliberately banal metre; "Ballad of Quislings," certainly among the weakest lines Klein has written and quite unworthy of his talent; and "Ballad of the Nursery Rhymes," where distorted snatches of popular verse help to convey the desolation of a world that is out of joint. As editor of the *Canadian Jewish Chronicle*, he wrote commentaries on the issues of the day; but as poet he could not draw much inspiration from the war. To write in favour of the fighting was not congenial to him, and, of course, he also lacked first-hand information. The poem "Not All the Perfumes of Arabia," published in 1943, showed that Klein could make vivid what he personally experienced. It describes the sensations of a man who, at home, listens to a news broadcast:

It is not words I hear,
Nor are they sights I see,
I smell the smell of fear.

War, as a subject for his art, only reclaims Klein's attention when it is again ethically possible to condemn it. In 1948, he writes an interesting short story, "And it Shall Come to Pass." A psychiatrist interviews a man who is tormented by a recurring dream. The man always sees himself in a plane which delivers the bomb that is to end all wars, but the psychiatrist is unperturbed. The dream is obviously only the memory of a wartime experience. But the frightening aspect, the man explains, is that the plane never makes it home. The dials all go crazy, and the plane descends and descends, and they never come anywhere near the ground. They can't land, and they can't crash. There is a foreign correspondent aboard the aircraft, and he reads from the Bible: "In the beginning God created the heaven and the earth. And the earth was without form, and void, and darkness was upon the face of the deep. . . . " In Klein's vision, man is undoing creation and is helplessly swept into chaos. The story shows that, quite apart from spontaneous humanitarian feelings which, no doubt, prompted his attitude, Klein condemned war because it counteracted the divine creative process.

The general mood of pessimism which gripped intellectuals in the 1950s, when the cold war combined with an escalation of atomic testing, moved Klein to revise and reprint an earlier poem, "Penultimate Chapter." Here he ironically foresees the day when a new species of earth-dwellers will excavate the remains of twentieth-century man and consider these an example of fauna that could not adapt to changing conditions and therefore became extinct. The specimens with their "lightning tusks" are labelled simply "The mammoths (circa 1951)."

To observe that Klein was better able to praise than to condemn is a commonplace by now. Critics are almost unanimous on this point.[77] Klein's poems on the theme of persecution written during the war are thought to have been composed from a sense of duty rather than from compelling emotions. Few think that Klein treated his theme adequately.

His first reaction to the rise of Hitlerism appears to be

contained in a quatrain, "Desiderata," which was published in 1932:

> Three things I long to see:
>   A lustrous moth
> Torment with envy bulky behemoth . . .
>   An elf and ant
> Conspire to affright an elephant . . .
>   A manikin
> Murder the superman of his own kin.

The lines seem to be written in the spirit of a political cartoon. They are to fulfil the same functions: they intend to ridicule, to discredit, and to give vent to indignation.

The subject is treated very differently a few years later when streams of refugees are trying to escape from Germany only to find that " . . . they have all been shut, and barred, and triple-locked, / The gates of refuge, the asylum doors." Klein devotes a long poem, "Childe Harold's Pilgrimage," to the plight of Central-European Jewry.[78] He feels that he must identify himself with the victims of persecution, and he speaks in the first person:

> What, now, for me to do?
> Gulp down some poisoned brew?
>
>   .   .   .   .   .
>
> No, not for such ignoble end
> From Ur of the Chaldees have I the long way come;

Clearly, the writing is rather poor. Klein is not inspired but driven by conscience. He wants to feel the emotions of the victims. But events take place far away in foreign lands and under conditions which are alien to him. He is bewildered, and he can only comprehend what is happening as he comprehends a lesson in a history book. Hence, there is no convincing outcry. He sees the persecutions in Hitler's Germany merely as part of a larger pattern. Experience has shown that periods of anguish pass eventually, and he is confident that the same will happen now.

> 'Tis not in me to unsheathe an avenging sword;
> I cannot don phylactery to pray;
> Weaponless, blessed with no works, and much abhorred,
> This only is mine wherewith to face the horde:
> The frozen patience waiting for its day,
> The stance long-suffering, the stoic word,
> The bright empirics that knows well that the
> Night of the *cauchemar* comes and goes away,—
> A baleful wind, a baneful nebula, over
> A saecular imperturbability.

These verses were published in 1938, but it is probable that they were written earlier, at a time when Klein's pacifist convictions were particularly strong. In view of our present-day knowledge of the holocaust, the lines seem intolerably complacent. But in the thirties, many shared Klein's hope that, somehow, political means would eventually bring amelioration and that current evils would pass away.

It is as if Klein were too stunned by the reports of savagery to visualize in realistic terms what was happening. He transforms his emotions into stylized, surrealist metaphor:

> Nuremberg tower-clock struck one:
> The Swastika clawed at the sun
>
> .   .   .   .
>
> A poet, at the hour of nine,
> Thought, in his cell, of the beautiful Rhine.

When the clock struck eleven, it expired, "as did human time."[79]

In a similar vein, "The Ballad of the Thwarted Axe"[80] tells of a victim who stands accused in the German People's Court. Haunting, but strangely impersonal like the true folk ballad, the refrain tells of the axe which is being prepared for the execution:

Headsman, headsman, whet your axe,
Against the sparking stone.
The blade that's eaten by the flint,
The better eats the bone!

In the end, there is the significant variation:

Headsman, headsman—cheated man!
Whom thorough judges mock.
You shall have no use for your axe,
A ghost stands in the dock.

In a metaphysical sense, the victims cannot be harmed; they cannot be reached. The murderers grasp the shadow, not the essential being. Thus Klein consoled himself, and, no doubt, he meant to console others in this way.

The well-known poem "A Psalm of Abraham, Concerning That which He Beheld upon the Heavenly Scarp," appeared in *Poetry* (Chicago) in 1942.[81] Here Klein brings himself at last to catalogue some of the Nazi atrocities. But, again, he writes in symbolist terms. The angels grow silent at what they see. One of them is weeping, and his tears are so bitter that they shrivel the flowers upon which they fall. Klein's imagination is appealing, but it detracts from the enormity of his subject. The symbolism has, however, another function here. It helps to make clear that Klein does not believe persecutions to be trials sent or permitted by God. God summons the angels of Sodom and sends them down to earth. In other words, Klein sees the persecutions as an evil which is counteracted by God. Klein here looks upon World War II, very much as he did in "Ballad of the Days of the Messiah": it is a mustering of divine energies; a purging of evil conditions which has divine sanction.

In 1944, he writes his poem "Address to the Choir Boys." They are about to sing the song of Rabbi Amnon, a martyr who accepted his lot. The boys, in their innocence, sing joyfully; the tragic phrases are not tragic on their tongue. With contemporary reports of new martyrdom on his mind, Klein fervently hopes the boys may never learn the meaning of the song. In the summer of 1944, he also publishes a Platonic tale of children who refuse to be born.[82] It is obvious that he is constantly trying to come to grips with the horror, the un-imaginable events of which he reads in the press and hears over the radio. But he remains, as it were, on the periphery. History and symbolism are summoned to help convey his feelings.

Klein evidently was longing to produce something more immediately relevant. Human beings were being destroyed; a civilization was being annihilated; and the victims were people of his own culture. His instinct of self-preservation and his intellectual principles demanded a supreme effort. He wanted to pillory the enemy; perhaps to unmask him for those who were too dull to know his true nature; he wanted to show that man was yet capable of passion in the face of injustice. It was certainly in this spirit that he wrote his long satire, *The Hitleriad*. The opening passage declares what drove him to this uncongenial task:

> I am the grandson of the prophets! I
> Shall not seal lips against iniquity.

The immediate inspiration for the poem came from Pope's *Dunciad*, and one can understand why Klein was attracted to this work. Like Pope, Klein felt that great disasters were caused by puny men, that it was precisely the littleness of mind in the many which permitted catastrophe to overtake mankind. Klein says, Hitler is strong

> For through him, magnified
> Smallness comes to our ken
> The total bigness of
> All little men.[83]

Some of Pope's lines must have appeared to Klein like a prophecy. Could a Hitler have come to power had there not existed an electorate teeming with dunces? Could Nazism have spread the way it did if the schools and universities of Germany had not been filled with non-entities who were

First slave to Words, then vassal to a Name
Then dupe to Party; child and man the same,[84]

and who were ever anxious to "bring to one dead level every mind"?[85] The final passage of *The Dunciad* seems to foretell the fate of Europe in the black-out of the early forties.

It was, no doubt, the topicality of *The Dunciad* that gave impetus to Klein's work. But Pope's duncas are, as individuals, comparatively innocuous. Klein dealt with evil men. The apocalyptic events at the end of Pope's poem were abstracta. Klein had to write about reality. *The Hitleriad*, in spite of the many good lines it contains, was doomed before it was written. Why did it fail?

The main reason is that the subject did not lend itself to satirical treatment; for satire cannot do without an element of the ridiculous, and the activities of the Nazi leaders defy laughter, no matter how bitter. A satirist like Swift could translate monstrous crimes into terms even more monstrous— until the exaggeration reached a point so ludicrous that it could elicit amusement. At the same time, the exaggeration illuminated the true nature of conditions which before had not been seen in their full crassness. This is the case, for instance, in *A Modest Proposal*. In the excesses of Hitler and his helpers, however, the absurd, the unimaginable, had become reality and thereby ceased to be comical. Exaggeration became impossible and, indeed, would not have been bearable. Evil had become so manifest that it froze all attempts to parody it. Literary devices could only diminish, not heighten, the impression made by reality. Where knowledge of real circumstances failed to rouse the emotions, a poet could not hope that his craft would draw forth the missing response. Satire is an ambitious art form. It always implies the hope that it may help to improve things. Where it cannot fulfil this function, it becomes futile.

One may then ask whether it was a weakness in Klein's ethical emotions that allowed him to treat humorously a subject so fraught with misery. In his defence, one may point to the political cartoons which appeared in the press throughout World War II and made sardonic comments on the leaders in the enemy camp. Many of Klein's passages are written in the spirit of the cartoon.

One might also remember that Jews much closer to the scene of horror continued to invent jokes about their oppressors. Although a form of defiance, it could be remarkably mild. I remember an anecdote which was circulating in Vienna in 1938, after the fall of Austria, when persecutions had become particularly virulent:

One Jew asked another for his dearest wish. The other replied he wished that both of them would grow very, very old, and that then, one day, they might go for a walk in the park and see a poor old tramp sitting alone on a bench; and that one of them might say to the other, Look at that fellow there; isn't that Hitler?[86]

Klein, possibly, knew this, or a similar joke, when he wrote Psalm 155 in "The Psalter of A. M. Klein." There he expresses the hope that an evil-doer (clearly, Hitler) might be remembered only as a name for some new, disgusting insect "Or in the writing on a privy wall."

Today, of course, witticisms concerning the era of National Socialism have ceased to appear funny. Our knowledge of the holocaust makes any reference to this topic in combination with comic elements offensive. But when Klein wrote his *Hitleriad* and other related poems, he did not have this knowledge. He had been told of atrocities, but he found it difficult to believe that what he heard could be true. Like so many, perhaps even most, he fervently wished that much of what was said might be war propaganda. We have his own word for this: "For the past six years, while the press was full of detailed description of the methods adopted by the Nazi extermination squads . . . while all this was being attested, both as to place and as to time, as to method and as to result, Jews, and all civilized beings, secretly entertained a hope, a wish, a concealed but cherished incredulity."[87] This incredulity, better than anything, explains why Klein could write as he did and why what was written concerning the persecutions could not succeed.

After the war, when the truth of the holocaust was before him in all its inescapable grimness, Klein wrote his "Elegy."[88] Here he abandoned the historical costume and the symbolism. His grief is personal and passionate. One may still maintain that no poetry, however sincere, can do justice to this subject because poetry is designed to give aesthetic pleasure, and one cannot convey ultimate horror and at the same time aim to please. Only the factual report, the documentary, may give us a glimpse of the reality. Nevertheless, Klein's "Elegy" impressed survivors of the holocaust, and they saw fit to include it in the *Ratno Memorial Volume*, which was published in Buenos Aires in 1954. The editors, Jacob Botoshansky and Isaak Yanasovitch, call it "the most powerful elegy on the holocaust of the century written in any language other than Hebrew or Yiddish."[89]

The true power to hand on to posterity an account of the holocaust is reserved for those who lived through it. Klein, having been spared the experience, could not hope to convey an authentic message. Nevertheless, his conscience continued to drive him on. He felt constantly that, somehow, he had to make mankind understand more keenly the enormity of murder and thereby, perhaps, make it understand more keenly also the true value of life.

In 1950, the poem "Meditation Upon Survival"[90] is still concerned with the fate of the six million:

> . . . I must live
> their unexpired six million circuits, giving
> to each of their nightmares my body for a bed—
> inspirited, dispirited—

The good action, in Klein's ethos, is always that which creates or preserves. Six million human lives, prevented from fulfilling themselves, are demanding continuity, and Klein strains to respond, even though he can do so only in a remote, metaphysical sense. It is, perhaps, the sign of a gathering spiritual darkness that Klein does not propose to live for the six million the happier existence that each of them craved; but that, instead, he feels he must continue within himself their unspeakable suffering.

THE SECOND SCROLL

Background, Religious Thought, and Ethics

In 1931, with the publication of "Out of the Pulver and the Polished Lens," Klein had emerged from religious doubts and had enthusiastically committed himself to Spinozan ideas. But if the arrangement of poems in *Hath Not a Jew . . .* is an indication of the sequence in which they were written, "Talisman in Seven Shreds" and "Design for Mediaeval Tapestry" suggest that his fervour was soon replaced by doubt and despair.[1] In 1939, in his "Psalm II," he firmly declares himself a believer; but the book *Poems* (1944), in which these lines of affirmation were published, contains also "Psalm XXXIV." Here, Klein begs Rashi to show him "Behind the veil the vital verity." The "metal beast" roars; the "steel bird screams." Klein longs for Rashi to tell him "that wine will issue from this bitter grape." He intones a Kaddish for Rashi, who had no son, and hopes that the prayer will also bring grace to himself: "To most unworthy, doubt-divided me." "The Cripples," a poem which appeared in the collection of 1948, also gives evidence of an absence of religious belief. With a sharp sense of privation, Klein envies the cripples whom he observes at their worship. He tells us that, like them, he once had faith; but he has lost it. Three years later, in 1951, in *The Second Scroll*, we find him in fervent prayer.

Did he, then, within the span of about twenty years, oscillate between fervent religiosity and agnosticism, atheism and renewed faith? The writings here referred to seem to indicate a repeated reversal in Klein's beliefs. I think, however, that they lend themselves to misinterpretation and that, after 1931, Klein's intellectual development was not marked by fundamental change. I do not think that after his encounter with Spinozan ideas, he was again troubled by questions concerning the existence of God. He did not adhere to Spinoza's uncompromising, mechanistic philosophy; there were certainly modifications in Klein's concepts; but the existence of the Deity was not in doubt once Klein had accepted the idea that God was present in nature: His existence was "The undebatable verity /.../ The simple *I am that I am.*"² Proof of divine existence was life itself. When Klein was tormented by doubts, he was concerned with the question whether the Divine was interested in the fate of humanity.

Contemporary history placed Klein's religious thinking in constant jeopardy. Was God concerned with mankind? Could one place one's trust in the ultimate goodness and beauty of creation? Could one speak of oneness and equality when a Hitler flourished beside an Albert Schweitzer? Could one proclaim the glory of a world which harboured Auschwitz? Anyone who tried to interpret modern life in terms of a religious philosophy which trusted in an essential perfection of the universe had to resolve these problems. The gap between faith and reality seemed unbridgeable.

In 1948, a political event at last indicated to Klein the possibility of a solution to his spiritual difficulties and led him to consolidate his ideas in a systematic statement. This event was the creation of the state of Israel. In the emergence of the new state, Klein found some of his most ardent beliefs vindicated. The self-proclaimed supermen of the Third Reich had been destined to realize their frailty, and a people close to annihilation now rallied to renew its nationhood. History seemed to prove that in the forces that govern human activities, the principle of justice played a part. The convulsions of the war had counteracted those trends which opposed the well-being of the species as a whole. Now, the setting up of the new state seemed to show a vital energy asserting itself in favour of those who were willing to serve it. Klein saw mankind involved in an evolutionary process. That an independent Jewish state could emerge after two millenia, and this at a moment when the Jewish people seemed most helpless, proved to Klein that the processes of the universe were not aimless. The creation of Israel, an event that was taking place contrary to all probability, became for him a divine manifestation, a modern miracle, meaningful beyond its national significance. He saw in it a proof that divine energy was struggling toward a finer mode of existence, toward an ultimate triumph of righteousness, no matter how hopeless this cause might seem. Evil was being eliminated by the counterthrust of the creative principle.

An opportunity to clarify his ideas and to gather material for a book in which they could be expressed came to Klein in 1949. He was to visit Israel and, on the way, to spend a few days in Europe and in North Africa. He sent home a series of dispatches which were published in *The Canadian Jewish Chronicle* between August and December 1949, under the title "Notebook of a Journey." In April 1950, another instalment, the essay "A Jew in the Sistine Chapel," was added.

Through his orthodox upbringing, Klein had acquired a detailed knowledge of Palestine, its geography and history. It had been the dreamland of his childhood days.[3] Later, as an active Zionist, he had seen in the Holy Land a haven for his disadvantaged brethren, a place where they could build a life of dignity.[4] In 1948 the symbolism of the ancient legends in which Zion is expected to herald the Messianic Age had become renewed in a reality of modern life. Klein's exuberance at the prospect of seeing at last the places that were hallowed in his imagination reverberates in his account of his departure from La Guardia airport.[5]

He landed at Lydda on 2 August 1949, at a moment of nationwide excitement. On the very first night he drove to the military cemetery of Beit Vegan at the outskirts of Jerusalem. Here, on a summit that overlooks the Judaean hills, a grave had been prepared for the body of Theodor Benjamin Herzl, the founder of modern Zionism. The grave was yet empty when Klein and his companion, Major A. Friedgut, who acted as his guide, "stood in silence upon that height, . . . grappling with justice and history," thinking of "tombs and resurrections," while a "great full moon shone in the heaven . . . a moon sublime, a great bronze gong waiting to be struck." Klein tells of his thoughts at Herzl's grave, which was yet a cenotaph:

> I thought of Rachel's tomb, Rachel lamenting her children's bitter fate, and of her tomb still in enemy hands. I thought also of that other sepulchre, emptied on the third day, and of how much good and how much evil it had brought to the world. I thought of them all, the many tombs and cairns with which this country was covered and of how the memory of the saints and sages whom they hid had kindled the minds of men for generations. Yet all these tombs, instead of being merely mementos of death, had been somehow, had been above all, signposts for life. Surely in this land always had there come out of the lion's fell—sweetness, and out of the very tomb— life and light.[6]

Klein's dispatch then gives an account of the welcome the nation had prepared for Herzl's body, which a delegation was bringing from Vienna. Masses of people stood watching at the shore when the El Al plane with Herzl's body approached Haifa. An escort of fighter aircraft rose to meet the incoming plane; thrice it circled the city while below in the harbour the guns of the Israeli navy fired salvos in salute. Herzl's body was then lying in state in Tel Aviv awaiting a cortege of cars that was to bring it to Jerusalem. In Tel Aviv, there were no salvos:

> . . . no shouting, no, and no mourning, but only a still small voice, uttering many languages, the languages of the Galuth giving the greeting of redemption. This is not a funeral but a reintegration, there is no sadness; this is not a triumph . . . but a vindication; there is everywhere solemnity and the knowledge that right has come into its own. There are tears, but pride, not softness shed them; there is, above all, thanksgiving.

While he contemplates the mass of people who have come to do homage to their modern prophet, Klein remembers an immigrant camp he had seen.

> ... they spoke varying tongues, they had customs unlike; and I thought as I beheld this debris, material and human, this wreckage of hearts once warm and domestic, that a great wind, a furious tempest it had been that had taken them, whirling and swirling aloft in the ether, them and their children and their pitiable impedimenta, a pell-mell confusion, Ashkenazi and Sephardi, of refined and uncouth, from the five continents and the seven seas, and had carried them helpless in its hold, through the air, suspended and afraid, at last to drop them, in confusion pell-mell here upon the coast of Haifa. No wonder, then, that the thousands who had known this experience now stood to welcome this latest flotsam of the air, the latest storm-tossed oylim, to welcome and to offer up their thanks to the man who had been the signator of all their passports, the author of the Idea that had become their Home.

It is clear from this passage that Klein considered Herzl an immigrant. Because Herzl came to Israel as a dead man, a rallying point and inspiration to the living, he appeared to symbolize the homecoming of all, of those who had died in exile and those who continued among the living. Herzl becomes the embodiment of the Jewish spirit and a representative of the Jewish people as a whole. In this sense, Klein found in him the prototype for the hero of his allegory. What he had felt at Herzl's grave helped him to create Melech Davidson, the King from the House of David. A clear echo of the passages he wrote pertaining to Herzl can be found in the description of Melech Davidson's funeral in *The Second Scroll*.

That the experience of those first days in Israel was of momentous import to Klein becomes evident when one reads the passionate lines which he addressed to Herzl in his dispatch published on 9 September. He writes with unabashed emotion:

> Hail, and farewell, then, O Prince of Israel! ... You have deserved well of your people, and at length you have been

granted what even to Moses was not granted—to rest, a king of the kings of Israel and Judah, in the Promised Land! You are yourself the fulfilment of Ezekiel's prophecy—have not the bones come to life? Is not a new breath breathed into the body of this people?

And he closes:

Rest well, rest easy, O Seer of Visions, Master of Fulfilments! To the high places of Israel are you lifted up to dwell in the heart and pinnacle of Hiersolyma the Splendid, Jerusalem the New! The hills of Judaea kneel before you, the plains lie prostrate before your coming! For all of us, and in especial for my generation, you dreamed a dream; it was the truth, and now you lie in its midst. Farewell, Majesty and Master of my days! I go, your word upon my lips. . . I shall not be to-morrow night upon the eminence of Beit Vegan. Whether the moon will shine upon it as it did that first night, I do not know. I know only that the great bronze gong has sounded.

The great bronze gong; what did it proclaim? The beginning of an age when the intent of Godhood could no longer be misunderstood and the Messianic condition had become a certainty? This, apparently, was how Klein interpreted the creation of the state of Israel, and in this spirit he wrote *The Second Scroll*.[7]

The book is prefaced by two quotations. The first reads:

. . . And ask a Talmudist
what ails the modesty
of his marginal Keri

that Moses and all the prophets
  cannot persuade him
to pronounce the textual Chetiv

As M. W. Steinberg, in his introduction to *The Second Scroll*
has pointed out, this is a passage from Milton's *Areopagitica*,
criticizing "those who would change words in the oral reading
of the Torah in accordance with the Talmudic precept 'that
all words which in the law are written obscenely, must be
changed to more civil words.'" This injunction, invoked for
modesty's sake, angered Milton, as he remarked "fools, who
would teach men to read more decently than God thought fit
to write."[8] Steinberg interprets the presence of the quotation
from *Areopagitica* as an indication that Klein accepted evil as
God-given and a phenomenon not to be questioned by man.[9]

It seems, however, that this quotation can assume also
another meaning when read with reference to a remark in *The
Second Scroll* made by the narrator of the story. This is a
Canadian who visits the Synagogue of Rabbi Isaac Luria in the
mountains of Galilee and there speaks with a venerable sage, a
Talmud scholar. He says: "Our conversation was in Yiddish,
for the old man was of those who held that Hebrew would be
profaned by secular use."[10] Many ultra-orthodox Jews feel that
Hebrew is a holy language and should be used solely to express
religious ideas. Its use in the motley communications of daily
living is offensive to them and they condemn it with un-
compromising vehemence. Some of the orthodox, known
chiefly by the name of Natore Karta (Guardians of the City),
go further: they believe that the creation of the new state of
Israel, which secularizes the use of Hebrew and Jewish culture
in general, is sinful because, according to tradition, the
kingdom of David is to be restored only with the coming of
the Messiah. Since Klein sees in the creation of the state of
Israel an event of religious significance, he cannot be com-
pletely indifferent to the attitude of those Jewish communities
who are most overtly concerned with religious issues. It seems

therefore probable that the quotation from *Areopagitica* is addressed to them. Klein seems to say: The creation of the new state of Israel as a political entity among the nations, the re-emergence of Hebrew as a living language and its use in both the elevated and baser contexts (including the Chetiv) which this necessitates, all this God has seen fit to "write" in terms of historical reality. Who may arrogate to himself the right to question when and how these events are to take place? It is as if Klein were saying, "Do not think that because the days of the Messiah are not yet here, it is too soon for Israel to emerge as an independent nation; rather maintain that because Israel is able to re-emerge, the days of the Messiah may be anticipated."

His gratitude and joy speak from the second quotation which prefaces *The Second Scroll*. This is a partly translated and paraphrased version of Rabbi Levi Yitschok's famous song "A Dudele."[11] Klein renders it thus:

> Rebono Shel Olam:
> 'Tis a Thou-song I will sing Thee—
> Thou . . . Thou. . . Thou . . . Thou
>
> Ayeh Emtzoeko, V'Ayeh Lo Emtzoeko
>
> O, where shall I find Thee?
> And where art Thou not to be found?
> Wherever I fare—Thou!
> Or here, or there—Thou!
> Only Thou! None but Thou!
> Again, Thou! And still, Thou!

"A Dudele," indubitably, was inspired by Psalm 139: "If I ascend up into heaven, thou art there; if I make my bed in hell, behold, thou art there." Ausubel draws attention also to the Rabbi's probable indebtedness to the Morning Prayer of Yehuda Halevi,

> Lord where shall I find Thee?
> High and hidden is Thy place!

And where shall I not find Thee?
The world is full of Thy glory![12]

Yet, we encounter here also a concept of Godhood which
accords with modern philosophies that are concerned with the
immanence of God. In the latter half of the twentieth century,
no one interested in religious philosophy can meet with such
emphasis on the word "Thou" and not connect it with Martin
Buber. Why did Klein use the archaic form in place of the
modern "you"? He was, by now, frequently emancipating his
diction from the archaisms of his early poetry. One may
remember, for instance, "Psalm XXIV" in *Poems* (1944).

As far as I am aware, all translations of Martin Buber's
writings use the word "Thou"; and to him it is of supreme
importance. Buber believes that God is found in all things;[13]
but He manifests Himself most clearly in relationships when
one entity approaches the other and recognizes in this other
the all-present. The "I" will then regard the other not as "it"
but as "Thou," and the relationship will be hallowed. "Meet
the world with the fulness of your being and you shall meet
Him," says Buber in his book *On Judaism*.[14] The Thou-song,
then, becomes an ideal motto for *The Second Scroll*. It may be
regarded simply as a paraphrase of a traditional song. On the
other hand, it could also be read as a proclamation of pan-
theistic ideology.

It does not appear that Klein ever declared himself Buber's
disciple. But Buber's love of Chassidic mysticism had, no
doubt, its appeal for Klein. There is a great deal in *The Second
Scroll* that is closely related to Buber's teachings. Buber believed
that love of the Creator and love of that which He has created
are finally one and the same.[15] He felt revelation to be con-
tinual.[16] It is not confined to biblical times. Man is constantly
struggling for knowledge of God's will.[17] Buber feels that "The
Jewish people are the most exposed point of modern mankind.
The venture and chance of civilization becomes concentrated
in their existence; their existence itself is an experiment."[18] It

is man's duty to "take part in the still uncompleted work of creation."[19] World history, for Buber, is "the battle-ground between false and genuine authority; each man of faith is obliged to take part in this battle and to contribute to the victory of the genuine authority...."[20] For Buber, the activities of individuals as well as of nations become an expression of religious significance. "A drop of Messianic consummation must be mingled in every hour," he writes.[21]

While *The Second Scroll* is steeped in such ideas, I do not suggest that the novel was consciously planned with Buber's ideas in mind. It is, however, clear that it expresses philosophical trends of which Buber was the most prominent modern exponent.

The Thou-song, which Klein chose as a motto for his novel is interesting not only for what it tells us and what it seems to imply but also for the words which Klein chose to leave out. Levi Yitschok's "Dudele" contains these words: *Is emitzen gut, is doch du, wecholiloh schlecht, oy du.*

In Ausubel's *Treasury of Jewish Folklore* this is translated thus:

If one prospers, it is because of You, and
if, God forbid, one has trouble, oy! it is also You.

It could, admittedly, be argued that Klein left out these words because he felt their meaning was sufficiently encompassed in the rest. It is, however, possible that he could not bring himself to say that evil could issue from God because such a statement would have been contrary to his belief.

Just as the First Scroll, the Old Testament, records the ancient history of the Jews and interprets it in religious terms, so *The Second Scroll* is to record recent Jewish history and to make the reader aware of its religious significance. To make this plain, Klein named each chapter after a Book in the Pentateuch. He then added chapters containing related material and called them "Gloss Aleph," "Gloss Beth," "Gloss Gimel," "Gloss Dalid," and "Gloss Hai." Steinberg, in his introduction to the novel, explains the glosses thus: "Just as the Torah comprises not merely the Bible, but also the commentaries on it—the Talmud, for example—which expand upon the events in the Five Books and explain them, completing the message, so too in Klein's *The Second Scroll* there are five glosses which elaborate upon or which help us elaborate events in the story."[22] In the following analysis, each chapter named after a Book of the Pentateuch will be discussed in conjunction with its gloss.

"Genesis," the first chapter, is concerned with the awakening consciousness of a child and, also, in broad outline, with the condition of Jewry as a whole as it emerged at the beginning of the twentieth century. The narrator of the story tells us how he grew up in an orthodox Montreal household, in the security of a western home, while his uncle, Melech Davidson, a renowned Talmud scholar lived "removed from wordly matters" in the backwoods of eastern Europe, "a flame tonguing its way to the full fire of God."[23] The boy hears his parents speak of Melech Davidson. He learns to think of his uncle with awe; but what he looks like he does not know, for the orthodox do not permit themselves to be photographed. Later we realize that here is an early clue to Melech Davidson's identity: his face can never be isolated from a larger concept that encompasses the mass of the people; he never appears as an individual; he is the searching, striving aspect of Jewry personified.

One day, the simple, pleasant life in the Montreal household is disturbed by news of a pogrom in Ratno (the place whence, according to Palnick, Klein's parents fled to Canada). Uncle Melech is among the survivors, but the massacre he has witnessed has roused him from his scholarly tranquility. The letters he now sends to his Montreal relatives make increasingly clear that he has abandoned his Talmudic studies. Then the letters cease altogether. Two refugees from Ratno, who arrive in Montreal, eventually tell the whole story. It transpires that uncle Melech, after a severe flogging he received for interceding on behalf of an old rabbi and after being called a Bolshevik by his tormentors, had decided to join the Bolsheviks.

The two emissaries from Melech Davidson are, themselves, not Bolsheviks. Indeed, they seem somewhat embarrassed, reluctant to speak of Melech's conversion. They represent the socialist segment of Jewish society; working-class people. In their pockets, the boy discovers, they carry sunflower seeds: they harbour ideas potentially nourishing; capable of producing something very beautiful and beneficial when planted in the right soil.[24] One is reminded of Buber's view that "the ancient Messianic dreams live on in the ideologies of Jewish socialists."[25]

Talmud scholars, deprived of their ancient, hereditary pursuit, seek new ways to bring about the millennium. Some go to extremes intolerable to the rest: Melech Davidson's name, we learn, is no longer mentioned in the orthodox household in Montreal. By and by, reports arrive of his total emancipation and secular activities, his polemical writings and success as a political agitator. His brother-in-law (the narrator's father) condemns him; his sister (the narrator's mother) accepts everything meekly as the will of God: everything—the pogrom, Melech's survival, his subsequent denial of his faith. Obviously, they stand for two kinds of orthodoxy, the militant and the resigned. But their son, as he grows up and enters university, tries to understand the various points of view with impartiality and takes secret pride in his uncle's independence and sense of social justice. The narrator, then, represents the intellectual of the 1930s. Klein tries to include in his story the broadest possible spectrum of Jewish thinking. Thus he introduces also the father's friend, the cabinet-maker who is a fervent supporter of the British Empire and always carries on his person a Union Jack. Critics have reproached Klein for not creating a novel with realistic, individualized characters,[26] and they are, of course, right in this: anyone who looks in his book for that combination of realism and symbolism which may be found, for instance, in *The Man of Property*, *Ulysses*, or *The Old Man and the Sea* will be disappointed. *The Second Scroll* has to be read as a modern parable; it does not attempt to be more than this.

As the narrator grows up, he becomes aware of the lack of homogeneity in the intellectual attitudes of his people. His uncle Melech comes to represent a wide intellectual spectrum, for he changes from extreme orthodoxy to extreme negation of the faith. When World War II breaks out, he is trapped in Europe, and his fate becomes representative of the fate suffered by his brethren irrespective of their individual persuasions. At the end of "Genesis," he is "enveloped by the great smoke that for the next six years kept billowing over the Jews of Europe—their cloud by day, their pillar of fire by night."[27]

The imagery in these concluding lines of the chapter "Genesis" makes clear that the tale is to be read and interpreted in the manner in which one appraoches symbolist poetry. When Klein speaks of billowing smoke, he refers, of course, to the smoke that rose above the crematoria of Hitler's concentration camps. This was the cloud that darkened the sun and embittered the day of the living; it was the pillar of fire that set passions ablaze in the general spiritual darkness. Steinberg has pointed to a connection between Klein's symbolism and the passage in Exodus, which reads: "And the Lord went before them by day in a pillar of a cloud, to lead them the way; and by night in a pillar of fire, to give them light."[28] When one keeps in mind the context in which the images of the pillar of cloud and the pillar of fire appear in the Bible, Klein's passage stirs the imagination and illuminates his own philosophical and religious position; for he seems to imply that the murdered millions—turned to smoke and transformed to dust, and towering above the land—harboured God and became the guides of the living.

This idea is more than the interpretation of gruesome contemporary facts in terms of poetic biblical legend: the full grandeur of Klein's idea can only be sensed if one recalls his lines from "Out of the Pulver and the Polished Lens":

> he who does violence to me, verily he sins against
> the light of day; he is made a deicide.
> Howbeit, even in dust I am resurrected, and even in decay I
>   live again.

If one accepts the Spinozan idea of the living, divine universe, one may see in the billowing dust God truly risen. Yet, even in other forms of pantheism, in Chassidic dualism, for instance, this interpretation of Klein's symbolism remains valid. If one accepts the idea of an all-pervasive *Anima* (a term which appears in "Gloss Gimel"), the cloud of dust and fire is still divine. God, the Creative, is murdered in the victims, but the smallest particle is still imbued with His presence. The highly developed organism is destroyed; but the particles, blown across the sky in their myriads, will reassert themselves. Their presence, or the memory of it, will make Jewry determined to seek the Promised Land of freedom and dignity. In the light of pantheistic thought, the tradition concerning the pillars of cloud and fire is turned into reality.

The commentary, "Gloss Aleph" is brief and consists of one poem which serves to establish beyond all question the auto-biographical character of the story. It is a reprint of Klein's poem "Autobiography" (1943); and it is as if Klein were saying: I am obviously not concerned with fiction but with a distillation and stylization of reality. The ending of the gloss, reminiscent of Plato's "Phaedrus" and Wordsworth's "Im-mortality Ode," tells of Klein's nostalgia for childhood days, for the intensity and vividness of childhood experience. Strongest in his imagination was then a vision of Jerusalem:

"It is a fabled city that I seek; It stands in Space's vapours and Time's haze."

In "Exodus," the narrator—now an adult and a writer by profession—is asked by his publisher to go to the new state of Israel and to produce a volume of translations of its latest poetry and songs. He is then undertaking his own pilgrimage to the Holy Land. The exodus, for him, as for a large segment of Jewry, is mainly spiritual; he is a Canadian who is determined to return to the country of his father's choice, to Canada. The Holy Land, for him, is the ideal, the inspiration, the other-wordly beacon that is guiding his spiritual life.

Shortly before his departure, he receives a heavily post-marked envelope from a displaced persons' camp in Bari, Italy. It comes from his uncle, Melech Davidson, and tells of Melech's fate. Gone is the Marxist jargon. Melech is once more conscious of his identity. He has survived the mass murders, and he is now trying to reach Israel. It is clear that Klein merges his own thinking not only with that of the narrator but also with that of Melech Davidson. Melech's letter, for instance, contains lines which are taken from Klein's poem "Meditation Upon Survival." "The numbered dead run through my veins their plasma. . . . I must live their un-expired six million circuits, . . . my body must be the bed of each of their nightmares."[29] The words help establish Melech as a personification of Jewry as a whole; of the dead as well as of those who survived. But there are many other clues to the scope of Melech's character. For instance, he represents the many Leftists who ceased ro be Marxist when Stalin signed his pact with Hitler and thus made possible Hitler's attack on Poland and the enslavement of Europe.

Melech's letter relates how the Jewish community of Kamenets is rounded up under a pretext, and how men, women, and children are murdered with sadistic ceremony. Klein here obviously drew on the many reports of eye-witnesses who somehow escaped similar massacres. Men and women are lined up along a pit and shot. At the first volley, a falling body pushes Melech into the pit where he lies motionless until the tired soldiers have lightly covered the bodies with earth and depart. At midnight he rises from the grave.

It becomes clear how Theodor Herzl inspired the creation of the character of Melech Davidson: Herzl, in a sense, had also risen from the grave when his body was flown to Israel, a representative of those who died and of those who, overcoming unimaginable odds, made their way to Jerusalem. Davidson, like Herzl, emerges from the grave and represents the dead as well as those who survived.

It may be suggested also that Melech represents the entire Jewry people because Jewry reasserted its strength at the moment when it seemed most weak, at the darkest moment of its history: it rose from the grave at midnight.

One can see here the various layers of Klein's symbolism. By analogy, one may say that not only Jewry but mankind at large has the capacity to overcome its difficulties and to triumph even when its condition seems desperate. In Melech Davidson, we may see not merely Jewry, but man. That Klein intended the wider interpretation will be seen later, especially in "Gloss Gimel."

Finally, it may be argued that Melech Davidson can be looked upon as a special agent of divine power, which expresses itself through living beings and is resurrected even when it is reduced to the very grave. Melech Davidson rises from the dead and slowly, patiently, relentlessly works his way toward the shores of the Holy Land, the Messianic condition.

Klein's oecumenism can be seen in a short episode which

occurs when Melech flees through the Polish forest and is befriended by a "good peasant family over whose house there presided the image of the man of Galilee,"[30] a family that hides and feeds and preserves him and thus has no small share in making his progress toward Jerusalem possible. Man's progress, Klein seems to say, must be a concerted effort.

The letter tells of how Melech, after the war, succeeded in reaching the displaced persons' camp at Bari, whence a flotilla of battered old vessels carried refugees to Israel. Melech calls the ships "a Navy of Redemption," which seems to indicate that the ships and their destination have, in addition to their physical being, an existence on the spiritual plane. The voyage is universal; the port, a condition of Grace to be reached in the future. Melech writes that he longs to board one of these ships, but that he must console himself with introspective hoping and sacred prophecies. Among them, there is the Cabalist's mystic view of evolution: "When the years were ripened, and the years fulfilled then was there fashioned Aught from Naught. Out of the furnace there issued smoke, out of the smoke a people descended. The desert swirled, the capital hissed: Sambation raged, but Sambation was crossed. . . ."[31] The strictly Jewish interpretation of these lines is relatively simple: out of the furnace of World War II, the Jewish people made its way to Israel. It crossed the Sambation, the turbulent river of Jewish legend on whose other shore live the lost tribes of Israel. In other words, Jews overcame every obstacle and were reunited with distant kinsmen; in Israel a reunion took place of many who had been lost to each other. A reunion, traditionally, is envisaged in the kingdom to come, in the Messianic condition.

Once again, however, a wider interpretation is possible. "Aught from Naught" clearly conveys the idea of being emerging from non-being. The words indicate that Klein is here concerned with evolutionary concepts. Humanity, quite literally, descends from the furnace, from the dust of volcanic smoke, and it may be expected to reach higher stages of physical and intellectual development. Klein seems confident that mankind, at last, will have crossed its "Sambation." He is intent on making clear that his symbolism is not confined to the home-coming of the Jewish people, for, in the very next passage, he refers to Israel as a "microcosm." One is reminded of Buber's view that Jews are the most exposed point of modern mankind. In their fate, one may see the fate of humanity.

"Gloss Beth," which pertains to "Exodus," consists of a single poem, the "Elegy," which was published in 1947. It mourns the six million victims.

The opening four verse paragraphs are a moving lament. Then follow three passages that cry for vengeance. They mar the poem because Klein insists on cataloguing various plagues wished upon the enemy and thereby diminishes the emotional impact. It would have been artistically preferable if the punishments for unspeakable crimes had remained abstracta. Two passages of prayer, Miltonic in tone and apparently traditional in spirit, end the poem. In them, one may well see a Job-like attitude toward fate and toward the workings of evil.

> O Thou who from Mizraim once didst draw
> Us free, and from the Babylonian lair;
> From bondages, plots, ruins imminent
> Preserving, didst keep Covenant and Law,
> Creator, King whose banishments are not
> Forever—for Thy Law and Covenant,
> Oh, for Thy promise and Thy pity, now
> At last, this people to its lowest brought
> Preserve!...

The Book of Leviticus contains details of legislation. Man is told how to live; how not to transgress; and what to do when transgression has been committed. The tribes are prepared for their life in the Promised Land. In the chapter "Leviticus," in *The Second Scroll*, too, there is something that could be called a preparation for entry into the Holy Land. Like the Israelites of Leviticus, who were wandering through the desert, waiting and learning, Melech Davidson makes his way through the world, learning, waiting for a cleansing process to be completed before he can enter Israel. Tracing his footsteps, his nephew, the narrator, to some extent seems to follow the same progress.

At the beginning of the chapter, the narrator is on his way to Israel. He is eager to collect there for his publisher the new melodies, the new poetry of the land. But his uncle's letter, which arrives shortly before his departure, makes him delay. Instead of flying to Jerusalem, as he had intended, he goes to the DP camp in Bari, Italy, hoping, at last, to meet Melech Davidson. When he arrives, he finds that he is too late. Davidson, he is told, has left—probably to join a friend, a Monsignor Piersanti, in Rome.

Yet another facet of Jewry is added to the composite portrait. Davidson, we find, also represents that part of Jewry that leans toward Christianity. In addition, the relationship between Davidson and Piersanti is representative also of Judaeo-Christian relations in the broadest historical sense. Davidson, it is said, at first acted as Monsignor Piersanti's guide through the DP camp. Now, the Monsignor does his best to guide Davidson, that is, he tries to win him to Catholicism.

The nephew, disquieted at the news, immediately sets out for Rome. He meets Piersanti and discusses with him Davidson's spiritual condition. The Monsignor describes Davidson as a man who is "climbing ever upward"; a man who is "wrestling valiantly with his doubts," and who will in the end "find the way."[32] Naturally, Piersanti assumes that this way will lead to Christianity. Davidson, he recalls, has sought spiritual guidance from the Gospels, from Marx and Freud,

among the economists and psychiatrists; he has been an
atheist, and also a fervent believer; but always he has been a
seeker after truth, and he has an innate instinct for righteous-
ness. Monsignor Piersanti says he does not know what has
become of Melech Davidson, but he produces a Hebrew letter
which Davidson had written after a visit to the Sistine Chapel,
and he encourages the nephew to borrow this letter and to
read it at leisure.

The passages that follow are climactic. Their position in the
story is noteworthy because, whether for reasons of aesthetics
or to emphasize his intent, Klein likes to follow the classical
pattern, and places statements concerning his fundamental
philosophical ideas at the centre of his work.[33] The technique
was clearly apparent in "Out of the Pulver and the Polished
Lens." Here, in *The Second Scroll*, we find it again. It is in
"Leviticus," the third of the five main chapters of the book,
that Klein states most clearly his attitude toward good and
evil, and it is here that the narrator of the story finds some of
Melech Davidson's philosophical conclusions.

The narrator, now in possession of Melech Davidson's letter,
walks through the sun-lit streets and sits down on a bench
"before one of the many sculptured fountains which add to
the beauty and music of Rome."[34] He dreams of a union of
religions and of a universal peace brought about by his uncle
Melech. Suddenly, his musings are interrupted by a group of
young men. He recognizes among them a Mr. Settano, whom
he had met at his hotel and with whom he had talked only the
night before. The fellow had shown himself very dogmatic and
unpleasant; contemptuous of any but his own materialistic
views. Now he seems affable enough; full of smiles; yet, in
spite of this, somehow wakening apprehensions.

Settano is full of banter, but his attitude soon becomes
menacing. For no apparent reason, he suspects (or pretends to
suspect) the innocent traveller from Montreal of being in-
volved in a mysterious plot, and derides his protestations that
he has come to Italy solely to search for his uncle Melech. At

last, the narrator tells us how he was forced away from his bench at the fountain and, at gun-point, made to accompany Settano and his gang to a Roman suburb. No one comes to his aid; no one notices his plight. In a doorway, he is robbed of Melech Davidson's letter. His tormentors, it seems, suspect that it contains some secret; a coded message opposed to their party. After this, they let him go. Humiliated and angry, he spends some time in a cinema, watching some tragedy and finding solace in the thought that his own misfortune was of a relatively minor nature. When he eventually returns to his hotel, he finds that the letter has been returned to him, slipped under the door of his room.

When one reads *The Second Scroll* as a realistic tale, this episode seems far-fetched, disconnected from the rest of the story, and altogether lacking in *raison d'être*. On the symbolic level, however, it is of prime importance. Evil, Klein seems to be saying, is not rational. It appears, takes its course, and disappears. Man suffers his fellow-men's ill-will because they suspect his intentions, misunderstand his actions, and enjoy tormenting him. Persecutions come and go. A man who does no harm is suddenly threatened with death: perhaps by a lone murderer out to enrich himself; perhaps by an atomic war that is to wipe out some nebulous, remote wrong. Evil defies logic. Settano, Satan, appears, gives vent to his hatred, which is inspired by no recognizable cause, does his evil work, and disappears. The important point is that Klein seems to think Satan will ultimately disappear.

Meanwhile—how is man to counter Settano? Klein's answer emerges from an image that brings his attitude to the entire question of good and evil into focus. We see the writer from Montreal sitting on a bench in Rome while he is being tormented by Settano for his possession of Melech Davidson's letter (as through the ages, the faithful have been tormented for their faith). At the same time, something very beautiful is in progress; something exquisite is happening before his eyes: the fountain continues "its brilliant introspection." When

Settano and his gang tempt and taunt the innocent traveller, he replies: "I think I will watch the fountain."[35] And he does so for as long as he can. In spite of evil, a pure, life-giving energy, a creative force, works ceaselessly. Klein wants man to look past evil, so that he may perceive the beauty of creation and understand the essential goodness of the universe.

Irving Layton once implied that Klein could not know true goodness because he had no knowledge of evil. "To know God truly," he wrote in his review of *Poems* (1944),[36] "one must also have known Satan. Klein gives no evidence of ever having been within a hundred yards of that versatile gentleman." The episode concerning Settano and the fountain reads like a reply to this criticism. Klein would say that, on the contrary, it is precisely our knowledge of Satan that tends to obscure our knowledge of God. When the Monsignor Piersanti spoke of Melech Davidson, he said that Davidson was blinded and deafened by his tragic experiences and therefore could not tell the direction whence came the Voice of God.[37] Settano and his gang force the traveller away from the fountain; they interfere with his contemplation of its loveliness. Experience of evil blurs our vision, prevents us from understanding the beauty of creation. Klein tries to redirect our attention. He reminds us that Settano's activities are transient and that the fountain continues to play, untouched, unsullied. In Klein's plea can be read the Chassidic influence, for to rejoice in the beauty of creation is the Chassid's piety.

It is noteworthy that, in Klein's book, Settano's hatred is based on a mysterious, unexplainable misunderstanding, since Settano mistakenly believes the traveller guilty of some dark, fantastic design. From this, perhaps, we may deduce that Klein considers evil not as something that has a legitimate place within creation, but rather as something that arises from man's misunderstanding of reality, from a malfunctioning in the natural process.

With his uncle's letter once more in his possession, the narrator now discovers how Melech Davidson's spiritual odyssey ended. The letter discloses that the man who explored the entire spectrum of religious thinking from orthodoxy to atheism finally reached port in the Sistine Chapel, under the auspices of Renaissance art, which in feeling and boldness of vision anticipates the modern age.

Contemplating Michelangelo's paintings, Melech Davidson seeks "to establish his basic premise: the divinity of humanity."[38] At this point, Klein offers a conciliatory hand to the orthodox Jew, for whom such a line must spell unmitigated affront. Klein, who in his teens was careful not to offend the sensibilities of his orthodox fellow-students, could not bear to insult the pious when he was about to make the most elaborate religious statement of his life. We find then, on the same page, another statement which seems to annul the pantheism of the first. Klein implies that man is divine because "Adam is created in the image of God." Perplexed, one may ask which is Klein's personal view. An answer may be found, but not until the end of "Deuteronomy," at the end of the story. Meanwhile, we are given merely a clue: when Melech Davidson contemplated the "divinity of humanity," he was "standing beneath the figure of Ezekiel." Why did Klein find it necessary to mention this? What, in Ezekiel's prophecies, was at this moment of particular importance to Melech Davidson? The answer may show that in Melech's philosophy the difference between an orthodox and a pantheistic view was resolved. But we have to wait until the end of the story to find out how this was achieved.

Michelangelo's paintings are seen not merely as an illustration of a biblical tale but as a general statement concerning the human condition. The various scenes of violence and bloodshed are thought to refer to violence perpetrated through the ages. In *The Expulsion from Eden*, Davidson sees a proleptic reference to the world's refugees. He notices that Michelangelo shows Adam and Eve put to flight, not by an angel, but by a double-headed serpent.[39] In other words, it is not by God that mankind is driven from the Eden of its prosperity.

"Since Adam is created in the image of God, the killing of man is deicide! Since Eve is a reproductive creature, the murder of the mortal is a murder of the immortal!"[40] Murder is heinous because it works counter to the life-producing tendencies of nature; counter to the divine. The more deeply Melech Davidson contemplates the paintings, the more convinced he is that they have prophetic significance. In Michelangelo's frescoes, he sees not only doom and slaughter but also "the sure promise of survival." He relates this to his own people. In spite of the holocaust, his people will survive. He reads it in the painting which shows *The Creation of the Sun and the Moon*: the dark heavens become bright; and he reads it in the seven colours used by Michelangelo: to him they appear "a rainbow pledging cessation of flood."[41] In the painting *The Separation of Light from Darkness*, Melech Davidson sees "God coming to the rescue of His chosen,"[42] and as he discusses the picture, he pours his emotions into one great affirmation of the Jewish creed, one great declaration of faith in which are uttered all the thirteen credos of Maimonides.[43] It is not difficult to find here certain contradictions. The credos include the belief in God's incorporeality. How can one, with this belief, speak of the murder of man as "deicide"? In accepting the credos, Davidson accepts Judaism; but it is a Judaism strongly tinged with pantheistic ideas. The two contradictory beliefs can only be reconciled if one considers the incorporeal, divine existence, not as something apart from nature, but as a quality inhabiting nature and, at the same time, as something transcending the levels of nature known to us.

For the actual text of Melech Davidson's letter, we have to turn to "Gloss Gimel," the third, the central one, of the five glosses. It is the essay which first appeared in 1950 under the title "A Jew in the Sistine Chapel" in the *Canadian Jewish Chronicle*, and it obviously recounts Klein's personal impressions. It is a bewildering *tour de force*; baroque in its ornate, poetic prose; its strange marginal mottoes of Vulgate Latin which, more often than not, seem only vaguely linked with the text; and its turbulent, grandiose emotions. Clearly, it was Klein's intention to reflect in his style the artistic tendencies of his subject. Whether or not his interpretations of Michelangelo's paintings are valid must remain a matter of opinion. He eloquently defended his right to impose his own ideas on the work of the Renaissance master:

> Such is the nature of art that though the artist entertain fixedly but one intention and one meaning, that creation once accomplished beneath his hand, now no longer merely his own attribute, but Inspiration's very substance and entity, proliferates with significances by him not conceived nor imagined. Such art is eternal and to every generation speaks with fresh coeval timeliness. In vain did Buonarotti seek to confine himself to the hermeneutics of his age; the Spirit intruded and lo! on that ceiling appeared the narrative of things to come, which came indeed, and behold above me the parable of my days.[44]

Some of the interpretations are truly ingenious. For instance, when Davidson looks at *The Fall of Man and the Expulsion from the Garden of Eden*, he notes that those who are driven into exile are without guilt: they had eaten no forbidden fruit. By design or through forgetfulness, perhaps with prophetic spirit, Michelangelo had eliminated the symbol of transgression. There is "subtle illusion of apples" but "there is no apple in that scene."[45] Again it is stressed that evil is not inflicted on Adam and Eve by a messenger of God; they are not driven from Paradise by an angel, but by a figure which in Michelangelo's painting seems, indeed, to rise from the body of the serpent, from "hermaphrodite evil."[46]

Many of Klein's readers will find it difficult to allow their imagination as much scope as "Gloss Gimel" demands, and in the area of art criticism, the value of the gloss may remain in doubt. Its passages, however, are of indisputable importance if one is trying to establish the nature of Klein's religious belief. In the chapter "Leviticus," the narrator, who had grown up in an orthodox Jewish home, had read in Melech Davidson's letter chiefly a prophecy of redemption of the Jewish people.

But this was only a paraphrase of Davidson's letter. "Gloss Gimel" represents part of the actual text of the letter, and here we find that the prophecy of redemption embraces all mankind. Here, too, the pantheistic influence is much more pronounced. It is thus as if Melech Davidson represented not only the incarnate spirit of Judaism but also the spirit of man in general. Klein, of course, speaks through both, the narrator and Davidson; and in the two characters he has isolated two facets of his own thinking. He is a conscious Jew, fervently concerned with the destiny of his people and convinced of the worth of its religious heritage; he is also conscious of an all-embracing reality into which Judaic thinking and the Judaic destiny fit as an archetypal part.

Melech Davidson sees in Michelangelo's paintings this double prophecy of redemption: in the four spandrels which depict *The Miraculous Salvation of Israel*, he sees God's promise that mankind shall never be utterly forsaken. Here he sees *David's Victory Over Goliath*, *Judith and Holofernes*, *Esther and Haman*. In each case, Israel, though weak, triumphs over a formidable enemy. Humanity is given power to overcome adversity. The fourth of the spandrels shows *The Brazen Serpent*, which Moses fashioned: the *Nebushtan*, at the sight of which the Children of Israel were healed. "Thus in the hour of brass, thus in the round of serpents, by God's grace Israel lives," writes Melech Davidson.[47] God overcomes evil. The serpent, symbol of evil, is transformed into a symbol of healing. It is Israel's story that is being told in the Sistine Chapel; but Melech Davidson sees in it the prototype of the history of mankind. He points out that "one colour dominates the ceiling." It is "the colour of the living skin; and behind the coagulation of the paint flows the one universal stream of everybody's blood." And again he writes: "It is the parable of the species that is pendent over me...."[48] In effect, he seems to say: Prophetically, Michelangelo has equated Israel's fate with the fate of mankind. Since, in history, Israel was saved, mankind as a whole may trust in a future salvation.

Pantheistic thought, in "Gloss Gimel," is more outspoken than in any of Klein's writings since "Out of Pulver and the Polished Lens"; but now there are indications that Klein also favours a dualistic concept: we find it in his description of "Adam anticipative." Here, Adam is not equated with the Divine. He receives life from God.[49] Klein, however, reiterates the idea that murder of the human is deicide. This time he does not seem to find it necessary to add the explanation that man is divine because he is made in God's image; he hopes, perhaps, that the orthodox reader will consider the relevant statement made in "Leviticus" to be valid for the rest of the book. Here, in the gloss, Klein refers to murderers as those who "denied the godliness of all flesh but their own."[50] By equating attacks upon life not merely with disobedience to the divine will but with an actual attack upon the Deity, Klein leads one to assume that he sees in the physical world a degree of immanent divinity.

Not only human life—all life is sacred. When Davidson contemplates the picture of the offering of the beasts, he refers to the raised index finger of Noah, who apparently gives the sign that the sacrificial slaughter of the beasts may begin; and he calls it "the finger now blaspheming life."[51] No killing, he feels, can possibly be performed in honour of God, for God is life.

To kill one creature is to commit perpetual murder, because within the organism elaborate preparation already exists for an entire chain of future creation. To interrupt this chain is to counteract God's hand "beckoning levitation"; it is to commit "eternal murder, murder immortal."[52] To kill a man is to commit "murder of the codes."[53] One may assume that Klein considers the laws of nature, the creative principle, as equatable with the Divine Law.

"Deicide," Klein says, is "the unspeakable nefas," the crime "possible only in its attempt."[54] Even when the higher organism has been destroyed, the creative energy begins once more its evolutionary process. Its activity can be counteracted, but it cannot be completely frustrated. In the Bible, the rainbow, of course, appears as a symbol of life, as God's promise to preserve the human race. Klein refers to the rainbow as the covenant which "stands between man and his destruction, the covenant of sea and sky: the bow in the cloud."[55] He thus seems to invite a realistic interpretation. Sea and sky or water and light, the component parts of the rainbow, signify regeneration, resurrection.

Almost at the end of "Gloss Gimel," Klein defines for us his concept of the Deity. Melech Davidson still refers to Michelangelo's paintings, implying that the master was able to convey in his art the idea of incorporeality; but, at this point, the paintings are no longer important. They merely provide the opportunity for a theological definition. Here Klein gives us what he now feels is

> ... the true concept—the form of formlessness, unphrasable, infinite, world-quickening anima, the shaped wind!—not in any manner image, not body, nor the similitude of body, but pure pervasive Spirit intelligential, the One (oh, musculature of flame!), the First, the Last (oh, uncontainable fire unconsumed!). Cloud luminous with Creation, Omnipotent, yes, and All-Compassionate, who in the heavens resides and in the heart's small chambers (beating little heart of Isaac on the faggots ...) magnanimous with Law, and who even to the latest of generations fulfils His prophets' prophecies, rebuking, rewarding, hastening for them who wait him who tarries, merciful-munificent with ascensions, aliyoth, resurrections, authorizing Days.[56]

The "world-quickening anima" may be thought of in terms of the God concept we find in Genesis. It may also be an immanent life-creating energy. The two concepts tend to fuse when we think of Genesis as symbolism expressing the idea of natural evolution. The word "anima" is inevitably linked also with Stoic philosophy. However, caution is indicated here. Agus, in *The Evolution of Jewish Thought*, differentiates very clearly between the Hellenistic "conception of *anima mundi*, the soul of the world, which pictured the Deity as the sum and substance of the laws prevailing in the universe," and the Talmudic analogy. "The rabbis," writes Agus, "did not think of God as the world's soul, in the sense of being the expression of the totality of its powers and functions."[57]

Klein's words "magnanimous with Law" may refer to God's gift of the Decalogue. Equally, Klein may be speaking about the laws of nature, the inexorable results of cause and effect. Again, one may also see in Klein's reference his conviction that Jewish tradition and natural religion do not contradict each other, that in its essential teachings, the Torah expresses natural law. To make man live benevolently, to make him respect the dignity of life, this, after all, is the aim and substance of the Torah's ethics. In a way, certain laws of nature may lead him to the same conclusions; human beings find that to respect the dignity of life is conducive to health, and the conduct of one generation affects the wellbeing of generations to come.

It appears that only one of the Judaic ideas in Klein's concept of God contradicts what is generally accepted in a religion that equates natural forces with the Divine. Klein speaks of God as "All-Compassionate." But God's compassion may be seen in the very fact that the universe exists, that life endures, that biological history—when it is viewed in broadest outline—appears to indicate an increase in both the duration and the intensity of life. God's compassion, one may say, expresses itself even in terms of evolution.

In the following chapters, Klein shows that he trusts in an evolutionary progress, that he considers the prophecy of the redemption of mankind well on the way to fulfilment. Utmost suffering is followed by unprecedented success. Abilities inherent in human nature, chances of war and politics, a myriad of different circumstances combined and made possible the return of Israel to the Promised Land, made possible the "ascensions, aliyoth, resurrections" of which Klein speaks as the gifts of a munificent Deity. In the Sistine Chapel he felt that the fate of the Jews indicated the fate of mankind. He is confident, therefore, that life as a whole is engaged in a process which eventually will lead to a superior, a Messianic condition. In *The Second Scroll*, the fusion of biblical ideas and evolutionary philosophy is implied. On a later occasion, Klein was more outspoken concerning his ideas on evolution. This will be discussed in the concluding section of the present study.

At the end of the chapter entitled "Leviticus," the narrator hears that his uncle has left Rome but that he did not embark for Israel. Melech Davidson felt he was not ready for the Holy Land. "He wanted to feel in his own person and upon his own neck the full weight of the yoke of exile. He wanted, he said, to be with his Sephardim brothers, the lost half of Jewry."[58] And so he left for Casablanca. His nephew, the writer from Montreal, follows him into the Sultanate of Morocco. It is as if Klein were saying that moral determination and an understanding of the direction in which one is to proceed, as well as confidence in the attainment of the ultimate goal, are prerequisites for the journey to the Holy Land. But they alone are not enough. There must be action before triumph is possible. Mankind must become more conscious of its responsibilities before it can reach a state of purification.

The Book of Numbers makes reference to various battles fought by the Israelites. It tells of various pagan tribes they had to conquer before they could enter the Promised Land. In Klein's analogy, too, there are battles to be fought before mankind can reach a Messianic age. In the chapter "Numbers,"

we hear how Melech Davidson went to Morocco to fight social injustice. He aids the inhabitants of the Casablanca ghetto, the mellah, where the poorest of Jews live, who are also among the poorest of all mankind. When his nephew arrives, he finds that Melech Davidson has left for Israel.

At first, when the young Montrealer arrives in Casablanca, the colours, the shapes and sounds, the sensuality of the city intoxicate him. His description of Moorish architecture would have delighted the heart of Ruskin. But soon the fascination gives way to contempt. Like the great English aesthete, he feels that beauty, when it thrives amidst social injustice, is tainted. Klein himself had visited Casablanca on his return journey from Israel, and the reactions of the Montreal writer in the story are, quite obviously, his own. One sees a man who is acutely sensitive to aesthetic experience, who is irresistibly drawn to beauty, yet who will reject art, no matter how exquisite, when it seems to ingratiate itself on behalf of a system or a person that must be condemned on moral grounds.

This Puritan streak is not new in Klein. It was evident in one of his very early stories, "The Meed of the Minnesinger," in which the Jewish Troubadour Susskind von Trimberg finds out that the world of splendid cathedrals and beautiful stained glass harbours also falsehood and cruelty. Klein feels that art cannot be divorced from ethics. The visual arts seem to lose their *raison d'être* when they exist side by side with iniquity. Literary art, of course, has a greater ethical responsibility than the decorative arts. This trend in Klein's thinking will be noted in his attacks on various writers, notably Ezra Pound and T. S. Eliot.[59]

The narrator in *The Second Scroll* relates in detail his impressions of the mellah. Klein himself had visited the mellah of Casablanca and published a report concerning the conditions prevailing there in the *Canadian Jewish Chronicle* of September 1949. One realizes with horror that the picture of degradation, filth, and disease which one finds in the novel is not the product of a writer's imagination but the factual account of a

newspaperman who wants to acquaint his readers with out-
rageous truth. Both the article in the *Chronicle* and the passages
in the novel depict an inferno. There is no water in the mellah.
"Across the boulevard in the hotel there is hot and cold
running water, all the time, and to spare."[60] It does not flow
through the mellah, whose alleys are its cloaca. Men here die
young. The death rate is fifty per cent in the first thirteen
years; and this is not surprising. We read of the butcher
behind a veil of flies who has but a single piece of meat to sell
and stands before it, fanning it; of the blind, deaf-mute,
filthily draped bag-o'-bones hag whose only shelter is a kennel.
The odour of refuse and ordure hangs heavily in the air.
Carcasses of animals are drying in the sun. "One turned aside
to be for a while sick against the wall," writes Klein in his
report. In the novel, Melech Davidson is sickened by the
mellah. When his nephew, the narrator, visits the place, his
guide tells him that Davidson was "nauseated, he actually
rejected."

The guide, a young Moroccan Jew, remembers Melech
Davidson well. Through the guide, we hear that Davidson was
vocal in his denunciation of the mental attitude, the resignation,
he found in the mellah. He saw the paupers squatting on the
steps of the synagogue, "intoxicated with the hashish of
katoob"; he saw the submissiveness of ghetto inmates who
accept evil with a simple piety: "Katoob! It is written"; and
he was angry. If one can have any doubt as to Klein's position
in this matter at the time he wrote *The Second Scroll*, this
passage must surely convince one that he did not consider evil
a trial sent from God. Melech Davidson, and through him, of
course, Klein, specifically rejects *katoob*. "You should have
heard him on Fatima, on the water question, on katoob," says
the young Moroccan guide to Davidson's nephew. "He moved
even me, truly.... Mr. Davidson was a very hysterical
man."[61]

We hear how Davidson gathered information on the diseases
prevalent in the mellah; how he tried in vain to rouse public

opinion; how, at last, he organized the beggars and cripples of the ghetto and led them to free a group of men who had been arrested for mendicancy and were being kept under inhuman conditions in a desert prison camp. Davidson succeeded in returning the prisoners to their homes; but he himself was arrested and freed only when his employers, the American Joint Distribution Committee, interceded on his behalf. To avoid further scandal, they put him on a ship bound for Israel.

The symbolism here is intricate. It moves on three levels: there is the personal experience of Davidson; there is the experience of the Moroccan Jews; and there is, finally, the analogous experience of mankind as a whole.

Davidson had worked to free the prisoners, and his effort was an important factor in his progress to Israel. But it is clear that his action was only a link in a chain of events which brings about his success. In the end he is being propelled toward Israel by the Joint Committee, in whose employ he works. Without the money and the ship supplied by the Joint Committee, he would hardly have reached his destination. While his rebellion against evil is instrumental in getting him to the Holy Land, the last leap in his odyssey requires the help of external powers.

To escape the mellah, the Moroccan Jews have to assert themselves. Their own innate capacity to survive, the biological and psychological traits which enable them to endure and to progress are an important factor. But individual will power would not get them far. We hear that the mellah slowly disappears. The young leave the place and migrate to Israel. Yet to do this, forces beyond their control have to create favourable conditions. Klein suggests that, imperceptibly, the social pressures of a modern age make themselves felt. By and by, many inhuman laws that oppressed the inhabitants of the mellah are abolished. Tyrannies have a tendency to wear themselves out. A liberalization brought about by a myriad of external factors is necessary before the inhabitants of the mellah can hope to escape their miserable condition. It is clear that he does not believe this evolutionary progress is an uninterrupted advance toward salvation. The inhabitants of the mellah, it is stressed, were once dons and hidalgos of the golden age of Spain. There are setbacks. Only gradually, life triumphs. Davidson eventually meets the inhabitants of the mellah redeemed in Israel, wearing white, the colour forbidden them in the troubled days of their exile. Since Klein has made clear he regards the Jewish fate as representative of the fate of mankind as a whole, one may perhaps conclude that here too, his symbolism refers to the larger issue.

"Gloss Dalid," which pertains to the chapter "Numbers," is a short play. It consists only of one act. There is occasional display of humour, but, on the whole, the tone is solemn, the language elevated. We find here the symmetry and frankly stated ethics which are typical of the medieval morality play. The chapter "Numbers," which makes the plight of the Moroccan Jews vivid in the reader's imagination, is apt to engender strife and bitterness. "Gloss Dalid" is designed to counteract this. It focuses attention on the unity of the human race. We are told that the play was written by Melech Davidson and that the manuscript later reached the hands of his nephew, the narrator.

The action takes place at the Gates of Justice in Baghdad; but, obviously, Klein had in mind other gates and a judge other than the cadi of an oriental sultanate. Three wise judgements are pronounced. In the last, the cadi decides that only the light is of the essence and that the name of those who sell the lamps is immaterial. Strongly reminiscent of the Ring Parable, the play constitutes Klein's final and unequivocal statement concerning the oecumenical position in religion: all faiths are good that bring the light of God.

In the last scene—like an answer to a cry demanding life— rain begins to fall. The words "Let lightening enlighten! Let thunder thunder Understanding! Let . . . " are drowned in the thunder from heaven. One cannot fail to be reminded of T. S. Eliot's "The Waste Land." But there, I believe, the thunder is pure metaphor. Here, in Klein's play, it may be regarded as a metaphorical device; but it may also be understood in an immediate pantheistic sense. Enlightenment and understanding are sought in the life-engendering forces of nature, and we are reminded that these forces transcend the comprehension of man.

In Deuteronomy, the tribes of Israel gather to honour Moses, who has led them to their goal, and the Promised Land is within sight. In Klein's chapter "Deuteronomy," there is a gathering of the tribes at the grave of Melech Davidson. The ending of Klein's story, like the ending in Deuteronomy, tells of limited achievement; of success that is not unalloyed; of happiness that is mixed with regret. But in Klein's story, as in the Bible, there is also at the end a great surge of anticipation. There is conviction that infinite good is within reach and that progress toward it is inevitable.

The narrator follows his uncle to the newly created state of Israel. On the way he is conscious of "Messianic, annunciatory" music in the roar of the aircraft that takes him to Jerusalem. Another passenger, a European Jew, philosophizes on the role of Jewry in world history. He is, of course, greatly elated at recent developments, and he proceeds to explain them in terms of an esoteric theory. The narrator interrupts him: "And what role does Providence play in your scheme?" he asks his fellow-passenger. "You have forgotten, in your thesis, to place God."[62]

These words may be considered evidence that Klein, after all, did abandon the philosophical approach and returned to a more or less orthodox faith which sees in historic events the arbitrary decrees of the Deity. In Klein's Judaism, as it had developed by the time *The Second Scroll* was written, the word "providence" may, however, be understood also in another way; namely, it may refer to a process that makes for good and is inherent in nature. Providence, in Klein's faith, could be seen as a tendency of the anima to act in a specific direction. Klein sees that this energy is evolutionary, not stagnant or aimless. In the *Oxford Universal Dictionary*, "providence" is defined not only as God's foreknowing but also as His beneficent care and government. Klein's use of the word, therefore, can be interpreted in the traditional or in the pantheistic sense.

The narrator of the story travels the length and breadth of the new state to fulfil his two-fold mission; to explore the new poetry of the land for his Canadian publisher and to find Uncle Melech.

The symbolic significance of Melech Davidson now assumes an additional dimension. Increasingly it becomes clear that he is a Messiah figure. Steinberg, in his introduction, points to a story in the Talmud where the Messiah joins the lame and the blind, and he connects this story with the episode in "Numbers" where uncle Melech leads a protest march in the company of the cripples from the mellah. Steinberg also points to the traditional Jewish view, set forth by Maimonides, which tends to identify the Messiah with the people in a purified state.

That Uncle Melech is symbolic of the people as a whole already emerged from the preceding chapters of the novel. In "Deuteronomy," great emphasis is put on the idea that his personality is diffused among the many. At the American Joint Distribution Committee office, the narrator had been shown a photograph of Uncle Melech. Unfortunately, the features were blurred because of double exposure. Now, in Israel, the narrator is looking everywhere for Uncle Melech's face, and again and again he feels he can discern a resemblance in a passer-by. On one occasion, it is a man "riding a donkey on Julian's way"[63] who faintly resembles Melech Davidson; but he turns out to be a stranger. This episode becomes significant when we remember Klein's early poem "Earthquake," in which it was suggested that the Messiah, on the Day of Resurrection, would use the mode of transportation which was typical of judges in biblical times, that is, he would arrive riding a white ass. Probably Klein also meant us to recall that Jesus entered Jerusalem on Palm Sunday, sitting on an ass's colt.

Davidson seems to be present wherever life is burgeoning. The narrator is reminded of him at Haifa, where he visits a painter who is engaged in a vigorous experiment. At Rospina, where he sees a farmer who places bees on his wrist to let their stings cure his arthritis, this too is "somehow evocative of Uncle Melech."[64] The connotation of the healing power in nature is very strong here. Again, at Kinnereth, when he listens to the boatmen "in the gaily painted boat singing Rahel's song," the narrator is reminded of Uncle Melech.[65] The Messiah concept seems to encompass not only the redeeming spirit within mankind but the divine healing energy beyond its manifestation in the individual human being.

Much emphasis was put on the diffusion of Melech's personality among the people of Israel.[66] Equal emphasis is put on the diffusion of the poetic spirit among the people:[67] the narrator, searching for the new poetry of Israel, acquaints himself with various groups of poets, only to discover that the true, living poetry is to be found in "the shaping Hebrew imagination," which springs from "the fashioning folk anonymous and unobserved. . . . Nameless authorship flourished in the streets. It was growth, its very principle, shown in prolific action! Twigs and branches that had been dry and sapless for generations, for millennia, now budded, blossomed—and with new flowers!" One may, then, perhaps, conclude that Melech Davidson's spirit can also be identified with the poetic spirit of the people. In turn, the poetic spirit can be identified as part of the healing energies of nature:

> It was as if I was spectator to the healing of torn flesh, or heard a broken bone come together, set, and grow again.

Wonderful is the engrafting of skin, but more wonderful the million busy hushed cells, in secret planning, stitching, stretching, until—the wound is vanished, the blood courses normal, the cicatrice falls off.

I had at last discovered it, the great efflorescent impersonality.

My hopes of finding uncle Melech revived.
And this discovered poetry, scattered though it was, had its one obsessive theme. It was obsessed by the miraculous.

A number of concepts are here intertwined. Uncle Melech, the Messiah figure, is linked with the healing power of nature, and he is sought as part of "the great efflorescent impersonality." This impersonality manifests itself in biological terms, in the cells which are "in secret planning"; and it manifests itself through the mind of human beings, in the poetic spirit. That its activity, the process of nature, is called "miraculous," seems to indicate that Klein considers it divine. The impression that a pantheistic view of nature is implied is very strong. Klein's use of the word "efflorescent" is an indication that he feels he is witnessing part of an evolutionary process which has now entered a highly auspicious phase.

That he does not think this evolution is one of uninterrupted progress is again made clear in the passages following, which recall that special determination on the part of those who fight on the side of life has repeatedly been necessary in the past. David slew Goliath. Jonah escaped the whale. That Klein believes the divine in nature to be involved in man's moral struggle can be read in his quotation from the song of Deborah, the prophetess, who refers to the war against Sisera, the Canaanite king of the twelfth century: *"They fought from heaven; the stars in their courses fought against Sisera."*[68]

In his search for Uncle Melech, the narrator reaches Safed, once the seat of the Cabalists. He visits the synagogue of Rabbi Isaac Luria and there meets an old man deeply immersed in the study of the Talmud. By his side, holding a heavy tome, sits a young scholar, a boy prodigy.[69] The old sage has not forgotten the prophecies which predict that the Messiah will lead mankind out of great agony. "Has any generation known deeper pain and bitterer agony than our own?" he asks.[70] He recalls the prophecy that in the days of the Messiah the cadavers and corpses would stand erect on the heights of Mount Carmel, on the hillocks of the Negev, and on the mountains of Galilee. It seems to him that this time has now arrived: from the dungeons of Europe, the skeletons have come to Israel. Finally, he speaks of a new immigrant, of one who, we know, literally rose from the grave. With growing agitation, the narrator hears that the newcomer is a teacher of religion who inspires those who hear him; who is able to make everything plain to them. As he listens, he realizes that the newcomer, the great teacher, is Melech Davidson. Klein thus shows us Davidson, the Messiah figure, as representative both of the power of nature and of resurrected humanity. The narrator is told that the new teacher has gone out to the border settlements, but that he is expected to return to the synagogue of Rabbi Luria for evening prayer. It is clear that he has reached his final conclusions, and that he has found spiritual peace in the mountains of Safed.

We see here the end of an intellectual odyssey. Since Melech Davidson's ideas (especially those expressed in "Gloss Gimel") manifestly represent Klein's own views, it may be surmised that Davidson's final resolution also represents Klein's own creed. In this context, it will be important to note not only what Melech Davidson was teaching, but also where he was teaching. We hear that he spread his ideas among the pioneers at the borders of Israel, and that he found his spiritual home in the mountains of Safed, once the illustrious centre of Cabalist learning. I am not suggesting that Klein, through Melech Davidson, tried to revive the complex theories of the original Cabalistic doctrine. I do, however, believe that he saw in the Cabala elements which can form the basis for a modern religious philosophy. This impression becomes more definite when we consider what Melech Davidson was in fact teaching.

The old man whom the narrator meets in the synagogue of Rabbi Isaac Luria, holiest place of worship in Safed, gives us an indication:

> Ah, if our Safed sage, our newcomer, were to explain it to you! ..." The old man was ecstatic. "A golden tongue he has! And such learning! You should hear him discourse on the *Maaseh Breshith*, explaining how the world was made.... And when he expounds the *Maaseh Merkabah*, it is as if the cherubim and the seraphim were with him holding up the celestial chariot, setting in motion its wheels within wheels, and you can almost see with your own eyes the composite creature, the lion, the ox, the eagle, and the human, moving in all directions at once, the brave, the plodding, the plumed, the inspired, all motion. Oh, he makes all Zohar and Bahir, brightness and light, to shine, to shine....[71]

When Agus discusses the problem of the immanence of the Deity in creation, he says, "We may assume that detailed speculations concerning this problem occupied no small part of the esoteric lore that was jealously guarded by the sages and designated as *Ma-asai Merkabah* and *Ma-asai Bereshith*, the former referring to Ezekiel's description of the divine carriage and possibly containing a theory of emanation, the latter referring to the first chapter of Genesis and possibly containing a Jewish version of the theory of ideas."[72] It was in the spirit of this tradition, then, that Melech Davidson spread *Bahir* and *Zohar*, clarity and splendour. *Maaseh Merkabah* seems to be of particular importance to him. Here one may find a theory which is anchored in the Bible and which, at the same time, proposes a concept which can be acceptable to a twentieth century writer. The genius of the ancient mystics appears to combine the belief in the oneness of all existence with a kind of dualism: the universe is an emanation of God and therefore of the same substance and divine; but it is not equated with that source of creation. God antecedes and transcends the world.

The theory of emanation of *Maaseh Merkabah* is based on the vision of Ezekiel (and we may remember that in the Sistine

Chapel, Melech Davidson was standing under the figure of Ezekiel when he spoke of "the divinity of humanity"). Creation, in the Book of Ezekiel, is seen as God's chariot and as consisting of a multitude of manifestations which seem to emanate from a divine fire and are imbued with the divine spirit:

> And I looked, and, behold, a whirlwind came out of the north, a great cloud, and a fire infolding itself, and a brightness was about it, and out of the midst thereof as the colour of amber, out of the midst of the fire.
>
> Also out of the midst thereof came the likeness of four living creatures. And this was their appearance; they had the likeness of a man. Their wings were joined one to another; they turned not when they went; they went everyone straight forward.
>
> As for the likeness of their faces, they four had the face of a man, and the face of a lion, on the right side: and they four had the face of an ox on the left side; they four also had the face of an eagle.
>
> And they went everyone straight forward: whither the spirit was to go, they went; and they turned not when they went.
>
> And the living creatures ran and returned as the appearance of a flash of lightning.
>
> The appearance of the wheels and their work was like unto the colour of a beryl: and they four had one likeness: and their appearance and their work was as it were a wheel in the middle of a wheel. (Ezek. 1:4–16, *passim.*)

The vision holds compelling fascination for anyone interested in a philosophy that equates nature with the Divine. The composite creature, seething with energy, moving in a myriad of directions, wheels within wheels, suggests the totality of nature. Incomplete and mysterious though the biblical words are, they indicate strongly that nature issues forth from a divine source.

When the Canadian visitor to the synagogue of Rabbi Luria has heard this teaching, he walks out into the winding streets of Safed elated, remembering a song of one of its Cabalist sages, Rabbi Solomon Halevi Alkabez. The song ends with the words,

> Arise! Arouse! Arise and waken!
> For it has come at last, the dawning!
> Lift up your voice your song to utter;
>   For on you is revealed God's glory.[73]

The joyful trust in the future and the deep contentment which at this point fill the heart of the narrator can surely not be due merely to the discovery that his uncle is teaching Cabala in the mountains of Galilee. His conviction that Melech Davidson's teaching augures "the dawning" seems to indicate the view that Melech Davidson is teaching Cabala in terms relevant to the modern age. Davidson's final credo is anchored in Ezekiel, in the Old Testament; but it seems that, at the same time, it could be understood also in terms of a religious philosophy according to which the universe is a manifestation of a great source of energy whose essence, being the cause of the creative process, is considered divine. In teaching such a creed, Melech Davidson proclaims that all life is one; that it is part of God, who in the fate of the Jews has shown that He favours life, survival, and that, therefore, life is to be held sacred. Such seem to be the thoughts of the narrator, and this, I believe, is the main idea Klein wants to communicate to his readers. In the fusion of Judaic teaching with a religious philosophy that seeks divinity in the life-engendering processes of nature Klein seemed to see a rejuvenation of the faith and a safeguarding of its traditional ethics.

The narrator in Klein's story never meets his kinsman. Melech Davidson is murdered by assailants whose identity is not known: the nature of evil remains a mystery. That he lives on, diffused among the people, is suggested in the gathering of the tribes which come to do homage to him. As they did at Herzl's grave, so they gather for the funeral of Melech Davidson. They come in clouds of dust.[74] And again, we hear the echo of Klein's earlier poetry:

> Howbeit, even in the dust I am resurrected,
> and even in decay I live again. . . .

In a universe where all is one and alive, the dead are part of the living whole.

It is said that Melech Davidson "had through the sheer force of his existence again in our life naturalized the miracle."[75] He had survived where survival seemed impossible. He had continued to strive toward a seemingly unattainable goal and, succeeding in this, had demonstrated the goodness of the divine universe. It is said of Melech Davidson that he was an *aspaklaria* of our time. In other words, his fate mirrored the Jewish fate, and with it, perhaps, also the larger destiny. Melech Davidson reached Israel. Though he became a prey to that mysterious phenomenon which men call evil, he is ultimately undefeated. In the Holy Land, we are told, tombs are "but antechambres to a new life, the *mis-en-scène* for an awakening."[76] His word, exalting the divinity of life, will go out from Safed, "holy city on whose hills once were kindled, as now again, the beacons announcing new moons, festivals, and set times."[77]

The joyful affirmation of life at the end of the story is found also in the last of the commentaries, "Gloss Hai." Here is a reaching out toward the divine, a pouring out of gratitude. A new era is anticipated, and the prayers, therefore, are intended in part to parallel the traditional Morning Service.

The Morning Service, which we find in the *Siddur*,[78] consists of the following parts: (1) preliminaries to the service, hymns and blessings, psalms and scriptural verses, songs and responses of adoration; (2) The Shema, which is the declaration of Israel's faith, preceded by benedictions on God, and followed by praises of God; (3) the Eighteen Benedictions (Amidah), which are pronounced standing and in silence, and some of which go back to the time of the Temple; (4) supplications, elegies and prayers and psalms. Then follow the Oleynu, Mourner's Kaddish, supplementary recitations, and voluntary readings.

Klein paraphrases a number of passages in the *Siddur*. His first passage is based on the preliminary blessing:

> Blessed art thou, O Lord our God, King of the universe, who hast formed man in wisdom, and created in him many passages and vessels. It is well known before thy glorious throne, that if but one of these be opened, or one of those be closed, it would be impossible to exist and stand before thee. Blessed art thou O Lord, who art the wondrous healer of all flesh.[79]

Klein renders the words of the *Authorized Daily Prayerbook* thus:

> Blessed art thou, O Lord, Who in Thy wisdom hast fashioned man as Thou hast fashioned him: hollowed and antrious, grottoed and gutted, channelled; for mercy's sake gifted with orifice, exit and vent! . . . Be blessed for the judgement of the eight great gates who dost diminish us to make us whole; for the piecemeal deaths that save; for wax and cerumen, which preserve all music, and for flux of the sinus, which gives the brain coolness, its space, and for spittle prized above the condiments of Asia; even for tears.[80]

In the benedictions which follow, and which to some extent parallel those in the *Siddur*, Klein inserts the phrase "For that he gave to a stone understanding to understand direction."[81] Gravity, magnetism, the tendency of minerals to crystallize, all this, summed up in the word "understanding," can be seen as a primitive manifestation of intellect. In turn, we are led to a concept of creation where all is alive.

Following the blessings, Klein inserts his poem "Grace Before Poison." The *Siddur*, here, includes Psalm 90, which contains the line "Make us rejoice according to the days wherein thou hast afflicted us, the years wherein we have seen evil."[82] In Klein's poem, the thanksgiving concerns specifically an acceptance of "The banes that bless," phenomena which seem inimical, yet have a healing effect in alleviating suffering. The poem is followed by "Of Remembrance," which probes the universe in terms of Cabalist mysticism.[83]

Klein's "Stance of Amidah" is based on the prayer of the same name. Among the passages in the *Siddur*, one reads:

> Thou favourest man with knowledge, and teachest mortals understanding. O favour us with knowledge, understanding and discernment from thee. Blessed art thou, O Lord, gracious Giver of knowledge.[84]

Klein writes:

> Favour us, O Lord, with understanding, who hast given to the bee its knowledge and to the ant its foresight, to the sleeping bear Joseph's prudence, and even to the dead lodestone its instinct for the star, favour us with understanding of what in the inscrutable design is for our doomsday-good.[85]

There follows a poem, "And in That Drowning Instant," in which Klein seems to say that the essential truth was contained already in the basic Judaic faith of the Bible and that subsequent achievements were only ephemeral variants of it.

The book closes with Psalm 30, which is a song at the dedication of the House of David. It is a prayer of gratitude. The fundamentalist will find it an expression of traditional faith. In adding this psalm, Klein stressed his allegiance to the mainstream of Judaism.

In *The Second Scroll*, ideas concerning the immanence of God are implied. How important these ideas were to Klein, can be seen in "Selected Poems." A typescript of this collection was found among the papers which the National Archives in Ottawa acquired after Klein's death in 1972. Most of the material assembled in the volume had been published previously, but there are also a number of poems which presumably were produced during the last decade of Klein's working life and did not appear in print.[86]

The best poem among them, and perhaps one of the best Klein wrote, is the "Sestina on the Dialectic." In it, he speaks of a law that "stirs the seasons" and "treads the tide," a law that is fundamental to all activity. Here is the last stanza:

> When will there be arrest? Accord? A marriage of the
> antipathies, and out of the vibrant deaths and rattles the life
> still?
> O just as the racked one hopes his
> ransom, so I hope it, name it, image it,
> the together living, the together-with, the final synthesis. A stop.
> But so it never will turn out, returning to the rack within,
> without. And no thing's still.

There are again, at the end of this poem, the pregnant words "no thing." The assumption that Klein used them in the Cabalist sense is strengthened by the fact that "Selected Poems" includes "Desideratum," with its unequivocal "I am no contradictor of Cabala," and a hitherto unknown poem, "Song of Innocence." I think the latter is not successful, in spite of much ingenuity. However, the idea which Klein here had in mind is that found in the impressive metaphor at the end of "Genesis" in *The Second Scroll*: The murdered millions are dust, but the dust is divine. They are "noughts." "Song of Innocence" is found also on a loose sheet among the typescripts, and here the last word, "Noughts," is capitalized.

We remember, then, that "no thing," in Cabalist usage, means that which cannot be described in terms of anything known to man, in other words, it means "the divine." When

Klein says, "no thing's still," he is saying that the divine is silent. He may have in mind the words of his "Psalm of Resignation," where he cried out, "He answers not." But "no thing's still" may also mean that the divine is (exists) still (nevertheless). Klein is thus expressing two thoughts simultaneously: God is silent. But, for all that, He exists.

Possibly, Klein may also have had in mind "the still small voice" that Elijah heard in the wilderness,[87] the divine guidance silently expressed in his conscience. But more obviously intended in the words "no thing's still" is the idea that the Deity is the still point, ultimate repose, the peace, the "life still" for which Klein was longing. Clearly, the Cabalist interpretation of the words "no thing" offers great richness of thought.

But that does not mean that the words cannot yield a great deal of meaning if we disregard the Cabalist usage. Most readers will probably assume that "no thing's still" may be rendered thus: everything is in motion, the entire universe is constantly changing. This interpretation, too, was indubitably very much in Klein's mind. But what must be remembered is that those who tend to believe in theories of emanation may consider the universe to be divine also; and it must be remembered that to a Spinozan, everything is part of God. In the words "nothing's still" (everything is in motion), Klein then says that the Lord is constantly active.

We see at last that the words "no thing's still," in their very simplicity, are resplendent with meaning; for Klein is proclaiming in one breath: the Lord is the still point and the Lord is constantly active. In God, Parmenides and Heraclitus are reconciled. Here is indeed a "marriage of the antipathies, the final synthesis."

In "Selected Poems," the arrangement of some of the titles, particularly toward the end of the volume, is of obvious significance. This strengthens the view that the sequence in *Hath Not a Jew* . . . was also intended to make a statement. The "Sestina" is followed by a vision of nightmare. In "Les

Vespasiennes,'' Klein is haunted by the fear

> . . . that we are not God. Not God. Why, not,
> not even angels, but something less than men,
> creatures, sickness, whose pornoglot
> identities swim up within our ken
> from *graffiti*. . . .

The vision looms before him, terrifies him in an "anxiety dream."[88] But like an answer, like an awakening, there follow the lines of "Spinoza: On Man, On the Rainbow." Here, Klein speaks of the dust that is "suffused by light." His trust in the divinity of creation is routing the nightmare after all. The spectres are creatures of his fear; but his faith is confirmed in the words of a great philosopher. I do not believe that Spinoza, in the end, replaced for Klein the teachers of the Cabala. He supplemented and in a way confirmed Cabalist thought. The idea of the divine universe was in harmony with a Cabalist view of creation.

Three poems that follow and conclude the volume "Selected Poems" are all well known. They show us that Klein did not profess that all his questions were resolved. In "Psalm XXXIV: A Psalm of Abraham to Be Written Down and to Be Left on the Tomb of Rashi," he speaks of "A time of murder and despising life," of "Giant wickedness," and there is much that he "cannot grasp." He longs for a teacher, for Rashi, to guide him. In the next poem, "Psalm" (which like the Psalm concerning Rashi had appeared in *Poems* 1944), he bemoans that no great prophets have risen in our day.

> Where in the dubious days shall one take counsel?
> Who is there will resolve the blotted doubt?

At the end of "Selected Poems," Klein placed once more his "Autobiographical," with its longing for the days of youthful strength and innocent certainty. In the last stanza of the poem, we find again these lines:

It is a fabled city that I seek;
It stands in Space's vapours and Time's haze.

This, perhaps, is Klein's last poetic message to the world.

That he abandoned neither his ideas concerning the immanence of God, nor his trust in the evolution of the universe, which is implied in *The Second Scroll*, may, perhaps, be surmised from an editorial in *The Canadian Jewish Chronicle* which appeared in 1954.[89] Here he was even more outspoken. Taking his cue from a report that Einstein, had he known the consequences of his science, would have rather chosen to be a plumber, Klein launched a lighthearted essay; but when he had amused his readers sufficiently to assure their attention, he turned to this serious theme. Einstein, as is well known, declared himself unequivocally a Jew.[90] He was a religious man. But he seemed to seek God in the workings of nature. He believed that the scientist was the only truly religious person in the modern world because "His religious feeling takes the form of a rapturous amazement at the harmony of natural law, which reveals an intelligence of such superiority that, compared with it, all the systematic thinking and acting of human beings is an utterly insignificant reflection. This feeling is the guiding principle of his life and work, in so far as he succeeds in keeping himself from the shackles of selfish desire."[91] Klein links Einstein's religious ideas with Tennyson's trust in the evolutionary power of nature. Writing about Einstein he says:

There in his own writings, he will find

> one law, one element
> And one far-off divine event
> To which the whole creation moves.

It is a law and an element which reduces all slings and slurs to the infinitesimally trivial, which renders negatory the outrages of politicians; which re-establishes right vision and true perspective; which gives the final accolade to the theory of relativity, for it insists, above all, upon the sense of proportion. It is thus that Einstein has expressed this law. "My religion," he has said, "consists of a humble admiration of the illimitable superior spirit who reveals himself in the slight details we are able to perceive with our frail and feeble minds. That deeply emotional conviction of the presence of a superior reasoning power which is revealed in the incomprehensible universe, forms my idea of God."[92]

It is as if Klein were saying to his readers, "Far from destroying the hope for salvation, far from diminishing the hope for a Messianic age, a belief in the immanence of God brings this hope within the realm of the possible: the Messianic condition may be brought about as a result of the natural evolutionary process, and this process is divine."

It is difficult to assess how future critics will view Klein's achievement as a writer. Whatever their verdict, I hope they will acknowledge that he faced bravely the challenge of his day. His writings are not without inconsistency; but we find in them a constant effort to serve on the side of life and an enduring concern with questions of ultimate reality. Einstein once spoke of a cosmic religious feeling. He thought that it was "the most important function of art and science to awaken this feeling and keep it alive in those who are capable of it."[93] If one surveys Klein's work as a whole, one realizes that it aspires with not inconsiderable strength to fulfil this great function.

Notes

INTRODUCTION

1. This has been noted especially by Thomas A. Marshall, "The Poetry of A. M. Klein."

2. Spinoza, *Ethica*, Part I, Prop. XIV.

3. Jacob B. Agus believes that the Baal Shem Tov proclaimed God's "very presence was to be found in the inner substance and vitality of all things." *The Evolution of Jewish Thought From Biblical Times to the Modern Era* (London: Abelard Schuman, 1959), p. 333.

Similarly, Martin Buber writes: "God, so the Baal-Shem teaches, is in each thing as its primal essence." *The Tales of Rabbi Nachman*, trans. Maurice Friedman (Bloomington: Indiana University Press, 1962), p. 12.

4. Agus, *The Evolution of Jewish Thought*, pp. 17, 72.

5. Ibid., p. 325.

6. E. D. Hirsch thus describes the pantheism of some of the nineteenth-century Romantics. He is one of the writers who call their belief "Immanence-Theism." *Wordsworth and Schelling; a Typological Study of Romanticism* (New Haven: Yale University Press, 1960), pp. 29–30.

7. *The Zohar*, trans. Maurice Simon and Harry Sperling (London: Sonico Press, 1934), 1:69 (I:16b). "*Light, And There Was Light.* These words imply that there had already been light. This word *awr* (light), contains in itself a hidden significance. The expansive force proceeding from the hidden recesses of the secret supernal ether opened a path and produced from itself a mysterious point (or rather, the *En sof* [Limitless] clave its own ether and disclosed this point), *Yod*. When this expanded, that which was left of the mysterious *Awir* (ether) was found to be awr (light). When the first point had developed from it, it showed itself upon it, touching and yet not touching it. When it expanded, it emerged into being."

8. Martin Buber, *I and Thou*, 2nd ed., trans. Ronald Gregory Smith (New York: Scribner and Sons, 1958), p. 129.

9. Mordecai M. Kaplan, *Judaism as a Civilization* (New York: Macmillan, 1935), p. 405. Among rough notes for a projected work, "The Time Issue," Klein wrote: "Theology: Caplan's book." I believe Klein meant to write "Kaplan."

10. Ibid., p. 401.

11. Mordecai M. Kaplan, *Questions Jews Ask: Reconstructionist Answers* (New York: Reconstructionist Press, 1956), p. 116.

12. Concerning Klein's work as an editor, see Elijah Ezekiel Palnick, "A. M. Klein: A Biographical Study," Thesis, Hebrew Union College, Cincinnati, Ohio, 1959.

13. Klein, "Bialik Thou Shouldst be Living at This Hour," *Canadian Jewish Chronicle*, 10 July 1942, p. 4.

14. Klein, "Writing in Canada," *Canadian Jewish Chronicle*, 22 February 1946, p. 8.

15. For remarks and bibliographical information concerning Klein's technique and interest in language, imagism, symbolism, and humour, see my doctoral dissertation, "A. M. Klein: Religious Philosophy and Ethics in His Writings," McGill University, Montreal, 1972, pp. 12–13.

16. Ibid., pp. 15–16. Bibliographical information on adverse criticism and critical interest in Klein's socialism and oecumenism.

17. Guy Sylvestre, Review of A. J. M. Smith, ed., *The Book of Canadian Poetry* (University of Chicago Press, 1943), *Le Devoir*, 17 February 1945, p. 8.

18. Among the critics who have emphasized Klein's interest in Judaism see, e.g., Roy Kervin, Review of *The Second Scroll*, *Gazette* (Montreal), 29 September 1951, p. 28. "The most irritating thing for me, a Gentile, in reading Klein, is that Klein is writing only for Jews. His talent is too great, too powerful, too fine, to be so jealously directed. Couldn't he write for us, too?"

19. See, e.g., Anonymous, "Canadian Poetry in English," *Times Literary Supplement*, 5 November 1954, p. 704.

Anonymous, "Canadian Writers Come Into Their Own," *Times Literary Supplement*, 5 August 1955, p. iii.

Malcolm Ross, Review of *The Second Scroll*, *Canadian Forum*, 31 (1952): 234.

CHAPTER ONE

1. Irving Layton, "Piety," *First Statement*, 3 (1945): 23–36.

2. Roberta Lyons, "Jewish Poets from Montreal: Concepts of History in the Poetry of A. M. Klein, Irving Layton, and Leonard Cohen," Thesis, Carleton University, Ottawa, 1966.

3. Jack Ludwig, "A Woman of Her Age," *Tamarack Review*, no. 12 (Summer, 1959), pp. 6–25.

4. Jack Ludwig, "Celebration on East Houston Street," *Tamarack Review*, no. 28 (Spring, 1963), pp. 20–28.

5. Florence Malus, for instance, says that, according to David Lewis, M.P. (with whom she discussed the topic on 17 July 1969), Klein was willing to ride a bus on the Sabbath during his high-school years. But, she adds, he would never emphasize such concessions to modern living before his more orthodox friends. One could feel, she says, that Klein was growing away from orthodoxy. When the topic was discussed, he would grow silent. But he was always careful not to give offence. (Personal interview with this writer, Ottawa, 18 July 1969.)

Klein never changed this attitude to orthodoxy. Years later, in a review of his *Poems* (Philadelphia, 1944), Jacob Glotstein remarked: "Without revolution or the iconoclastic beating of drums, he has turned a new leaf in the annals of English Jewish literature here." "The English Jewish Poet A. M. Klein," *Yiddisher Kemfer* (New York), 4 May 1945, p. 16; trans. by David Rome, *Jews in Canadian Literature*, 1:61.

6. Palnick, "A. M. Klein: A Biographical Study," Part I.

7. Ibid., p. 2.

8. The false hair orthodox women used to put on after their wedding day on which they parted with their own cherished tresses.

9. Harriet Schneider, in a personal interview, Ottawa, 22 May 1969.

10. Palnick, "A. M. Klein," p. 8.

11. One hears, strangely, an echo of Ludwig Uhland's "Des Sängers Fluch." *Des Königs Namen meldet kein Lied, kein Heldenbuch;* | *Versunken und vergessen! Das ist des Sängers Fluch.* (No song, no heroic tale proclaims the king's name; | Sunk into oblivion and forgotten! That is the minstrel's curse.)

12. Klein, "Portraits of a Minyan," *Menorah Journal*, 17 (1929): 86–88.

All of Klein's published poetry quoted here may be found in *The Collected Poems of A. M. Klein*, compiled by Miriam Waddington (Toronto: McGraw-Hill Ryerson, 1974), and only where bibliographical details of earlier printings seem important, do they appear in the Notes.

13. That the poem "Sophist" contains a portrait of Rabbi Simcha Garber is generally accepted. Harriet Schneider mentioned it to me, and Palnick writes about it in "A. M. Klein." Not only is the name Simcha chosen; some of the rabbi's outstanding qualities, such as his exceptional memory, are also referred to.

14. Palnick, "A. M. Klein," Part I.

15. See, e.g., "Exultation," in "Sequence of Songs," *Poetry* (Chicago), 35–36 (1929): 22–24:

My blood shouts very joyous news
    Into my heart; and then
Hurries upon a lively cruise
    To come and shout again.
Whose is the gladness that can vie
    With mine? Once more, for spite,
Who is so happy as am I? . . .
    I see my love tonight!

16. Exod. 39:12.

17. Palnick, "A. M. Klein," p. 8.

18. Klein, "The Parliament of Fowls," *McGilliad*, 2 (November 1930): 10.

19. Ibid., p. 11.

20. A. H. McNeile and Theophile J. Meek, "Ecclesiastes," *Dictionary of the Bible*, ed. James Hastings, rev. ed. Frederick C. Grant and H. H. Rowley (New York: Scribner and Sons, 1963), p. 228.

21. Buber, *The Tales of Rabbi Nachman*, p. 15.

22.   Let the sky and let the sod
       And all between now praise our God!

CHAPTER TWO

1. Klein, "Out of the Pulver and the Polished Lens," *Canadian Forum*, 11 (1931): 453–54. Reprinted in *Hath Not a Jew* . . . .

2. For example, see Spinoza, *Ethica*, Part V, Prop. XVII, Corollary.

3. Arrangement of poems in "Out of the Pulver and the Polished Lens":

1	5	9
BIOGRAPHICAL	SPINOZA'S	BIOGRAPHICAL
Spinoza	PHILOSOPHY	Spinoza
persecuted		serene

2	6
PUBLIC POETRY	PUBLIC POETRY
The despised	The revered
apostate	innovators

3	7
PERSONAL POETRY	PERSONAL POETRY
Torments of	Ecstatic certainty
doubt	

4	8
ARGUMENT	ARGUMENT
Religion re-	Religion and
jected in	philosophy
favour of	harmonized
philosophy	

4. Frank Sewall, "Introduction," to Benedict de Spinoza, *Improvement of Understanding, Ethics and Correspondence*, trans. R. H. M. Elwes (Washington: M. Walter Dunne, 1901), p. vi.

5. E.g., Eccl. 1:5–7.

6. E.g., Eccl. 3:18–19.

7. See Introduction, lines pertaining to note 7.

8. According to Agus, the phrase "suspended in mid-air" was used in the Talmud in regard to issues on which the rabbis could not reach agreement. *The Evolution of Jewish Thought*, p. 106.

9. E.g., Spinoza, *Theologico-Political Treatise*, chap. 4, *The Chief Works*, trans. R. H. M. Elves (New York: Dover Press, 1955), vol. 1.

10. Ps. 29.

11. Ps. 65.

12. Relevant discussions concerning the Lurianic Cabala are found, e.g., in Agus, *Evolution of Jewish Thought* or Gershom G. Scholem, *Major Trends in Jewish Mysticism*, 3rd ed. (New York: Schocken Books, 1954).

13. Prov. 6:6.

14. Lev. 19:18.

15. Spinoza, *Theologico-Political Treatise*, chap. 14, *The Chief Works*, 1:183.

16. Klein, *The Second Scroll*, p. 110.

17. Marshall, "The Poetry of A. M. Klein," p. 38.

18. Klein, "Design for Mediaeval Tapestry," *American Caravan*, 4 (1931): 351–57. Reprinted in *Hath Not a Jew* . . . .

19. Spinoza, *Political Treatise*, chap. 2, secs. 8, 18, *The Chief Works*, 1:295, 297.

20. Spinoza, *Theologico-Political Treatise*, chap. 14, *The Chief Works*, 1:181, 183.

21. Spinoza, *Theologico-Political Treatise*, chap. 12, *The Chief Works*, 1:165.

22. Deut. 30:6; Jer. 31:33; Ps. 40:8.

23. Klein, "Talisman in Seven Shreds," *Menorah Journal*, 20 (1932): 148–50. Reprinted in *Hath Not a Jew* . . . .

24. Gershom G. Scholem, *Major Trends in Jewish Mysticism*, p. 99.

25. Nathan Ausubel, ed., *A Treasury of Jewish Folklore* (New York: Crown, 1948), pp. 603–4.

26. Egon Erwin Kisch, *"Dem Golem auf der Spur," Der Rasende Reporter* (Berlin: Erich Reiss, 1925), pp. 262–76.

27. Klein mentions one Johann Silvester "in his scarlet cap," presumably Silvester III, the anti-Pope, who reigned from January to May in 1045 and about whose activities the standard works of reference are silent; and Havlíček, a Czech journalist of the mid-nineteenth century, who was a known anti-semite and roused the bitterness of Jewish-Czech patriots by maintaining that they could not be considered a genuine part of the Czech nation. Klein calls him "the butcher," an appellation which in the perspective of World War II seems hardly appropriate, unless, indeed, one may consider it poetic clairvoyance that allowed Klein to recognize the looming disaster in human attitudes of seemingly lesser importance.

28. One may discern here a similarity between "Tetragrammaton" and "Exorcism Vain."

29. Max Brod, *The Redemption of Tycho Brahe*, trans. Felix Warren Grosse; with a foreword by Stefan Zweig (London: Alfred A. Knopf, 1928).

30. Ibid., p. 270.

31. Isaac Broydé, "Moses Ben Maimon," *Jewish Encyclopaedia* (New York, 1905), 9:80.

32. Maimonides, *The Guide of the Perplexed*, abridged ed., trans. from the Arabic by Chaim Rabin, introd. Julius Guttman (London: East and West Library, 1952), bk. 2, chap. 1, p. 93.

33. *Nicomachean Ethics*, bk. 1, chap. 10, (1100^b).

34. Maimonides, *The Book of Knowledge*, ed. according to the Bodleian (Oxford) Codex, transl. and introd. Moses Hyamson (Jerusalem: Boys Town Jerusalem Publishers, 1962), p. 92b.

35. Josh. 12:4.

CHAPTER THREE

1. See, e.g., Mark Zborowski and Elizabeth Herzog, *Life is with People. The Jewish Little-Town of Eastern Europe*, foreword by Margaret Mead (New York: International Universities Press, 1952).

2. Klein, "A Chassidic Anthology," *Canadian Jewish Chronicle*, 3 December 1948, p. 12.

3. Meyer Waxman, *History of Jewish Literature* (New York: Yoseloff, 1960), 5:179.

4. Bibliographical details of the first printing are not certain.

5. Klein, "The Ballad of the Dancing Bear," *Jewish Daily Eagle*, 8 July 1932, pp. 13–14. Reprinted in *Hath Not a Jew* . . . .

6. See, e.g., Zborowski and Herzog, *Life is with People*, pp. 181–82.

7. Klein, "Diary of Abraham Segal, Poet," *Canadian Forum*, 12 (1932): 297–300.

8. Buber, *The Tales of Rabbi Nachman*, p. 23.

9. Ibid., pp. 24–25.

10. Ibid., p. 99.

11. Alan Crawley, "The Poetry of A. M. Klein," *Contemporary Verse*, no. 28 (Summer 1949), p. 23.

12. Klein had much admiration for J. I. Segal. He translated his poems (see e.g., *Canadian Jewish Chronicle*, 23 October 1940, p. 4), and he wrote reviews of his work which show that he saw in him a brother-poet with whom, in some respects, he could identify himself. (Klein, "The Poetry Which is Prayer," *Canadian Jewish Chronicle*, 2 November 1945, p. 8; Klein, "Poet of a World Passed By," *Canadian Jewish Chronicle*, 9 June 1950, p. 5.)
When Segal died, Klein wrote a tribute ("In Memoriam J. I. Segal," *Canadian Jewish Chronicle*, 12 March 1954, pp. 3, 6) in which he drew attention to Segal's Chassidic heritage: "Poetry for him was not only a calling to be followed; it was a call to be answered. That call came to him across the generations by way of an unbroken sacred legacy, bequeathed at first by the

Baal Shem Tov, cherished by the Bratzlaver, and at last transmitted from his favorite Koretz to this latter-day Levite 'making great songs for a little clan.' "

Klein included in his tribute to the memory of Segal his translation of one of Segal's poems. Here are some of the lines:

World, I would take and lift you up
  Like a sheep lost in the dell,
And bear you to the high hill-top,
  To the golden well!

.   .   .   .

O, high upon the sunlit hill
  That well is cool and deep . . .
The sun washes her face in it
  Before she goes to sleep.

The style of Segal's poem is lyrical, quite different from that of Klein's "Diary of Abraham Segal, Poet." Yet, the essential longing in both poems is the same. Segal and Klein both sought dignity in everyday existence, while all around they saw a life debased and blighted. Both know of a cleansing experience that can be reached by those who climb to the top of the hill.

The kinship between the two poems strengthens the thought that Klein had J. I. Segal in mind when he wrote his "Diary of Abraham Segal, Poet."

13. Klein, *Hershel of Ostropol*, *Canadian Jewish Chronicle*, 31 March 1939, pp. 19–27; 13 September 1939, pp. 19–26. For a discussion of this play see my article "A. M. Klein's Forgotten Play."

14. S. A. Horodecky, *Leaders of Hassidim*, trans. Maria Horodecky-Magasanik; foreword by M. Gaster (London: Hasefer Agency for Literature, 1928), p. 96.

15. The word "Maskil," which appears in the Bible, is a term "usually thought to describe the character of a Psalm" and "may be held to denote a carefully composed, didactive or meditative poem; but its precise meaning is uncertain." James Hastings and others, eds., *Dictionary of the Bible*, p. 817.

16. A translation appears in Ausubel, *A Treasury of Jewish Folklore*, pp. 726–27.

17. Spinoza, *Political Treatise*, chap. 2, sec. 8, *The Chief Works*, 1:295.

18. Klein, "The Yiddish Proverb," *Canadian Jewish Chronicle*, 2 January 1953, p. 4.

19. S. A. Horodecky, *Leaders of Hassidim*, pp. 96–97.

20. See, e.g., "Song of Toys and Trinkets," "Song of Exclamations," or "Baal Shem Tov": "That rabbi of infants, man of children's love / Greybeard and leader of tots, the Baal Shem Tov!" Poems like "Wandering Beggar" or "Ballad for Unfortunate Ones" contain motifs typical of Chassidic imagination.

21. Louis Dudek, "A. M. Klein," *Canadian Forum*, 30 (1950): 12; reprinted in T. A. Marshall, ed., *A. M. Klein*.

22. Ps. 137:3.

23. Abraham Stilman, *Healer of All Flesh* (New York: Whittier, 1959), p. 43.

24. Ausubel, *Treasury of Jewish Folklore*, p. 104.

25. *War and Peace*, trans. Constance Garnett (New York: Modern Library, n.d.), p. 477.

26. June Rossolatos told me that Greeks still remember this when they speak of the fall of Mesolongion. Ottawa, 22 March 1970.

27. It may be interesting in this context to recall that English literature does not lack instances where dancing is equated with a religious or metaphysical concept. One may think of Yeats's "Among School Children" ("How can we know the dancer from the dance?") or the first poem in Kathleen Raine's "Northumbrian Sequence," *Collected Poems* (London: Hamilton, 1956), p. 111 ("I was the lonely dancer on the hill").

28. Roy Daniells, in the Milton Lectures, University of British Columbia, 1954/55.

29. *Zohar*, 3:202 (II, 64b). This passage refers to Exod. 17:7.

30. Gershom G. Scholem, *On the Kabbalah and Its Symbolism*, trans. Ralph Manheim (New York: Schocken Books, 1969), p. 103.

31. Agus, *The Evolution of Jewish Thought*, pp. 340–41.

32. Reprinted as "Psalm IV" in *Poems* (1944).

33. In "Psalms of Abraham," *Menorah Journal*, 29 (1941): 280–85. Reprinted as "Psalm XIV" in *Poems* (1944).

34. In "Psalms of Abraham" (Psalm 175).

35. In "Psalter of A. M. Klein," *Poetry* (Chicago), 58 (1941): 6–8. Reprinted in *The Second Scroll*.

36. John Sutherland, "The Poetry of A. M. Klein," *Index*, 1 (August 1946): 9.

37. Klein, "Saadyah Gaon," *Canadian Jewish Chronicle*, 22 May 1942, p. 4.

38. A "sennet," in stage directions, is a signal call on the trumpet. Gheel is a small city in Belgium, about thirty miles east of Antwerp. Its Gothic

church is dedicated to Dymphna, the patron saint of the insane, who, it is said, was executed there in A.D. 600. For hundreds of years, the city has contained a colony of farms and houses where insane persons were housed and treated. *Encyclopaedia Britannica* (1929), 10:323.

39. The word "hundemonium" is an example of Klein's inventiveness, suggesting the words "pandemonium," "Hun," and the German "Hunde," dogs.

40. "Zuruck" means "back." Yiddish. Cf. German, "zurück."

41. See, e.g., Gershom G. Scholem, *Major Trends in Jewish Mysticism*.

42. One is reminded of the Brazen-head in Greene's *The Honourable History of Friar Bacon and Friar Bungay* and its mysterious reference to Time.

43. "Psalms xv–xx."

44. "Shiggaion" is a word which appears in the Bible. It may mean a "wild, passionate song, with rapid changes of rhythm." James Hastings and others, eds., *Dictionary of the Bible*, p. 817.

45. Randall Jarrell, "These are not Psalms," *Commentary*, 1 (November 1945): 89.

46. See above, note 18.

47. Klein, "A Psalm of the Bratzlaver," *Canadian Jewish Chronicle*, 24 October 1947, p. 6.

48. Martin Buber, "The Seven Beggars," *The Tales of Rabbi Nachman*, pp. 149–78.

49. Ibid., pp. 154–56. (One is reminded, inevitably, of Plato's "Phaedrus.") "He was a man as old as the seas who spoke with a voice that came out of the distance, 'What shall I tell you? I remember the day when one broke the apple from the branch.' Then the next oldest arose and said, 'But still I think of the time when the light burned.' And the third, who was still younger, cried, 'I can recall the day when the fruit began to form.' 'But my thoughts,' joined in the fourth, 'reach unto the hour when the seed fell into the flower-cup!' 'And to me is still present,' said the fifth, 'how the flavor of the fruit entered into the seed.' 'And to me,' interjected the sixth, 'how the fragrance of the fruit entered into the seed.' 'And I still have within me,' spoke the seventh, 'how the shape of the fruit joined with the bud.' But I, who at that time was still a boy," spoke the blind beggar further, "was also with them. And I said to them, 'I recollect all these occurrences and I recollect nothing at all.' They were all greatly astonished that the youngest had the earliest memory and the child knew of the most ancient happening.

"Then came the great eagle, rapped on the tower, and bade them all step outside in the order of their ages: the boy he bade go before all, for he was really the oldest in memory, and the oldest he led out last, for he was really the youngest. And the great eagle spoke, 'Can you remember how you were detached from the body of your mother, or how you grew in your mother's body? Can you recollect the hour when the seed fell into your mother's womb? Can you recall your spirit before it entered into the seed, or your soul, or your life before it entered into the seed? This lad is above you all, for there still stirs within his inward mind the shadow of the primordial beginning, and the breath of the great night has not withdrawn from him. Thus he stands on the abyss of eternity as on native ground.'. . ."

CHAPTER FOUR

1. See, e.g., "Five Characters"; "Ballad of Signs and Wonders"; or "Legend of Lebanon." This is the story of a beautiful woman of Galilee who is made queen but vanishes when her prince is defeated by wicked enemies. Echoes of Keats mingle with a legend concerning Rachel:

From stanza 29. He took her to his tent and set for her
                 Sweetness of figs and dates, and toothsomeness
                 Of almonds . . .
From stanza 39. Her spirit wanders in the valley, and
                 Calls blessings on the lovers of the land.

2. Klein, "The Tale of the Marvellous Parrot," *Canadian Zionist*, April 1937, pp. 106, 108.
3. Klein, "Three Candle-Lights," *Judaean*, 2 (1928): 8.
4. Klein, "Haggadah," in *Hath Not a Jew* . . . .
5. Klein, "Thirty Plots and Holy Writ," *Canadian Jewish Chronicle*, 15 April 1938, pp. 35–38.
6. Klein, "Marginalia," *Canadian Jewish Chronicle*, 11 June 1948, pp. 8–9. Since Klein was deeply interested in the work of James Joyce (see "The Oxen of The Sun," *Here and Now*, 1 (January 1949): 28–48; "The Black Panther," *Accent*, 10 (Spring 1950): 139–55; "A Shout in the Street," *New Directions*, no. 13 (1951), pp. 327–45), we may surmise he applied to the Bible ideas which were inspired by Joyce's *Portrait of the Artist as a Young Man*. Parallels in the writings of Joyce and Klein have been noted on various occasions. An

interesting study may be found in Solomon Spiro's "The Second Gloss."

Not all of Klein's essays on aesthetics are concerned with subjects of Jewish interest. See, e.g., "Marginalia," 25 June 1948, p. 8. Klein here develops, *inter alia*, the theory that there are circular poems which make one look back at the poem for its central meaning, and centrifugal poems, where the last line reaches out toward other experiences. He illustrates this theory with examples from Rilke and Keats. See also "Marginalia," 24 December 1948, p. 6, and 28 January 1949, p. 6; and the satirical essays "A Definition of Poetry," *Canadian Jewish Chronicle*, 19 April 1946, pp. 8, 12; "Book Reviewing in Seven Easy Lessons," ibid., 10 December 1948, p. 18; or the exceedingly funny parody of a report from a conference on literary criticism: "On Criticism—And the Mome Raths Outgrabe," *Here and Now*, 2 (1949): 31–37; etc.

7. Klein, "The Bible's Archetypal Poet," *Canadian Jewish Chronicle*, 6 March 1953, p. 7.

8. Ibid., 13 March 1953, p. 4; 26 March 1953, p. 4.

9. Earl Birney, "Canadian Jewish Poet" [Rev. of *Hath Not a Jew* . . . .], *Canadian Forum*, 20 (1941): 354–55.

10. W. Bacher, "Hillel," *Jewish Encyclopaedia*, 6:398.

11. S. Mendelsohn, "Johanan," *Jewish Encyclopaedia*, 2:213–14.

12. Isaac Broydé, "Meir," *Jewish Encyclopaedia*, 8:432–35.

13. Klein, "Yehuda Halevi—His Pilgrimage," *Canadian Jewish Chronicle*, 19 September 1941, pp. 9–12. Reprinted in *Poems* (1944).

14. John Fredrick Nims, "Tares and Wheat," *Poetry* (Chicago), 66 (1945): 104–5.

15. Stanzas 34–39 inclusive are a translation of Halevi's "Ode to Zion."

16. Maurice Evans, in an informal discussion connected with his lectures on Literary Criticism, McGill University (1965/66).

17. A parallel may be noted here between the imprisoned Rabbi Yom-Tob and Byron's Prisoner of Chillon, who saw how

> The fish swam by the castle wall,
> And they seemed joyous each and all;
> The eagle rode the rising blast,

An echo of Coleridge's "Ancient Mariner" may be found in the blessings pronounced by Rabbi Yom-Tob on the cellar floor and the stones of the prison when he has heard "the still small voice."

18. The stories of Yom-Tob of Joigny and Amnon are included in Ausubel's *A Treasury of Jewish Folklore*, pp. 146–48.

19. See "The Seventh Scroll." The story of a scribe.

"Kapusitchka." A simple story, masterfully told. The Jewish background is lightly sketched in.

20. For a list of Klein's translations see the bibliographies of Usher Caplan and David Rome.

21. See, e.g., his articles "Humbert Wolfe" (in which Klein draws attention to his biting phrase, the pregnant epigram, the ironic twist); "Leon Feuchtwanger" (which shows that Klein, at the time, thought Feuchtwanger was "probably the most distinguished novelist of his generation"); [Stefan] Zweig's "Hail and Farewell"; "*The Dybbuk*" (Text of a trans-Canada radiotalk on Ansky's play); "Poems of Yehoash"; "New Writers," Rev. of *Here and Now* by Irving Layton.

22. Klein studied Law at the University of Montreal. He was called to the bar in 1933. He retired from legal practice in 1954. Norah Story, *The Oxford Companion to Canadian Literature* (Toronto: Oxford University Press, 1967), p. 407.

23. Klein, "The Draft Constitution of Israel," *Canadian Jewish Chronicle*, 11, 18, 25, February 1949.

24. *Ethica*, Part III, Prop. VI. See also Part IV, Prop. VIII, Note.

25. Klein, "A Psalm Touching Genealogy," in *Poems* (1944).

26. From a letter, written in 1913 to Dr. Israel Abrahams, the Anglo-Jewish scholar (1858–1925). It is quoted in Leon Simon, *Ahad Ha-Am; a Biography* (Philadelphia: Jewish Publications Society of America, 1960), p. 229.

27. Ibid., p. 311.

28. Ibid., pp. 311–12. See also Jacob B. Agus, *Modern Philosophies of Judaism; a Study of Recent Jewish Philosophies of Religion* (New York: Behrman's Jewish Book House, 1941), p. 40. Agus explains that "shocked by the brutality of the pogroms in the years 1880–1881, many Jewish intellectuals were overcome with remorse at their former disdain of their national culture" (p. 31), and that the teachings of Ahad Ha-Am (One of the People, pseudonym for Asher Ginsberg) were the product of the reawakened Jewish national consciousness.

29. See, e.g., J. S. [Jesse Schwartz], "Creative Judaism," Rev. of the *Reconstructionist Papers*, ed. Mordecai M. Kaplan, *The Canadian Zionist*, December 1936, p. 54.

30. Kaplan, *Judaism as a Civilization*, p. 328.

31. Ibid., p. 514.

32. Klein, "Of Jewish Existentialism," *Canadian Jewish Chronicle*, 5 November 1948, p. 8.

33. Stephen Leacock, *Economic Prosperity in the British Empire* (Toronto: Macmillan, 1930), pp. 195–96.

34. John Porter, *The Vertical Mosaic; an Analysis of Social Class and Power in Canada* (Toronto: University of Toronto Press, 1965), p. 67.

35. Leon Edel, "Abraham M. Klein," *Canadian Forum*, 12 (1932): 300.

36. This sonnet was included in "Sonnets Semitic" in *Hath Not a Jew* . . . .

37. Klein, "A Notable Historical Event," *Canadian Jewish Chronicle*, 19 February 1943, p. 4.

38. E. W. Mandel, "Introduction," to Gwendalyn Graham, *Earth and High Heaven* (1944) (Toronto: McClelland and Stewart, 1960), p. xi.

39. Canadian Jewish Congress, "The Impact of the Canadian Jewish Congress on Antisemitism in Canada," *Congress Bulletin*, 7 (1951): 7.

40. Klein, "Notes on a Court Jew," *Canadian Jewish Chronicle*, 12 December 1941, p. 15.

The topic is raised also in "Memoirs of a Campaigner," *Canadian Zionist*, May 1937, p. 25, where Klein quotes Shakespeare in support of the idea that adherence to one's native culture does not present a threat to one's wider political allegiance: "to thine own self be true/And it must follow as the night the day/Thou canst not then be false to any man."

41. Klein, "Jewish Self-Hatred," *Canadian Jewish Chronicle*, 14 January 1944, p. 4.

42. Klein, "Annotation on Shapiro's Essay on Rime," *Northern Review*, no. 1 (October–November 1946), p. 37.

43. Klein, "Talents Which Should Have Been Ours," *Canadian Jewish Chronicle*, 10 May 1946, p. 6.

44. Ibid., p. 15.

45. Ibid., p. 6.

46. Ronald Sutherland, "The Body-Odour of Race," *Canadian Literature*, no. 37 (Summer 1968), p. 46.

47. Clearly, the story is reminiscent of Huxley's *Brave New World* (1932) and of Briussov's "The Republic of the Southern Cross" (1919).

48. Klein, "The Mystery of the Mislaid Conscience," *Canadian Jewish Chronicle*, 17 July 1942, p. 4.

49. Desmond Pacey, *Creative Writing in Canada* (Toronto: Ryerson Press, 1967), p. 143.

50. E.g., A. J. M. Smith, "Abraham Moses Klein," *Gants du Ciel*, 11 (Spring 1946): 78; John Matthews, "Abraham Klein and the Problem of Synthesis," *Journal of Commonwealth Literature*, 1 (1965): 157; Merirose Bell, "The Image of French Canada in the Poetry of William Drummond, Emile Coderre, and A. M. Klein," Thesis, McGill University, Montreal, 1967, p. 83.

51. Albert Regimbal, "Artistes Israélites au Canada Français," *Relations*, no. 90 (June 1948), pp. 184–85.

52. See, e.g., Arthur Leonard Phelps, *Canadian Writers* (Toronto: McClelland and Stewart, 1951), p. 117. "In Klein is the comprehensive catholicity of human understanding which gives its authority to noble verse."

John Anthony Scullion, "Abraham Moses Klein, Poet and Novelist," Thesis, University of Montreal, 1953, p. 16. "It is strange that a man not of the Catholic religion could... so realistically express what Catholics firmly experience."

B. G. Keyfetz, "Immigrant Reaction as Reflected in Jewish Literature," *Congress Bulletin* (October 1962), pp. 4–5. "He has accepted both worlds and is one of the few in North America writing to epitomize this dual harmony, a very rare kind of phenomenon, for it is generally the very conflict and turmoil that makes for creativity."

53. Northrop Frye, "English Canadian Literature," *Books Abroad*, 29 (1955): 270.

54. Klein, note to "Parade of St. Jean Baptiste," *Canadian Forum*, 27 (1948): 258.

55. Camillien Houde, to whom the poem is "dedicated," was immensely popular. Léon Gauthier described him as "un homme du peuple... en ce sens qu'il connait mieux que beaucoup d'autres la vie des petites gens qui doivent peiner pour gagner leur subsistance." "Le Maire de Montréal," *L'Écho de Saint-Justin*, 9 (April 1930): 1. During World War II, Houde was, for a time, interned. He was re-elected after his release. Klein predicted that he would be remembered only "in a shamefaced footnote" to Canadian history. "Commentary," *Canadian Jewish Chronicle*, 16 August 1940, p. 4.

56. According to Palnick, Klein fell into a cellar when he was five years old and was taken to the Hôtel-Dieu.

57. Klein, "The Thirteenth Apostle," *Canadian Jewish Chronicle*, 18 February 1944, p. 4.

58. He remained active in the support of Jewish organizations and Jewish causes. The degree of his involvement may be seen in an anecdote reported by Mordecai Richler in "The War, Chaverim and After," *Canadian Literature* no. 18 (Autumn 1963), pp. 21–29. Concerning the independence of Israel, a prominent Montreal doctor made a speech in which he expressed his fear that the creation of the new state would cause Jewish loyalties to be divided. The (Montreal) *Star* printed his complete speech; whereupon the Habonim collected money from door to door so that Klein could reply to the doctor's allegations on radio. That Klein was convinced a Jew could be a Zionist and, at the same time, be truly at home in a land other than Israel can be seen in "A Reply to Dr. I. M. Rabinovitch" and "In Praise of the Diaspora," *Canadian Jewish Chronicle*, 9 January 1953, p. 4. See also above, lines pertaining to note 40.

59. "The Sugaring," in *The Rocking Chair and Other Poems*, is dedicated to Guy Sylvestre, whom Klein never met but who introduced Klein's poetry to French Canada and in whom, Klein felt, he had found an understanding friend. (Interview with Guy Sylvestre, Ottawa, at the National Library, 11 February 1969.)

60. Shloime Wiseman, Review of *Hath Not a Jew . . .*, *Canadian Jewish Chronicle*, 14 June 1940, p. 6.

61. See Klein, "Grain Elevator," in *The Rocking Chair and Other Poems*. This is the third stanza:

Sometimes, it makes me think Arabian,
the grain picked up, like tic-tacs out of time:
first one; an other; singly; one by one;—
to save life. Sometimes, some other races claim
the twinship of my thought,—as the river stirs
restless in a white Caucasian sleep,
or, as in the steerage of the elevators,
the grains, Mongolian and crowded, dream.

62. In this essay, Klein tries to prove that the idea of universal equality, at least in inspiration, was already present in Hebrew legend and that modern science furnishes further proof of its correctness. He points to the tale of David who loathed the spider but was saved by a spider; and he recalls that penicillin is manufactured from a seemingly insignificant mould.

63. Palnick, "A. M. Klein: A Biographical Study," p. 3.

64. Ibid., p. 2.

65. See "Manuscript: Thirteenth Century," *Canadian Forum*, 14 (1934): 474–76.

66. Klein, "Dress Manufacturer: Fisherman," *Contemporary Verse* (Fall 1947), p. 3. Reprinted in *The Rocking Chair and Other Poems*. Thoreau MacDonald, whose drawings illustrate this volume, provides an interesting little comment when he shows us the silhouette of the fisherman who casts his line into empty waters while two fishes swim away beneath his boat.

67. Klein, "Psalm IX: A Psalm to Be Preserved Against Two Wicked Words," *Poems* (1944).

68. Prov. 30:8.

69. G. B. Shaw, "Socialism for Millionaires" (1896), *Essays in Fabian Socialism*, rev. ed. (London: Constable, 1932), p. 120.

70. Klein, "Beggars I Have Known," *Canadian Forum*, 16 (1936): 20.

71. Klein, "Of Faith, Hope and Charity," in "Barricade Smith," *Canadian Forum*, 18 (1938): 210.

72. Klein, "The Jewish Unitarian," *Canadian Jewish Chronicle*, 28 August 1942, p. 16.

73. Palnick, "A. M. Klein: A Biographical Study," chap. 2.

74. In 1926, there was a design competition for a war memorial to be erected in Ottawa. It was won by the English sculptor Vernon March. He died in 1930, but his brother and a sister completed the work in 1932. The federal government delayed erecting the monument until a fitting site could be purchased and cleared. It was at last unveiled by George VI on 1 May 1939. Canada National Capital Commission, *Statues and Monuments in Ottawa and Hull* (Ottawa, n.d.), p. 14.

75. Klein, "To One Gone to the Wars," in "Of Castles in Spain," *Canadian Forum*, 18 (1938): 79. The man addressed in this poem, according to Palnick, is Sam Abramson, a childhood friend.

76. Klein, "The Issue is Clear," *Canadian Jewish Chronicle*, 8 September 1939, p. 4.

77. E.g.: Randall Jarrell, "These are not Psalms," *Commentary*, 1 (1945): 90 ("Mr. Klein, understandably and even laudably, has been drawn to a type of writing and a subject that are not only uncongenial to him but completely beyond the scope of his gentler talents"); Irving Layton, "[Rev. of] *The Hitleriad*," *First Statement*, 2 (1944): 17–20; Pacey, *Ten Canadian Poets*, p. 279 ("As always Klein is more successful in celebration than in condemnation"); A. W. Steinberg, "The Stature of A. M. Klein," *The Reconstructionist*, 29 November 1957, p. 17 ("Klein fails to suggest the scope

of the horror and the evil." *The Hitleriad* "shares the general inadequacy of all literary attempts to come to terms with Hitlerism"). One of the few favourable reactions comes from E. J. Pratt who, in reviewing *The Hitleriad*, speaks of Klein's "masculine thrust against the common foes of humanity." *Canadian Forum*, 24 (1944): 164.

78. Klein, "Childe Harold's Pilgrimage," *Opinion*, 8 (1938): 15–16. Reprinted in *Hath Not a Jew. . . .*

79. Klein, "Ballad of the Nuremberg Tower-Clock," *Saturday Night*, 8 November 1941, p. 10.

80. Klein, "Ballad of the Thwarted Axe," *Canadian Forum*, 21 (1941): 212. Reprinted in *Poems* (1944).

81. Klein, "Psalm VI: A Psalm of Abraham, Concerning that which He Beheld Upon the Heavenly Scarp," *Poetry* (Chicago), 59 (1942): 315–16. Reprinted in *Poems* (1944).

82. Klein, "We Who Are About to be Born," *Canadian Jewish Chronicle*, 2 June 1944, p. 4.

83. Klein, *The Hitleriad*, part 3.

84. *Dunciad*, book 4, 501–2.

85. Ibid., book 4, 268.

86. This I heard in 1938 from my aunt, Julia Diamant, who came to Olomouc, Czechoslovakia, as a refugee from Vienna.

87. Klein, "The Jews of Europe," *Canadian Jewish Chronicle*, 3 August 1945, p. 8.

88. Klein, "Elegy," *Canadian Jewish Chronicle*, 25 April 1947, pp. 8, 9. Reprinted in *The Second Scroll*.

89. This quotation and the bibliographical information on the Ratno Memorial Volume appear in David Rome's bibliography *Jews in Canadian Literature*, 1:97.

90. Klein, "Meditation Upon Survival," *Contemporary Verse*, no. 32 (Summer 1950), pp. 9–10.

CHAPTER FIVE

1. See Chapter Two.

2. "Psalm II," *Poems* (1944).

3. See, e.g., "Autobiography," *Canadian Forum*, 23 (1943): 106.

4. See, e.g., "Greetings on This Day," *Menorah Journal*, 18 (1930): 1–4.

5. Klein, "Notebook of a Journey," *Canadian Jewish Chronicle*, 12 August 1949, pp. 3, 6.

6. "Notebook of a Journey," 9 September 1949, pp. 5, 16.

7. For a brief annotated survey of critical opinion see my dissertation on A. M. Klein, pp. 293–94.

8. *The Second Scroll*, p. viii.

9. Ibid., p. xiv.

10. Ibid., p. 88.

11. The word "Dudele" derives from the Yiddish "Du"— you or thou.

12. Ausubel, *A Treasury of Jewish Folklore*, p. 721.

13. Martin Buber, *I and Thou*, p. 129.

14. Martin Buber, *On Judaism*, ed. Nahum Glatzer (New York: Schocken Books, 1967), p. 213.

15. Buber, *The Tales of Rabbi Nachman*, p. 109.

16. Martin Buber, *A Believing Humanism*, trans. and introd. Maurice Friedman (New York: Simon and Schuster, 1967), p. 113.

17. Buber, *On Judaism*, p. 163.

18. Buber, *A Believing Humanism*, pp. 184–85.

19. Buber, *On Judaism*, p. 209.

20. Buber, *A Believing Humanism*, p. 114.

21. Buber, *On Judaism*, p. 209.

22. *The Second Scroll*, p. ix.

23. Ibid., p. 19. In this context, it may be well to recall the teachings of the Cabalist Rabbi Luria, which tell of a prehistoric catastrophe that caused sparks of divine light to be scattered and exiled from the Godhead. It is man's task to help reintegrate the sparks of light until their final restoration may take place, *tiqqun*, a state in which the entire universe is completely redeemed. Every good act, every act that accords with the Law, contributes to the return of the exiled sparks of light. See, e.g., Gershom G. Scholem, *On the Kabbalah and Its Symbolism* (New York: Schocken Books, 1969), pp. 111–17.

24. Klein here refines an image which seems to originate with T. S. Eliot. One is reminded of Mr. Eugenides in "The Fire Sermon," "the Smyrna merchant / unshaven, with a pocketful of currants." The unpleasant image of the unhygienic, sticky, sweet, dried-up currants in Eugenides's pockets is used to discredit an uncongenial type.

25. Buber, *On Judaism*, p. 157.

26. See, e.g., Miriam Waddington, *A. M. Klein*, p. 118.

27. *The Second Scroll*, p. 26.

28. Exod. 13:21. Steinberg, "Introduction," *The Second Scroll*, p. xiv.

29. *The Second Scroll*, p. 30. Added here is also a remark which appeared in "Meditation Upon Survival" and which, incidentally, shows how much Klein had to rely on other people's reports, and how little personal knowledge he had of European Jewry, with whose fate he was so frequently concerned. I am referring to the words "Then, sensing their death wish bubbling the channels of my blood, then do I grow bitter at my false felicity—the spared one!"

Klein here evidently refers to twisted rumours, fairly widespread after World War II, according to which Jews marched into gas chambers because their will to live had actually broken down. While it is, of course, not impossible that this was the case in individual instances, it would certainly be erroneous to conclude that such was the attitude of appreciable numbers. Anyone familiar with the psychology of European Jews will attest to this. I discussed the problem with a survivor of Auschwitz (Stan Lenga, Vancouver, Yom Kippur, 1952). To my question how it was possible that people entered the gas chambers without each putting up a physical struggle, he had this, in my opinion completely plausible, explanation.

Being completely isolated from any possible help, the inmates of concentration camps did their utmost not to give offence. Each hoped that he himself would survive if he remained as inconspicuous as possible. Therefore, when prisoners were ordered to enter the "shower house," they walked into the gas chambers without resistance. They knew that opposition to an order would mean that they would instantly be gunned down. Since they felt completely innocent, they were persuading themselves that the building they entered might indeed contain only a shower.

30. *The Second Scroll*, p. 36.

31. Ibid., p. 38.

32. Ibid., p. 42.

33. In *Oedipus Rex* and *Antigone*, the chorus proclaims the author's fundamental philosophical ideas exactly half way through the play.

34. *The Second Scroll*, p. 44.

35. Ibid., p. 48.

36. Irving Layton, Review of "*Poems* (1944)," *First Statement* 2 (1945): 35.

37. *The Second Scroll*, p. 42.

38. Ibid., p. 51.

39. Ibid., p. 51.

40. Ibid., p. 51.

41. Ibid., p. 52.

42. Ibid., p. 52.

43. Carol Klein, in *The Credo of Maimonides* (New York: Philosophical Library, 1958), p. 117, writes: "Maimonides describes these *ikkarim*, or root beliefs, as ideas that must be accepted a priori, but still can be fully expounded by reason." To deny even one of them means that one is no longer part of the Jewish community. The thirteen credos pertain to the existence of God; His Unity; His incorporeality; His eternity; His exclusive right to be worshipped; the fact of prophecy and acceptance of the words of the prophets; Moses as the greatest of the prophets; divine origin of the Torah; eternity of the Torah; omniscience of God; divine reward and punishment; the coming of the Messiah; resurrection.

44. *The Second Scroll*, p. 106.

45. Ibid., p. 109.

46. Ibid., p. 108.

47. Ibid., p. 112.

48. Ibid., p. 105.

49. Ibid., p. 110.

50. Ibid., p. 107.

51. Ibid., p. 108.

52. Ibid., p. 110.

53. Ibid., p. 109.

54. Ibid., p. 110.

55. Ibid., p. 110.

56. Ibid., pp. 111–12.

57. Agus, *The Evolution of Jewish Thought*, p. 74.

58. *The Second Scroll*, p. 55.

59. In his article "Robinson Jeffers—Poet Fascist?" Klein upbraided this American writer for not seeing the difference between Roosevelt and Hitler, or between Britain and Germany; and he said he associated himself with the idea that "a poet must possess a sense of humanity."

It was, no doubt, considerations of this nature that prompted him to write his verses against Ezra Pound, whose offence, Klein said in his poem "Cantabile," was "usura." "[Pound] thought to extract an exhorbitant interest from a limited talent." (*Northern Review*, 2 (1949): 30–31.) Evidently,

Klein felt that Pound's talent was short of a vital ingredient: the sense of humanity. In "Old Ez and His Blankets," he deplores bitterly the decision of the committee which awarded Pound the Bollingen Prize.

When T. S. Eliot received the Nobel Prize, Klein courageously spoke out against him, in spite of the obvious artistic debt he owed him. "Perhaps the final test to a man's religion and humanity is his attitude to minorities," wrote Klein. (*Canadian Jewish Chronicle*, 26 November 1948, p. 8.)

In the same year, he wrote also "That Rank Picture," an article attacking the Rank Organization's film production of *Oliver Twist*, noting that the character of Fagin had worried Dickens, and that to make up for it, Dickens later created the idealized Jew Mr. Riah of *Our Mutual Friend*.

In *The Jews of England*, a mimeographed pamphlet (Montreal, undated) issued by the Hadassah Organization of Canada, Klein analyses *The Merchant of Venice* and points out that the play is full of absurdities. In view of the title of Klein's first collection of poems, it may be interesting to note that Klein feels the court scene is guilty of "crass stupidity." E.g., the idea of the pound of flesh comes from the Twelve Tables of Roman Law, not Jewish law; Shylock's speech "Hath not a Jew eyes . . ." "is hardly the thing Shylock would have argued, for the same plea even to the detail of laughter can be made of a hyena."

It has to be emphasized here that Klein went out of his way to bring to the notice of his readers those works of English literature which point to harmony between Gentiles and Jews, works like Browning's "Rabbi Ben Ezra." He published them under the title "Jewish Themes in English," and we find them scattered, especially during 1953, in the pages of the *Canadian Jewish Chronicle*.

60. *The Second Scroll*, p. 65.

61. Ibid., p. 67.

62. Ibid., p. 73.

63. Ibid., p. 75.

64. Ibid., p. 78.

65. Ibid., p. 78.

66. Ibid., pp. 76–77.

67. Ibid., pp. 84–85.

68. Ibid., p. 85; Judg. 5:20.

69. It is not by chance that Klein pictures the old man in the company of a boy scholar. Tales of prodigy scholars abound among the traditions connected with Rabbi Luria. For information on this subject, I am indebted to Anny Plaschkes-Scharf of Jerusalem.

70. *The Second Scroll*, p. 88.

71. Ibid., p. 89.

72. Agus, *The Evolution of Jewish Thought*, p. 73.

Writers have reported that the rabbis would not expound the chapter of the Chariot before anyone unless he was a sage and already had an independent understanding of the matter. One history (ascribed to a first-century writer) tells of a child who read the Book of Ezekiel, apprehended what it meant, and was consumed by fire. See "Kabbalah: Historical Development of the Kabbalah," *Encyclopaedia Judaica* (Jerusalem, 1971) 10:498; "Merkabah Mysticism," ibid., 11:1386.

73. *The Second Scroll*, p. 90.

74. Ibid., p. 91.

75. Ibid., p. 92.

76. Cf. above, lines pertaining to note 6.

77. *The Second Scroll*, p. 93.

78. *The Authorized Daily Prayer Book*, rev. ed., Hebrew text, English translation with commentary and notes by Joseph H. Hertz (New York: Bloch, 1948). (*Siddur.*)

79. Ibid., p. 11.

80. *The Second Scroll*, p. 136.

81. Ibid., p. 137.

82. *Siddur*, p. 71.

83. This poem was discussed in Chapter 3. Lines pertaining to note 47.

84. *Siddur*, p. 137.

85. *The Second Scroll*, p. 139.

86. Klein, "Selected Poems," National Archives, Ottawa, n.d. Usher Caplan, who, at present, is engaged in the sorting of Klein's papers, has found evidence among Klein's hand-written notes that one of the poems, "Sestina on the Dialectic," existed in 1946. He suggests that the volume "Selected Poems" was ready in 1955, and that this was probably the manuscript of poems Klein unsuccessfully submitted to a publisher in that year.

Klein was in the habit of refining and improving and reprinting his poems. After *The Second Scroll*, he continued printing poems in the *Canadian Jewish Chronicle*. We find there, for instance, "Ni la mort ni le soleil," "The Library," and the rather attractive poem "Beaver." According to Alan Rose, he left the employ of the *Canadian Jewish Chronicle* in June, 1955. (Letter addressed to the writer by Alan Rose, Assistant Director of Canadian Jewish Congress, 14 July 1969.)

After 1955, Klein lived in retirement, a stranger to his friends. This mysterious, apparently self-imposed isolation has given rise to much speculation. Palnick suggested that Klein's acute depression was brought about by a number of professional disappointments. I draw attention to a passage in *The Second Scroll* (p. 50), where the narrator, clearly Klein's *persona*, says he has experienced an "unidentified melancholy, a sadness that refused to give its name."

87. I Kings 19:12.

88. This rather awkward word combination appears to be a literal translation of the German "Angsttraum," the common German term for "nightmare."

89. [Klein,] "Einstein, his Eternal Verities and his Relative Conveniences." This editorial is based on lecture notes on the "Three Greatest Jews of Modern Times," Einstein, Freud, and Herzl. (National Archives, Ottawa, n.d.) According to Klein's notes, his quotation of Einstein's words appears to have been taken from a manuscript at the Hebrew University. It is most likely that Klein saw this manuscript when he was in Jerusalem, and that the lecture notes post-date his journey to Israel. In the notes, Klein equates Herzl with the "Jewish will-to-live." Here he expresses also the conviction that literature becomes life. Oscar Wilde's playful suggestion that nature imitates art may have inspired Klein. But in the present context, the approach is serious.

90. Albert Einstein, *The World as I See It* (*Mein Weltbild*), trans. Alan Harris (New York: Philosophical Library, 1949), p. 90.

91. Ibid., p. 29.

92. Klein, "Einstein, . . ."

93. Einstein, *The World as I See It*, p. 27.

Selected Bibliography

THE WRITINGS OF A. M. KLEIN

BOOKS

The Collected Poems of A. M. Klein. Compiled with an introduction by Miriam Waddington. Toronto: McGraw-Hill Ryerson, 1974.

Hath Not a Jew .... Foreword by Ludwig Lewisohn. New York: Behrman's Jewish Book House, 1940.

The Hitleriad. New York: New Directions, 1944.

Poems. Philadelphia: Jewish Publication Society of America, 1944.

The Rocking Chair and Other Poems. Toronto: Ryerson Press, 1948.

The Second Scroll. New York: Knopf, 1951; with an introduction by M. W. Steinberg, Toronto: McClelland and Stewart, 1961.

PROSE

"And It Shall Come to Pass." *Canadian Jewish Chronicle*, 29 October 1948, p. 4.

"Annotation on Shapiro's Essay on Rime." *Northern Review* 1 (1946): 30–38.

"Beggars I Have Known." *Canadian Forum*, 16 (1936): 19–20.

"Bialik Thou Shouldst be Living at This Hour." *Canadian Jewish Chronicle*, 10 July 1942, p. 4.

"The Bible Manuscripts." *Canadian Jewish Chronicle*, 28 September–26 October 1951.

"The Bible's Archetypical Poet." *Canadian Jewish Chronicle*, 6–20 March 1953.

"A Chassidic Anthology." *Canadian Jewish Chronicle*, 3 December 1948, p. 12. Review of Martin Buber's *Tales of the Chassidim*.

"Commentary [on David Croll and Camillien Houde]." *Canadian Jewish Chronicle*, 16 August 1940, p. 4.

"The Draft Constitution of Israel." *Canadian Jewish Chronicle*, 11–25 February 1949.

"The Dybbuk." *Canadian Jewish Chronicle*, 23–30 July 1948.

"Einstein: His Eternal Verities and His Relative Conveniences." *Canadian Jewish Chronicle*, 19 November 1954, p. 1. Editorial.

"Feuchtwanger, Zionist." *Canadian Jewish Chronicle*, 20 December 1940, p. 4. Review of *Josephus*.

"Friends, Romans, Hungrymen." *New Frontier*, 1 (1936): 16–18.

"The Golem of Prague." *Canadian Jewish Chronicle*, 20 January 1939, p. 4.

"Humbert Wolfe." *Canadian Jewish Chronicle*, 12 January 1940, p. 4.

"In Memoriam J. I. Segal." *Canadian Jewish Chronicle*, 12 March 1954, pp. 3, 6.

"In Praise of the Diaspora." *Canadian Jewish Chronicle*, 9 January–27 February 1953.

"The Issue is Clear." *Canadian Jewish Chronicle*, 8 September 1939, p. 4.

"A Jew in the Sistine Chapel." *Canadian Jewish Chronicle*, 28 April–12 May 1950.

"Jewish Folk Songs." *Canadian Jewish Chronicle*, 2 September 1944, pp. 6–7.

"Jewish Self-Hatred." *Canadian Jewish Chronicle*, 14 January 1944, pp. 4, 15. Review of *Person, Place and Thing* by Karl Shapiro.

"The Jewish Unitarian." *Canadian Jewish Chronicle*, 28 August 1942, pp. 4, 16.

"The Jews of England." Montreal, n.d. A mimeographed pamphlet issued by the Hadassah Organization of Canada. It contains Klein's analysis of *The Merchant of Venice*. Jewish Public Library, Montreal.

"The Jews of Europe." *Canadian Jewish Chronicle*, 3 August 1945, p. 8.

"Kapusitchka." *Canadian Jewish Chronicle*, 15 October 1948, p. 4.

"Marginalia; Towards an Aesthetic." *Canadian Jewish Chronicle*, 11 January, 25 June, 24 December 1948; 28 January 1949.

"The Meed of the Minnesinger." *Jewish Standard*, 30 March 1934, pp. 16, 75-78.

"Memoirs of a Campaigner." *Canadian Zionist*, May, 1937, pp. 21, 25.

"The Mystery of the Mislaid Conscience." *Canadian Jewish Chronicle*, 17 July 1942, p. 4.

"New Writers Series, No. 1." *Canadian Jewish Chronicle*, 8 June 1945, p. 8. Review of Irving Layton's *Here and Now*.

"A Notable Historical Event." *Canadian Jewish Chronicle*, 19 February 1943, p. 4. Review of Stephen Leacock's *Canada; The Foundations of Its Future*.

"Notebook of a Journey." *Canadian Jewish Chronicle*, 12 August–23 December 1949.

"Notes on a Court Jew." *Canadian Jewish Chronicle*, 12 December 1941, pp. 4, 15.

"No Traveller Returns." *Canadian Jewish Chronicle*, 30 June 1944, pp. 4, 16.

"Of Hebrew Humour." *Canadian Jewish Chronicle*, 25 January–15 February 1946.

"Of Jewish Existentialism." *Canadian Jewish Chronicle*, 5 November 1948, p. 8. Review of Jean-Paul Sartre's *Antisemitism and Jew*.

"Of Lowly Things." *Canadian Jewish Chronicle*, 23 June 1944, p. 4.

"Old Ez and His Blankets." *Canadian Jewish Chronicle*, 4 March 1949, pp. 4, 13. On Ezra Pound.

"One More Utopia." *Canadian Jewish Chronicle*, 7 September 1945, pp. 5, 87-88.

"The Parliament of Fowles." *McGilliad*, 2 (1930): 9–11.

"Poems of Yehoash." *Canadian Jewish Chronicle*, 26 September 1952, p. 4.

"Poet of a World Passed By." *Canadian Jewish Chronicle*, 9 June 1950, p. 5. On J. I. Segal's *Sefer Yiddish*.

"The Poetry Which is Prayer." *Canadian Jewish Chronicle*, 2 November 1945, p. 8, 16. Review of J. I. Segal's *Lider un Loiben*.

"A Reply to Dr. I. M. Rabinovitch." *Canadian Jewish Chronicle*, 16 October 1946, pp. 3–5.

"Riddle Me This Riddle." *Canadian Jewish Chronicle*, 31 March 1944, p. 4.

"Robinson Jeffers—Poet Fascist?" *Canadian Jewish Chronicle*, 6 February 1942, p. 4.

"Saadyah Gaon." *Canadian Jewish Chronicle*, 22 May 1942, p. 4.

"The Seventh Scroll." *Jewish Standard*, 22 September 1933, pp. 119, 163–67.

"Talents That Should Have Been Ours." *Canadian Jewish Chronicle*, 10 May 1946, pp. 6, 15.

"The Tale of the Marvellous Parrot." *Canadian Jewish Chronicle*, 11 April 1941, p. 5.

"That Rank Picture." *Canadian Jewish Chronicle*, 17 September 1948, p. 8. On the film of Charles Dickens's *Oliver Twist*.

"The Thirteenth Apostle." *Canadian Jewish Chronicle*, 18 February 1944, p. 4. Review of Sholem Asch's *The Nazarene*.

"Thirty Plots and Holy Writ." *Canadian Jewish Chronicle*, 15 April 1938, pp. 35–38.

"T. S. Eliot and the Nobel Prize." *Canadian Jewish Chronicle*, 12–26 November 1948.

"The Value That is Prayer." *Canadian Jewish Chronicle*, 20 December 1940, p. 4.

"We Who Are About to be Born." *Canadian Jewish Chronicle*, 2 June 1944, p. 4.

"Writing in Canada." *Canadian Jewish Chronicle*, 22 February, 1 March 1946.

'The Yiddish Proverb." *Canadian Jewish Chronicle*, 28 November 1952–2 January 1953.

"Zweig's Hail and Farewell." *Canadian Jewish Chronicle*, 6 March 1942, p. 4. Review of Zweig's *Amerigo*.

UNPUBLISHED MANUSCRIPTS IN THE NATIONAL ARCHIVES, OTTAWA, NOT DATED

"The Golem." [Notes.]

"Selected Poems."

"Three Greatest Jews of Modern Times." Lecture. [Notes.]

"The Time Issue." [Notes.]

WRITINGS CONCERNING A. M. KLEIN: BIBLIOGRAPHY, BIOGRAPHY, CRITICISM

Anonymous. "Canadian Poetry in English." *Times Literary Supplement*, 5 November 1954, p. 704.

Anonymous. "Canadian Writers Come Into Their Own." *Times Literary Supplement*, 5 August 1955, p. iii.

Anonymous. "Poems of French Canada." *Les Carnets Viatoriens*, 13 (1948): 62–63. A Review of Seven Poems from *Poetry* (Chicago).

Avison, Margaret. Review of *The Rocking Chair and Other Poems*. *Canadian Forum*, 28 (1948): 191.

Bell, Merirose. "The Image of French Canada in the Poetry of William Henry Drummond, Emile Coderre, and A. M. Klein." Thesis. McGill University, Montreal, Quebec, 1967.

Benjamin, Louis. "A. M. Klein." *Canadian Jewish Yearbook*, 1940–41, 160–63.

Birney, Earl. "Canadian-Jewish Poet." *Canadian Forum*, 20 (1941): 354–55. Review of *Hath Not a Jew* . . . .

Brown, Edward Killoran. "The Development of Poetry in Canada." *Poetry* (Chicago), 58 (1941): 34–47.

———— *On Canadian Poetry.* Toronto: Ryerson Press, 1943.

———— Review of *Hath Not a Jew. . . . University of Toronto Quarterly*, 10 (1941): 286–87.

———— Review of *The Hitleriad* and *Poems* (1944). *University of Toronto Quarterly*, 14 (1945): 261–62.

———— Review of Seven Poems from *Poetry* (Chicago). *University of Toronto Quarterly*, 17 (1948): 262–63.

Bruce, Charles. Review of *The Rocking Chair and Other Poems. Canadian Poetry Magazine*, 12 (1948): 32–33.

Caplan, Usher. "A Bibliography and Index to Manuscripts." Seymour Mayne, ed., *The A. M. Klein Symposium* (1974). University of Ottawa Press, 1975. Gives details of all available earliest printings and pagination of serialized prose.

Collin, W. E. "The Spirit's Palestine." *The White Savannahs.* Toronto: Macmillan, 1936, pp. 205–31.

Crawley, Alan, "The Poetry of A. M. Klein." *Contemporary Verse*, no. 28 (1949), pp. 20–23. Review of *The Rocking Chair and Other Poems.*

Dudek, Louis, "A. M. Klein." *Canadian Forum* 30 (1950): 10–12.

Dudek, Louis, and Gnarowski, Michael. *The Making of Modern Poetry in Canada; Essential Articles on Contemporary Poetry in English.* Toronto: Ryerson, 1967.

Edel, Leon. "Abraham M. Klein." *Canadian Forum*, 12 (1932): 300–302.

———— "Beautiful Tale of a 20th Century Wandering Jew." *Compass*, 23 September 1951, p. 29. Review of *The Second Scroll.*

———— "Poetry and the Jewish Tradition." *Poetry*, 58 (1941): 51–53.

Fisch, Harold. "Poets of Hebraic Consciousness." *Judaism*, 14 (1965): 485–90. Review of *The Second Scroll.*

Fischer, Gretl Kraus. "A M. Klein's Forgotten Play." *Canadian Literature*, no. 43 (1970). pp. 42–53.

———— "A. M. Klein: Religious Philosophy and Ethics in His

Writings." Thesis. McGill University, Montreal, Quebec, 1972.

Frye, Northrop. "English Canadian Literature." University of Oklahoma, *Books Abroad*, 29 (1955): 270–74.

Glotstein, Jacob. "The English Jewish Poet, A. M. Klein." *Yiddisher Kemfer* (New York), 4 May 1945, pp. 15–17. Translated by David Rome in his bibliography on Klein, 1:61.

Gotlieb, Phyllis. "Klein's Sources." *Canadian Literature*, no. 26 (1965), pp. 82–84.

Hirano, Keiichi. "Abraham M. Klein." *Studies in English Literature*, English number. Tokyo, Literary Society of Japan, University of Tokyo, 1964, pp. 71–103.

Jarrell, Randall. "These Are Not Psalms." *Commentary*, 1 (1945): 88–90. Review of *Poems* (1944).

Kennedy, Leo. Review of *Hath Not a Jew*. *Canadian Poetry*, 5 (1940): 39–40.

Kervin, Roy. Review of *The Second Scroll*. Montreal *Gazette*, 29 September 1951, p. 28.

Keyfetz, B. G. "Immigrant Reaction as Reflected in Jewish Literature." *Congress Bulletin*, Canadian Jewish Congress, Montreal, October 1962, pp. 4–5.

Kreymborg, Alfred. Review of *Poems* (1944). *Saturday Review of Literature*, 24 March 1945, p. 35.

Layton, Irving. Review of *The Hitleriad*. *First Statement*, 2 (1944): 17–20.

——— Review of *Poems* (1944). *First Statement*, 2 (1945): 35–36.

Lewison, Ludwig. "The Jew as a Poet." *Canadian Jewish Chronicle*, 2 March 1945, p. 6.

Lyons, Roberta. "Jewish Poets from Montreal: Concepts of History in the Poetry of A. M. Klein, Irving Layton, and Leonard Cohen." Thesis. Carleton University, Ottawa, 1966.

Mackay, L. A. "Klein's Latest Verse Collection an Event in Canadian Letters," *Saturday Night*, 6 November 1948, p. 17. Review of *The Rocking Chair and Other Poems*.

Mandelbaum, Allen. "Everyman on Babylon's Shore." *Commentary*, 12 (1951): 602–4. Review of *The Second Scroll*.

Marshall, Thomas A., ed. *A. M. Klein*. Critical Views on Canadian Writers series. Toronto: Ryerson, 1970.

―――― "The Poetry of A. M. Klein: A Thematic Analysis of the Poetry of Abraham Moses Klein in the Light of the Major Themes of *The Second Scroll*." Thesis. Queen's University, Kingston, Ontario, 1964.

Matthews, John. "Abraham Klein and the Problem of Synthesis." *Journal of Commonwealth Literature*, 1 (1965): 149–66.

Nims, John Frederick. "Tares and Wheat." *Poetry* (Chicago), 66 (1945): 104–5. Review of *Poems* (1944).

Pacey, Desmond. *Creative Writing in Canada: A Short History of English Canadian Literature*, revised edition. Toronto: Ryerson Press, 1961.

―――― *Ten Canadian Poets: a Group of Biographical and Critical Essays*. Toronto: Ryerson Press, 1958.

Palnick, Elijah Ezekiel. "A. M. Klein: A Biographical Study." Thesis. Hebrew Union College, Cincinnati, Ohio, 1959.

Park, Julian, ed., *The Culture of Contemporary Canada*. Toronto: Ryerson, 1957.

Phelps, Arthur Leonard. *Canadian Writers*. Toronto: McClelland & Stewart, 1951.

Pratt, Edwin John. Review of *The Hitleriad*, *Canadian Forum*, 24 (1944): 164.

Rashley, R. E. *Poetry in Canada: the First Three Steps*. Toronto: Ryerson, 1958.

Regimbal, Albert. "Artistes Israélites au Canada Français." *Relations*, no. 90 (1948), pp. 184–85.

Richler, Mordecai. "The War, Chaverim, and After." *Canadian Literature*, no. 18 (1963), pp. 21–29.

Rome, David. *Jews in Canadian Literature*, revised edition. Montreal: Canadian Jewish Congress, 1964, 2 vols. A bibliography.

Ross, Malcolm. "*The Second Scroll*." *Canadian Forum*, 31 (1952): 234.

Samuel, Maurice. "The Book of the Miracle." *Jewish Frontier*, November 1951, pp. 11–15. Review of *The Second Scroll* by the reader who appraised the manuscript of the novel for Alfred E. Knopf.

Sanderwell, B. K. "About Eternal Murder." *Saturday Night*, 13 October 1951, p. 27. Review of *The Second Scroll*.

Scherr, Julian M. Review of *The Second Scroll*. *Library Journal*, 15 September, 1951, p. 1420.

Schultz, Gregory Peter. "The Periodical Poetry of A. J. M. Smith, F. R. Scott, Leo Kennedy, A. M. Klein, Dorothy Livesay, 1925–1950." Thesis. University of Western Ontario, London, 1957.

Scullion, John Anthony. "Abraham Moses Klein, Poet and Novelist." Thesis. University of Montreal, 1953.

Smith, Arthur James Marshall, "Abraham Moses Klein," *Gants du Ciel*, 11 (1946): 67–81.

———— The Original Preface to *New Provinces* (1936). *Canadian Literature*, no. 24 (1965): pp. 6–10.

Spiro, Solomon. "The Second Gloss: An Exegesis of *The Second Scroll* by A. M. Klein." Thesis. Sir George Williams University, Montreal, 1971.

Spurgeon, D. C. "Whither Green-Haired Poet?" *Saturday Night*, 23 May 1950, pp. 12, 46. Interview with Klein.

Steinberg, M. W. "Poet of a Living Past: Tradition in Klein's Poetry." *Canadian Literature*, no. 25 (1965): 5–20.

———— "The Stature of A. M. Klein." *The Reconstructionist*, 29 November 1957, pp. 15–18.

———— "A Twentieth Century Pentateuch." *Canadian Literature*, no. 2 (1959), pp. 37–47.

Stern, Harry J. "Far More than I Have Read Is in That Scroll," *Canadian Jewish Chronicle*, 25 January 1952, p. 12. Review of *The Second Scroll*.

Sutherland, John. "Canadian Comment." *Northern Review*, 2 (1949): 30–34. Review of *The Rocking Chair and Other Poems*.

———— "The Poetry of A. M. Klein." *Index*, 1 (1946): 8–12, 20–21.

Sutherland, Ronald. "The Body-Odour of Race." *Canadian Literature,* no. 37 (1968), p. 46.

Swados, Harvey. "A Work of Splendour." *The Nation,* 3 November 1951, pp. 379–80. Review of *The Second Scroll.*

Sylvester, Harry. "Pathway to Israel." *New York Times Book Review,* 25 November 1951, p. 58.

Sylvestre, Guy. Review of A. M. Smith, editor. *The Book of Canadian Poetry* (Chicago, 1943). *Le Devoir,* 17 February 1945, p. 8.

Tallman, Warren. "Creation Beyond Perception." *Canadian Literature,* no. 11 (1962), pp. 72–73. Review of *The Second Scroll.*

Waddington, Miriam, *A. M. Klein.* Toronto: Copp Clark, 1970.

Wiseman, Schloime. "Review of *Hath Not a Jew.*" *Canadian Jewish Chronicle,* 14 June 1940, pp. 6, 14.

Index